ADV[illegible]

With passion and courage [illegible] *Turkey* [illegible] *story of* [illegible] *Armenian family's dislocation, separation, immigration, struggle and survival. By the end of this saga, narrated chiefly by the author's uncle, there emerges a picture of a family sorely tried by Turkish tyranny but unbroken in spirit.*

Though highly partisan, this grim account of the Yessaian's odyssey from a once-peaceful village in central Turkey to an industrial city in the American Mid-west has the ring of bitter truth, balanced by moments of joy, humor, and reconciliation. The book as a whole commands attention through its ominous and stunning immediacy.

Leo Hamalian
City College of New York

Out of Turkey *is must reading for every Armenian, and indeed for every American who should know more about the Armenian genocide. It's more than a book of recollections about the life of Donik Yessaian and the people of Efkereh, an Armenian village decimated by the Ottoman Turks.*

As I read each page, I felt the pain and suffering the Yessaian clan had been forced to endure more than 75 years ago. It has a chilling effect that refuses to fade away because present-day Turkey still denies the first genocide of the 20th century.

Some might suggest Harry Yessaian's chilling memoir is just another book for the bookcase. I beg to differ. The family memoirs of the Yessaians of those dark days that befell Efkereh and the burning of Smyrna, could also have been a story about the massacred Tarpinians of Erzeroum, the Sarkisians of Moush, the Manoogians of Sepastia, or the Bedrosians of Van. Out of Turkey *is about the depopulation of historical Armenia, and the will of the Yessaian clan to survive and preserve a heritage antedating the birth of Christ.*

Should present-day Turkey be held responsible for the crimes of its predecessors? Read Out of Turkey *and judge for yourself.*

Mitchell Kehetian
The Macomb Daily

ADVANCE PRAISE

Harry Yessaian's story of his family during the Armenian genocide is analogous to the story of almost every Armenian who went through a similar ordeal but somehow miraculously survived. Harry put his family's suffering on record as testimony, while most of the others who suffered similar fates have been consigned to oblivion. This story is important not only for the Yessaian and Kouradjian families, but for history as well.

Antranig Chalabian,
Author

A remarkable and moving book. . . Intrinsically very worthwhile and timely.

John Davies,
British Writer and Book Critic
Award Winning Editor

A very moving story . . . can be read in one breath.

Artem Haroutiunian
Professor of American Literature
University of Yerevan
Yerevan, Armenia

OUT OF TURKEY

Photograph of Donik "Haji Bey" Yessaian, in Smyrna, Ottoman Empire (Turkey), 1919.

Out of Turkey

*The Life Story Of Donik "**Haji Bey**" Yessaian*

A family memoir as recollected by Harry Yessaian

With Introduction, Footnotes, Afterword, and Bibliography for Reading by

Dennis R. Papazian, Ph.D.

The Armenian Research Center
The University of Michigan-Dearborn
1994

1998 1997 1996 1995 1994 5 4 3 2 1

Library of Congress Catalog card number: 94-071057
ISBN: 0-8142-2556-4 (pbk.: alk. paper)

Cover design and photo layout by Nazareth Hadjian, assisted by Morris Johnson.

Cover illustrations: Background photo is of the St. Stepanos [Stephen] Armenian Cathedral of Smyrna. Foreground photo is of Efkereh. Inset photo is of Donik "Haji Bey" Yessaian.

To all Armenians
especially to the 1.5 million
who were innocent victims
of the first genocide of the 20th century.

Also to my father's grandchildren

Dan and Mark

Chuck and Diane

Victoria

TABLE OF CONTENTS

Acknowledgements

This book could not have been written or published without the generous support of many wonderful relatives and friends. I would like to extend to all of them my heart-felt gratitude. In particular, I would like to thank:

My dear wife Joyce, whose encouragement and support sustained me over the many difficult days, months, and years of writing.

My Uncle Nazar, who spent innumerable hours relating to me the exciting story of my father, his brothers, and his family.

My mother, Victoria, who told me the stories of Sarkis Aga, my great-grandfather, of my great-grandmother Sultan Hanim, and of the Kouradjian family in Smyrna.

My Uncle Krikor [George], who finally shared with me the horrors he experienced during the Turkish reoccupation of Smyrna.

My late brother Charles and his wife Rose; my sister Alice Papazian-Teberian; my aunts Rose Torosian, Sarah Torigian, Artemis Torosian, and Arous Waterian; and my Uncle Jim Kouradjian and his wife Betty, for their personal accounts.

My nephew Chuck, the son of Charlie and Rose Yessaian, and his wife Tulie. It is because of Chuck's enthusiasm for the manuscript that he brought together the team which finally produced this book. Chuck also underwrote the cost of the first printing so that the proceeds could be used to aid the children of Armenia. Without his energy, drive, and determination — so much like his grandfather's — this book would not have been published.

My cousin Rosemary Torigian, the late Tom Charles, La-Nona Robinson and her husband Carl, Gladys Craemer, Vahakn Dadrian, George and Lena Chacker [Chackerian], Antranig Chalabian, Edward Korkoian, the late Coulet Wooster, Gerald Ottenbreit, Jr., Luben Christoff, and the late Asadoor Sarajian and his wife Mary, all of whom helped in various ways.

Special thanks are due to Alice Nigoghosian, Associate Director of the Wayne State University Press, for her untiring labors, valuable editorial contributions, and the unselfish gift of her time and book-publishing experience to the project.

And to Dennis Papazian, Professor of History at the University of Michigan-Dearborn and Director of the Armenian Research Center, and his wife Mary. Dr. Papazian generously provided the introduction, footnotes, afterword, and bibliography for the book and made a trip to Efkereh and Smyrna to verify several items in the manuscript.

I am deeply indebted to Ms. Nigoghosian and Professor Papazian for devoting their total energies over a period of several months to see the book through publication.

Without the gracious generosity of all these people, this book would not have seen the light of day. I have tried my best to reflect accurately the information so kindly shared with me by my family and friends. I hope I have fulfilled their trust.

Harry Yessaian,
1994

Foreword

by the First Grandson

Why this book? Why this subject? Why me? Those were the unanswered questions that raced through my head after reading the initial manuscript written by my uncle Harry Yessaian.

Haji Bey was my grandfather, yet the closest I ever came to the man was at the age of sixteen when I helped carry him in his casket to his final resting place in Detroit, Michigan. I, unlike most grandchildren, never knew who my grandfather was, what his life was all about, how he survived, how he lived, and why he came to America.

Although I had heard bits and pieces of how my father Garbis [Charlie] survived the massacres, at best the story was fragmented and incomplete. This book opened the door to my ancestral past.
I had to read a manuscript in order to meet my grandfather. I had to read a manuscript in order to know substantially more of my own genetic workings and why possibly "I am what I am." I had to read a manuscript in order to understand the tragic ordeal that my father and our family suffered.

Through this manuscript, I have been afforded the opportunity to step into a time machine, a treat few mortals ever experience. Through this manuscript, I learned of my grandfather's exploits as my great-uncle Nazar whispered the true story to my uncle Harry over sixty years ago.

There are several reasons for publishing this book. This story is too important to the Armenian spirit to let it remain unpublished and silent forever.

Even more important, I wanted to share this story with my darling daughter Georganna Rose, who speaks, reads, and writes Armenian; and to my son Chuck Gregory, whose many years at the A.G.B.U. Alex Manoogian School, in Southfield, Michigan, imbued him with a total commitment to the Armenian cause.

Also, I wanted them to know about their own grandfather (who died many years before they were born) and how he survived the

Armenian genocide and worked in the Detroit area selling *madzoon* [yogurt], marrying Rose Margosian, my mother, and raising my sister Diane and me.

Finally, I also felt that the Turks should read this book and know that I am educating my children as Armenians and will never allow them to forget what the Turkish government did to our countrymen and our own family. My revenge is, in part, publishing this book and bringing into this world two children who will carry the spirits of Haji Bey and Charlie Yessaian into the twenty-first century.

Chuck Yessaian,
1994

INTRODUCTION

When I was first asked to examine Harry Yessaian's manuscript, I must confess that I was a bit hesitant because I am asked to review so many survivor memoirs. Once I began to read it, however, I was immediately captivated by the exciting story and stayed up all night absorbing every word.

It is difficult to classify this book. Harry Yessaian's memoir reads like a novel, yet it is history. It is in one sense the biography of an unusual man. The story of a life. In another sense, it is the history of a family. An exciting and wondrous family at that. In yet another sense, it is a dramatic adventure story. The story of escape from Turkey to the New World.

We can also view it as a survivor *memoir*, even though the survivors' accounts are related to us through an intermediary, Harry Yessaian. We may also see it as a portrait of the immigration experience of an Armenian family. The movement of an extended family from the Old World to the New, with all of its challenges, traumas, and joys.

In still another sense, we have before us a classical tragedy. The chronicle of "Donik" [Donagan] Yessaian, a heroic man, who in his adult years was addressed by the honorific title of "Haji Bey." A man who by virtue of stubborn self-confidence, an indomitable will, irrepressible spirit, and restless imagination, overcame innumerable obstacles and met all challenges until he was finally brought low by changing times and the very character traits that originally accorded him his successes.

In the broadest sense, this book is a story of mankind, with all its virtues and vices, its victories and defeats, and the unyielding determination of people to survive under arduous conditions and harsh circumstances.

The Story

The Yessaian story begins in Detroit, Michigan, with a flashback to a *pogrom* in 1885 in Efkereh, a village in the interior of Anatolia (present-day Turkey). These random raids on the Armenians were encouraged by the paranoid Sultan Abdul Hamid (Abdulhamit) II, who saw the Christian Armenians as an alien and disruptive element in his Empire.

It tells of the adventures of bold young Donik Yessaian who led his four brothers to the exciting city of Smyrna (present-day Izmir), an international seaport on the Mediterranean, to start a new life. And it continues with the voyage of two of the brothers, led by a still irrepressible Haji Bey (Donik), to America.

Haji Bey returns to Turkey after World War I to seek his family. He learns that his entire family had been deported from Efkereh by the Young Turk government and sent on a death march to the Syrian desert. Some members of the family apparently survived to return to Efkereh following Turkey's surrender to the Allies after World War I, only to be driven out a second time by the Turkish nationalists. Haji Bey's son, Garabed, and his young brother-in-law, Kourken, were the only members of the large family to survive the second expulsion. After being married a second time, Haji Bey returns with his new bride, sons, and his first wife's young brother to safety in America.

The story goes on through the dreadful burning and sacking of Smyrna in 1922 by the Turkish nationalists and the escape of other members of Haji Bey's new family. It is carried through World War II in Detroit, Michigan, and ends in 1988 with the death of Harry Yessaian's mother in Florida.

The Style

Some readers might question Yessaian telling his story through dialogue. Certainly he could not have remembered the exact words of all the conversations he had with his uncle, or even with his mother for that matter. To believe that would be to stretch credulity. Memory is fallible.

Yet in reading Yessaian's story we are reminded of Herodotus, the classical Greek historian, who graced his narrative with tales and stories he had heard from local residents and far-off travelers, things which he could not personally verify. We can only imagine how impoverished his history would be without those colorful stories and details, some of which may or may not have been true.

We are also reminded of the great classical Greek writer Thucydides, credited with being the first political scientist, who readily graced his story with long quotations. What student has not been thrilled by Thucydides's account, ostensibly verbatim, of Pericles's great speech in defense of democracy?

While these conversations and speeches reported by Thucydides may not be factual in the sense that they are verbatim transcriptions, they are certainly true inasmuch as they capture the spirit and meaning of events which would have been lost in a simple narrative or a mere self-conscious paraphrasing.

Clearly, Harry Yessaian's dialogue meets the same criteria: it is a true reflection of reality, although perhaps not entirely a precise representation. The spirit is true even if the conversations have been recreated and some of the stories possibly exaggerated.

The Voices

In this work, we hear Harry Yessaian's own voice, as well as those of his uncle Nazar, his mother Victoria, and other members of the family. The uncle's melancholy voice relates the tragic yet often rich story of life for the Armenians in the old Ottoman Empire and the journey of Haji Bey, Mardiros, and himself to safety in America.

Harry Yessaian's mother describes the splendid life of an upper-class Armenian family in Smyrna, the beautiful and exciting port on the seacoast, and the exodus of some members of her family to America. She goes on to tell the story of her own mother, Sultan Hanim, and her dramatic escape from the burning city of Smyrna to Greece and eventually to America.

Harry's own voice primarily relates what he was told by the various members of his family over a period of years, beginning from the time he was about thirteen years old. He masterfully weaves the various threads into one story. Harry Yessaian committed these stories to memory and began to write them down in his adult years.

Harry's uncle Nazar spoke to him in Armenian and Turkish, both of which Harry understands and speaks. His half-brother Garabed also spoke to him in a mixture of Armenian and Turkish, while Harry's mother Victoria chiefly used Armenian and English.

The authentic voice of Harry Yessaian derives from the fact that he is not a scholar and has not delved into the academic literature on the life of Armenians in Turkey, the Armenian genocide, or the burning of Smyrna. He sees the events through the personal accounts of his own relatives, the very people who lived through them. Indeed he includes a few of the *misconceptions* of his informants; not of what happened to them, which they would remember only too well, but of the larger context of their tragedy. Like most of the innocent victims, they did not always understand the larger picture.

Family Memories

I have studied the Middle East, the Armenian people, and the Armenian genocide for over thirty years. I have also known scores of men and women who were survivors of the Armenian tragedy of 1915-22. I have listened attentively to hundreds of stories from the "old folks" — in coffee houses, in living rooms, and at political gatherings. More recently, I have directed an oral history project that recorded the interviews of a few hundred survivors. I have also read most of the published survivor memoirs.

Just as importantly, perhaps, I have known the Yessaian family since my pre-teen years. Harry Yessaian's dialogue accurately expresses the mode of conversation, the ideals and beliefs, and the hopes and fears of his family and people like them. I can personally testify that this book is absolutely authentic in that sense. Every word rings true.

I met "Haji Bey" Yessaian in his old age, when he was no longer in his prime. Although it was many years ago, I recall accompanying my family to some of the lively Saturday night parties at the Yessaian home. I was awed by the rich oriental carpets, the seemingly opulent furnishings, the lavish decorations, the unending supply of delicious foods, and the free flow of drink.

I vividly remember the singing and dancing, the laughter and merriment, the love and affection, and the occasional absentminded overindulgence in the fruit of the vine and the sometimes sharp exchanges of tipsy merrymakers.

Harry Yessaian's portrait of his family and their friends is authentic. Readers of William Saroyan will recognize many of the colorful types. I am afraid, we may never see the likes of such full-blown characters again.

Unexpurgated

Some readers will be shocked by the blunt language and the many graphic scenes in Harry Yessaian's story. Yet what makes the present work more authentic than most others of its type is that it has not been sanitized: it has not been expurgated to please a cautious publisher or a timid reader.

The story is an accurate reflection of real life. I can testify from my own childhood experience that recent immigrants, particularly those from the villages or the poorer sections of towns, often used vulgar expressions in Turkish to spice up their conversation. We can find such vulgar usage even in English, although not polished to such an art form as in Turkish, in some neighborhoods in America today. Yessaian has rightly preserved these expletives in their original Turkish, their authentic language, and has obligingly provided English translations.

There is a saying that "English is the language of business, French of love, Armenian of prayer, and Turkish of profanity." As a matter of fact, when I was a child I thought nothing of it when people in my circles, who usually spoke English, Armenian, or Greek, would spice up their conversation with salty Turkish expressions. It seemed to my boyish mind a part of the natural order of things, just as the men calling out their numbers in a Median dialect when they played *tavlu* [backgammon] in the coffee houses.

I recall picking up a few Turkish phrases, which I took to be exclamations of joy, in the Armenian coffeehouses. One night at a Yessaian party, when the singing and dancing were reaching their peak, I shouted out my new expressions in an innocent but loud voice. There was dead silence and all-around embarrassment. I thought I would die. Then Victoria, that grand lady, said simply, "He doesn't know the meaning of those words," and the party went on as before. That was the last time I attempted to use my limited Turkish vocabulary. I have never dared to ask anyone the meaning of these expressions. Now, I have finally learned them from Yessaian's text. As I reminisce, I blush anew at my childish indiscretion.

Cultural Changes

Yes, times change. During the early years, the Armenian-American community held lavish picnics just like the outdoor feasts in the old country. I can remember in the old days driving out to Cass Benton Park on Saturday or Sunday afternoons where scores of families came with large quantities of food and other refreshments.

Each family would stake out an area for themselves and their relatives. They would unload the food, sometimes starting with breakfast, and cook and serve all day. The children would mix and play games, carefully watched over by several "grandmas" and "grandpas," just as in the picnic of Harry Yessaian's story.

Once or twice a year a grand picnic would be held at the State Fairgrounds in Detroit. Not only would the food and drink be plentiful, but Middle Eastern dance bands would be hired, sometimes two or three, to play music all day and later into the night.

While I never attended the weekend dances at the Yessaian farm, I can imagine them. They were probably like our own picnics writ large. Truly, those were the good old days.

Furthermore, the party music in those days in that milieu, including the Yessaian home, was made up of Greek, Turkish, Arabic, and Armenian songs and dances. To sing in Turkish or Greek in those days seemed as normal as to sing in Armenian, that is, until the late 1960s when the Armenian community of America once more became preoccupied with the genocide.

Turkish music, which in earlier days of immigration had reminded people of "the homeland" and the joys of their childhood, became proscribed at public gatherings. At a feast or a wedding reception, dance bands were stopped in the middle of a Turkish song by self-appointed "culture monitors," often with a harsh exchange of words in Armenian or English — Turkish no longer being allowed in Armenian-American circles even for swearing!

Those Armenians who spoke only Turkish, the ones who were not allowed to use their native Armenian tongue in their part of Turkey, now had to learn Armenian to be accepted by the community. One almost never hears Turkish expressions in Armenian-American circles today. Thus the Yessaian conversations, with the lavish sprinkling of Turkish expressions, and their use of Greek and Turkish music, were manifestations of a passing era.

A Story from the Armenian Genocide

Harry Yessaian does not tell the story of the Armenian genocide. For instance, he does not discuss Abdul Hamid's massacres of Armenians during the years 1894-96. These tragedies are ignored probably because by that time his father, Haji Bey, and uncles were safe in Smyrna and their native town, Efkereh, was spared.

These killings, which took the lives of some 300,000 Armenians, were well-known in informed circles in the Ottoman Empire and all over Europe and America. But Harry's father and uncles were simple young working men — blacksmiths — and not intellectuals. Apparently they were not connected with the more erudite Armenian or Turkish elites, the men of affairs. Yes, they did know "Sarkis Aga" Kouradjian, one of the wealthiest and best connected men in Smyrna, but while Sarkis Aga knew and did business with many high-ranking Turks and Armenians, he would not be the type of man who would discuss "unpleasant, transient matters" involving his Turkish "friends" with the young Yessaian brothers. In any case, these massacres are unreported in Harry's narrative.

Yessaian does report the Young Turk genocide of the Armenian people in 1915-16. First, through the letter that his father and uncles received in America from their "adopted" Turkish brother Hashim, who had been left behind in Smyrna, and then by other informants.

Harry Yessaian's half-brother Garabed [Garbis, Charles] survived the expulsion and death march of the Armenians from Efkereh, as did Haji Bey's young brother-in-law Kourken [George] Chackerian.

Of all the numerous members of the Yessaian and Chackerian clans who were driven out of Efkereh, only these two boys finally survived. The boys were traumatized by their experience (after all they were both under ten years of age) and, after they were found in an orphanage, would tell little to Haji Bey and the others except of the cruel death of Garabed's mother Siranoush, Haji Bey's first wife. Kourken Chackerian is alive at the time of this writing, but he is an old man in ill health and refuses to talk about his experiences and relive the trauma.

The general story of Harry's "Uncle Nazar" about the Armenian genocide must have been taken from other survivors who resided in the Detroit area. It was not at all unusual for the survivors, in the early days, to exchange stories about their suffering and the suffering and deaths of their loved ones.

In a sense, this sharing of tragedy in order to come to terms with it, reminds us of present-day support groups. Most of the survivors, we know from academic studies, never came to grips with the genocide. Most of them merely repressed the past and tried to make a new life for themselves. It is no wonder. How can one come to terms with genocide?

Surprisingly, at least to me, the survivors rarely told their full story to strangers or even to their own children. In general Harry Yessaian's story coincides with evidence we have from many other sources. It should be remembered, however, that most of the immigrants did not even know the year of their birth, much less the exact chronology of events. Harry's dates, therefore, must be viewed with caution.

The Armenian victims were shot, butchered, starved, and marched to their death. There are as many personal stories about the Armenian genocide as there were victims and survivors. Nearly 1.5 million people died and only some 0.5 million, mostly young children, survived. The recounting of only a few of the stories of the 1.5 million victims, or the scarred survivors, can cloy the mind. Repetition even of only a dozen of these stories eventually takes on a patina of macabre unreality. The human mind can absorb only so much horror at one time. After a while, we block it all out. Too much horror is no horror at all.

Characters

The main characters of this story are Armenians, although it does include Turks, Greeks, Americans, and people of a host of other nationalities. The personalities, relationships, and events for the most part are readily understandable. Others might benefit from a bit of explanation.

Some people might question the "adoption" of Hashim, a Turkish waif, by Haji Bey as his Turkish "brother." I do not.

My own uncle, Kamer Pehlivanian, remained in Constantinople after the Armenian Genocide and after my mother, Armenouhe, was brought to America by my father Nahabed. On one of his several visits to America, I taped an interview of my uncle's experience.

My uncle told me that he was poverty-stricken after World War I, a virtual orphan, and went about looking for a job, any type of job, just to keep alive. He was taken in by a Turkish blacksmith who treated him well. A few years later, when my uncle wanted to get married, he had almost no money and not even a clean suit of clothing to wear.

The Turk — I was never given his name — bought my uncle a new suit of clothing and lent him an automobile for his wedding day. As my uncle told this story, he broke down in tears. I remember his words clearly. "How can I hate the Turks?" he sobbed. "It was a Turk who put me on my feet in life. He treated me like a son. He taught me a trade, and through this trade and my investments, I am a rich man today." My uncle Kamer echoes the words of Sarkis Aga Kouradjian.

Yes, Armenians and Turks were often close friends on a personal level. These friendships extended from among people in the villages to among many in high places. The pogroms, massacres, and the genocide of the Armenians was not the work of friends and neighbors, but rather that of warped-minded intellectual elites, unjust rulers, cruel brigands, deluded and misguided rabble, and corrupt officials. Neighbors rarely, if ever, participated in the killings.

Others might question the "friendship" between Haji Bey and Ibrahim Pasha, a young Turkish aristocrat, in Smyrna. While certainly this kind of rapport between two young and high-spirited men might be unusual among Armenians and Turks, it was certainly not unheard of. Many Armenian leaders were "friends" of Young Turk leaders. And, after all, Haji Bey was an unusual man, independent minded and self-willed, a lover of life and adventure. Ibrahim Pasha was an enlightened man, one who believed in Ottomanism, the equality of all people in the Ottoman

Empire under the rule of law. Certainly a friendship between these two types is plausible. I am reminded, in this context, of a line from one of Rudyard Kipling's poems, "East is East and West is West, and never the twain shall meet/ . . . But there is neither East nor West, Border, nor Breed, nor Birth/When two strong men stand face to face. . . ."

The friendship between the two young men, of course, did not extend to involve their families. That would have been quite unusual, and even unbelievable, considering the differences in their social status, culture, religion, and traditions. We are told nothing of Ibrahim Pasha's family. What we are told about him is never quite clear. Undoubtedly, Ibrahim Pasha did not discuss his personal affairs with the Armenian youth.

What the friendship amounted to was two young men, and their companions, carousing together in cafés, drinking, eating, laughing, telling stories, enjoying music, and wenching. In other words, it was made possible by an unfettered Haji Bey adopting the lifestyle of young Turkish playboys under the patronage of Ibrahim Pasha, a young Ottoman of high rank and status.

Once Haji Bey was married, the deep rapport remained, the friendship of two strong young men, but was expressed on a more sporadic and episodic basis.

Two other stories warrant further analysis. One is the tale of Ibrahim Pasha's treatment of the Turkish highwaymen who dominated the road between Smyrna and Efkereh.

This story is quite believable to me. Upper-class Turks, particularly reformers, were often disgusted with the Turkish rabble. In fact, upper-class Turks considered themselves "Ottomans," not "Turks." The Turks, in the minds of the upper classes, were beneath society. Similarly, the Russian nobility considered the Russian peasants as less than human. Ibrahim Pasha, being from the aristocratic class, could easily treat the brigands as if they were animals.

The other story that might be questioned is the story of the murder of Bedri's father, the Turkish police official. This story might indeed be the offspring of a too vivid imagination. Yet, it is possibly true, particularly in its core. There was a great deal of intrigue in Turkish official circles, just as there is in most authoritarian societies, where success was most often based on birth, connections, luck, and/or scheming. If Bedri's father had stepped out of line once too often, he might have been made by his superiors to pay the price.

One might even question facets of Krikor's [George] story. Krikor tells of his arrest, incarceration, release, and what he witnessed on his return home. While Krikor's story is certainly plausible in terms of what we know happened to Armenians in Smyrna, some of his details are cloudy. But after all, Krikor did not want to tell his story and, when he was finally persuaded to do so after the lapse of more than ten years, perhaps his account was incomplete. What he actually saw and heard we will never know for sure.

Verification

As I began to analyze Harry Yessaian's manuscript carefully, many questions entered my mind about Efkereh and Smyrna. By coincidence, I had the opportunity to visit historic Armenia (eastern Anatolia) in the summer of 1994, just before this book went to press, with the professor of Armenian studies at Harvard, James Russell, and other seasoned travelers.

In a private vehicle we traveled to Ankara, Cappadocia, Kayseri (and the surrounding villages), the valley of Muş, Aktamar, Van, Doĝubayazit, Kars, Ani, Erzurum, İstanbul, and Smyrna. The trip was made under trying circumstances inasmuch as heavy fighting was taking place in the east between the Turks and the Kurds. Twenty-nine Kurds were killed in battle near Bingöl the day after we passed through, and nine tourists were killed near Smyrna the week before we arrived. We could not visit Diyarbakir or Digor, between Doĝubayazit and Kars, because of the heavy fighting in those regions. The minority problem has not yet been solved in Turkey.

We spent almost a full day in Efkereh. The village, which has been designated a historic site by the government, is partially in ruins. The St. Garabed Monastery [Garabed=Forerunner: St. John the Baptist], a few miles outside of town, is now a military installation and inaccessible. With the help of some local Turks, however, we were able to identify the foundation of the Yessaian home on the hillside and were able freely to inspect the church of which only the shell remains.

We spent a great deal of time investigating the numerous caves which pocket the cliffs on both sides of the stream. Some of the caves could still be accessed through the basement of the houses. We were told by a local official that the larger caves had been sealed off by the government, particularly those that could hold upwards of a hundred people in one of their caverns. Other locals told us that the network of caves and caverns reached to the St. Garabed Monastery three miles away, thus confirming the information in Harry Yessaian's story.

Three of us were invited into a Turkish home in a display of genuine hospitality. As one travels east of Ankara, the society becomes more conservative. The women and children of the household stood next to our table as we men enjoyed the refreshments the women had prepared. Their behavior, typical of eastern Turkey, reminded me of the reticence of Dudük Hanim, the widow of Arabagee, to sit and eat with the Yessaian brothers. In fact, in the city of Van, for example, one rarely saw women on the streets, and those who moved about were usually veiled.

We also discovered the "picnic grounds" of Efkereh, upstream of the village, described by Harry Yessaian in his story. It is located in a small valley and is still in use. When we visited, we saw what seemed like hundreds of people, in groups of tens or twenties, who were enjoying their meals and recreating at the lake which had been formed by the damming of the stream.

Of special interest were the large "pigeon coves" which peppered the hillsides surrounding the village for what seemed to be miles around. These fascinating structures were made of finished stone and were approximately six by six feet at the base and ten to fifteen feet high. One can only wonder why and how they were originally built.

The city of Smyrna, the last stop on our trip, has grown considerably since 1919. Yet the esplanade is still there as are one or two of the old wharves. We found the area of Sarkis Aga's homes, but the Armenian church nearby had been destroyed. We did, however, see a synagogue. We rode on the elevator (built in 1902) to the upper level of the hill. This elevator, described by Harry Yessaian, serviced Sarkis Aga's summer house and the other residences which covered the hillside. From that level, as reported, the harbor and surrounding area could be clearly seen.

Only four long streets of stone houses remain of the Armenian quarter which began only a city block from the dock area. All the wooden houses, covering many square blocks, had been destroyed in the great fire of 1922 and have been replaced by apartment buildings. Only the stone houses still stand. "One can still smell the stench of burning flesh inside those houses," we were told by a local Turkish informant. Here again, Yessaian's story stands the test of verification.

■ ■ ■ ■

Yet, when all is said and done, we see that this book is not the story *of* the Armenian genocide. That story is told better in systematic studies, some of which are listed in the Bibliography. It is rather a story *from* the Armenian genocide. And an exciting story at that.

More particularly, it is the story of Armenians, Greeks, and Turks who lived together in relative peace until ambitious, misguided, and unscrupulous leaders with their grand illusions and abstract schemes tore apart a traditional society that was slowly and painfully groping toward modernization.

It is a story of social change that was not really understood by those involved and to which, in one way or another, they all — Armenians, Greeks, and Turks — fell victim. Harry Yessaian's informants intuitively understood that the Young Turk genocide of the Armenians was not caused primarily by religious animosity, although that was used to incite the masses, but rather by the uneven rate of modernization of Armenians, Greeks, and Turks in the Ottoman Empire which aroused envy, jealousy, and resentment with tragic results.

But perhaps we get ahead of our story. We should let the characters speak for themselves and allow the reader to gain his own insights and reach his own conclusion. For those, however, who want a more precise overview of the Armenians and the Armenian Genocide, we have provided the Afterword to satisfy that interest.

Dennis R. Papazian
Professor of History
The University of Michigan-Dearborn

CHAPTER ONE
A Village Still Sleeping

The picnic was in my family's backyard, in Detroit, Michigan. It was in celebration of the Fourth of July, 1933. My mother and my aunts carried food from the house to the tables in the yard, while my father and his friends sang songs from the old country. Over the porch we had proudly hung an American flag. It was the object of great admiration, on all our parts. On the steps, beneath the flag, sat my dear *Emmï* [Uncle] Nazar, crying softly to himself.

I sat down beside him and wanted to know what was wrong. As always, of course, I spoke to him in a mixture of Turkish and Armenian, which of course was the way our family spoke in the Old Country. The people of Efkereh had their own patois. Uncle Nazar leaned back with a grunt and propped his elbows up on the step behind him, his compassionate, honest face heavy with the weight of the past. He turned to stare at me for a long moment, his eyes still wet.

"How old are you now, my boy?"

I looked at him in surprise. "Aw, come on, Uncle Nazar, you know I just turned thirteen last month!"

He nodded, still staring. Then, as if having made an important decision, he said, "Go in and ask your mother to make us a couple of cups of Turkish coffee. I have much to tell you about another picnic in another time."

When I got back, I asked if it was a long story. He nodded sadly. "Yes. A very long story. You know, right now I'm broke, I don't have a business or a job — yet I've got a lot to tell you about the family — about your father and the rest of my brothers, our mother, and my other nephews.

He began crying again. I felt sad but didn't know what to do to comfort him.

"I'm going to spill out what is in my heart. Maybe someday, when you're old like me, you'll think back and remember what I tell you today."

What follows are my recollections of the stories Uncle Nazar began to tell me on that very special Fourth of July long ago when he became my link with the past.

■ ■ ■ ■

We Yessaians were born of Armenian parents in the Ottoman Empire (in an area now called Turkey), in a town called Efkereh, about ten miles east of Caesarea.[1] Our little village was located in a high valley between two cliffs in the foothills of Mt. Erciyes. This mountain rose out of a plateau area and dominated the plain. Running through the center of the village was a small, rapid mountain stream which powered the only flour mill. Around four hundred and fifty Armenian families, large extended families, lived there. There were around fifty Turkish families and five or six Kurdish families. The Armenians lived comfortably in the bosom of their Christian faith and ancient culture. This was our ancestral home.

The more wealthy Armenians built their houses on the slopes of the gorge, while the others built on the plateau above the gorge. The center of town, along the banks of the stream, was filled with small shops — tailors, shoemakers, blacksmiths, and the like — which provided services for us and the surrounding hamlets as well as for summer visitors who came to escape the hot weather of Caesarea on the plains below. Vegetable plots abounded on the plateau. Horses, donkeys, sheep and goats grazed all around. The older women worked around the homes as the younger children played. There were two Armenian schools, one for the boys and one for the girls. We learned to read and write Armenian and some Turkish. The Armenians of Caesarea spoke mostly Turkish. Our life was good in our beautiful village.

Your father, Donik, arrived in our tiny village waving his little arms wildly and screaming. He demanded attention, and he wanted it right away. That was the way he was then, and that is the way he remains. The year was 1880. He was the last of five

---

1 Called Gessaria by the Armenians. Present-day Kayseri.

sons and much younger than the rest of us. We brothers fondly teased him that he was nothing but an accident. He was only two when our father died, and so we were indulgent with the little guy — to compensate for his lack of a father's loving care.

I still remember the day our father died. I can still see the look on my mother's face as she came out of the bedroom to speak with me. She was so pale. She was exhausted and drained of all vitality. Her eyes were swollen from crying.

She motioned me to her side. "Go to your father," she whispered, "he's asking for you. Your father will leave us soon, Nazar." She started to cry again.

I closed my ears, trying to block out what I had just heard. I was only nineteen then, and Donik was still a toddler. My mind reeled with anxiety. With our father gone, my brothers and mother would be depending on me for leadership and guidance. As the first son, I would be the head of the household.

Dr. Oskan, who served our village, had already told us father's kidneys were failing, and that there wasn't much he or any other doctor could do for him. We accepted his word. Even though he was a Turk and a Moslem, he was a man of great decency and compassion.

I entered my parents' bedroom hesitantly. Mother had lowered the kerosene lamp to keep the glaring light out of father's eyes. Although he tried to sit up as I came to his bedside, he was too weak to move. He motioned with his frail hand for me to come closer. I could barely hear his last words, uttered in a raspy whisper.

"Your brothers are God-fearing young men. They will obey you. But this last one to enter our family has a way about him that I haven't seen in any of you. See to it that he walks a virtuous path and brings no shame to our family name."

I choked up and could only nod my assent. I was grief-stricken.

"Now," father murmured, "tell your brothers to come to me."

My brothers were waiting on the other side of the door. I motioned them in. They carried little Donik in with them. I took the baby boy and held him so father could kiss him. Father's tears flowed onto his pillow as each of us kissed him in turn. In less than an hour, he was gone forever.

The entire village turned out for the funeral. Father's casket was carried on a two-wheeled cart drawn by our donkey as mourners followed on foot. The mourners intoned a solemn wail as they accompanied the procession.

As my grandfather was a priest, he performed the burial services. We were afraid he would break down with grief. It is hard on a parent when a child predeceases him. So we stood close to grandfather to give him moral support. Because his hands trembled so much, it was impossible for him to read from the Book of Offices. He slowly closed the book and simply spoke from his grieving heart.

For the next forty days, by tradition, our neighbors visited us daily and brought us prepared food. Mother was vexed at being confined to the house; she was a vibrant woman. Her philosophy was to take what came and to get on with life.

Mama Yessaian was also very religious. In her mind, her loss was temporary. She believed she would be reunited with her husband in a better place. When the period of mourning finally passed, she was happy to get back to work. All of us were.

Mother had her hands full trying to keep up with little Donik. She allowed no one but herself to punish him. She took care of that task very well, spanking his bottom several times a day. She complained that she'd never had problems raising the four of us, but this last child was different — he wanted his own way.

After she gave Donik his last spanking for the day, Mother would pick him up, give him his bath, cuddle him with great affection, and put him in bed.

All of us in the family worked very hard. Each of us had a job. I was a woodworker and could make or repair furniture, cabinets, and also build or repair houses. Your Uncle Hovsep [Joseph] was a skilled metal worker. And your Uncle Mardiros was a good designer. Your Uncle Artin — you're his namesake — was also good at designing things. He and Mardiros would draw something up, and then we other brothers would make the thing, just like it was depicted.

In our iron-working shop, we made plowshares, shovels, hoes, rakes, and kitchen utensils — almost anything — and sold our products to the townspeople and visitors. We also made different kinds of fasteners, long bolts and nuts to thread onto the bolts. Merchants sold us many sizes of threading dies which had been imported through Smyrna — the great seaport on the Mediterranean. The harbor there was a gathering place for all nations bringing new products and ideas to Turkey. That's why your father became obsessed with the idea of going there to live.

During the winter months, life was more relaxed. In our village, that was when the weaving was done and babies were made. We would sit around the fire in the evenings, speaking in rhymes, trying to outdo each other with our poetry. Donik was good at that — he was quite the poet. Mardiros would compose dance music, songs, and tunes.

Mother would occasionally visit our neighbors in the evening. She had her own personal transportation, Aram, our cantankerous donkey. Mother was the only one he'd let near him and would kick anyone else within striking distance of his hind legs, even if you were just trying to feed him. Yet all mother had to do was call him and he'd trot right over. She'd mount him and talk to him in Armenian. *"Aram, anoushigus, aisor inchbes yes? Haideh, kich mé bdédink."* [Aram, my sweet, how are you today? Come, let us go visiting.] And off they would go.

We realized only later why mother was so busy socializing around the village. She was shopping for brides for us older boys. With our father dead, it was time for us to marry. We all knew that our father had wanted at least one of us to carry on the family tradition by becoming a priest. None of us was cut out for that life, however, and mother knew it. So married men we would be.

"Maybe we can make little Donik a priest," mother would think. "But no, he'd probably sit down and try to rewrite the Bible. It wouldn't work."

It was common for the majority of Efkereh's young men, both Armenians and Turks, to leave the little hamlet by age thirteen or fourteen and head for Caesarea, the district capital about ten or twelve miles away, to seek work as apprentices. The trail passed through another village and then along the foot of the monastery of St. John the Forerunner. From there, it went along the edge of a precipice below which rushed a brisk mountain stream. Finally, the trail emerged on a broad, windy plateau which was inhabited by wandering herdsmen. From the plateau, it ran straight down to the plain of Caesarea.

People generally traveled on foot, or, if they were wealthy, on a donkey or on horseback. The trail was more or less safe for adults, especially those who traveled in groups and in daylight. Young people, however, were especially vulnerable.

Donik, even at a young age, was bored with our little village. From childhood he pestered us to leave. We paid little attention to his idea, considering it foolish child's talk. He would look down the dusty trail leading away from Efkereh, hands in pockets, angry, kicking the dirt with his sandals. If he must live in Turkey, he would say, why did it have to be in this part of it? He kicked hard, raising a cloud of dust, stared longingly at the long road stretching before him — lying between him and his dream. Dear God, he would wail, why couldn't I have been born in an exciting city like Smyrna?

Smyrna was a great cosmopolitan seaport on the Mediterranean. It took several days to get there. I'm sure that today in your school they call it İzmir. When Mustafa Kemal Pasha[1] took over the country, Nephew, he changed the city's name to İzmir, although for me it will always be Smyrna.

■ ■ ■ ■

As Donik grew up, we often kidded and teased him; yet we loved him dearly. Early on, it was clear to us that the youngster was gifted. Even at the tender age of ten, he had a broader view of things, with a knack of expressing his thoughts in a way that forced those around him to listen even though they might disagree with him. It slowly dawned on us that this kid that we thought of as rebellious, one who wouldn't conform to our way of thinking

---

[1] He later took the surname, Atatürk, which means "Father of the Turks."

and doing things, was really a visionary. He instinctively understood things that we could hardly grasp.

Sometimes our lack of foresight made him wild with impatience and he would explode. "Are you crazy," he would yell at us, "why is it taking you fellows so long to see something as clear as day? Efkereh is a stagnant village, we are going nowhere here, the Yessaians have to move on to meet their destiny!"

I was seventeen years his elder, and supposed to be respected as the head of the household, so I sometimes exploded right back at him: "Shut up, you little runt! What makes you so smart?"

"You fellows treat me as if I'm stupid," Donik would complain, "just because I'm the youngest. That's not fair! Age has nothing to do with it. How come you don't listen to ***me*** once in a while? Why can't ***I*** sit in on your meetings when you make plans? ***I*** might have something important to say, too!

"Nazar, you know I respect you and understand that you have the responsibility for the family. Yes, ***you*** have the responsibility to see that we eat, are clothed and have shelter. But since my mind isn't cluttered with these everyday concerns, I have time to think of the future. We're missing opportunities to better ourselves.

"Look at our talents — there isn't a thing we can't do. We are natural iron workers and carpenters. Mardiros is a fine composer, just like our grandfather, and we all play musical instruments. We could make good money playing at wedding receptions in Smyrna, if nothing else."

Oh, Nephew, I would fume with impatience when your father carried on and on like that.

"Listen, boy," I would shout, "you're asking for nothing but trouble! How many times do I have to tell you about the dangers out there beyond our village. Moving to Smyrna is not that easy, you know. There are murderous highwaymen lurking in the hill country and on the plains, waiting for an Armenian boy like you to come along. After they finish playing with you, they pluck your balls off!"

When I saw the pained expression on my youngest brother's face, my heart melted. "All right, little man, let's just say, for the sake of argument, that we were lucky and made it to your precious Smyrna. Don't you see that things could be worse for us? Armenians are not welcome in the big cities. Can't you get that through your thick skull? The Turks don't like Armenians. The Turks will make it hard on us. Here, in Efkereh, we live among our own people. Can't you leave well enough alone?

"Anyway, what would we do there? How could we find jobs, shelter, money to live on? We don't know anyone in Smyrna."

I could see your father felt he was making headway. He was pleased that at least I was asking questions. Nephew, you should have seen him, standing there, poking an accusing finger at each of us.

"What you guys don't understand is that you have to have guts!" He stabbed us with another poke in the chest after each word, "Guts! *Guts!* ***Guts!***"

Well, we four brothers looked at each other. We didn't know if we should laugh at the boy's bravado or give him a good hard smack on his impudent face.

The seeds of his idea ***were*** taking hold. As the months of that year passed, a change came about in the thinking of the Yessaian boys. We were more ready to listen to Donik, and with much more sympathetic ears.

■ ■ ■ ■

Much to my annoyance, Uncle Nazar went off on a tangent at this point, pontificating about duty to the family and other such boring subjects.

■ ■ ■ ■

Over the years, mother set up arranged marriages for each of us, except for Donik who was still too young. We didn't date in those days. We hardly knew the girls mother had chosen. Our wives were surprise packages we received *after* the wedding.

You see, Nephew, we each had a role in life to fulfill. It was important for families to produce offspring from good stock. The bride was expected to be a good homemaker, a loving mother, and to take care of her in-laws. Children were the "social security" for the elders in their later, unproductive years. That's why a male baby, in particular, was considered a blessing. Boys earned a living and provided daughters-in-law.

Of course, these matchmaking practices are fading away in America. You want to marry for love. What is love? You make too much of it! America is becoming decadent as mutual respect disappears and people seek cheap thrills.

I became impatient with his lecture.

"Oh, sure, Uncle, and what if they didn't get along? What then?"

His face turned red — I was stepping on my uncle's toes when I questioned him about what I considered the Armenians' old-fashioned marriages.

He glared at me. "Listen, if you want to hear the rest of this story, you're going to have to shut up!"

"I'm sorry, Uncle," I said, chastened. "Please go on. I'll keep quiet."

He hesitated for a moment. Not because he was angry with me. I could see that wasn't it. He was fighting with himself. He was undecided about whether or not he could continue. He was afraid to bring back a scene that was repressed in the back pages of his memory — a thorn in his flesh that had pained him all these years. His eyes grew misty again. He brought his nicotine-stained fingers up to his lips and dragged long on a Lucky Strike.

■ ■ ■ ■

We Yessaian brothers had become the village musicians. We played at baptisms, weddings, and *khunjuks* [community festivals] where the families would come to dance, sing, and eat. These celebrations would be held at our picnic ground upstream from our village. Everyone would come.

Men would set up tables and benches; the barbecue pits would be cleaned out and fires started. The women would bring their specialty dishes, and plenty of them. The tables would overflow with the abundance of food. Oh, the marvelous food!

At one end of the picnic grounds, an area was set aside with swings and playthings for the children. This is where you would find the grandparents attending the toddlers.

During the festivals, those who couldn't afford large wedding receptions would get married that day and share in the merrymaking. These brides and grooms were always a welcome sight. Sometimes two or three couples would marry.

It was on these occasions that we brothers would try out the songs which we had composed and practiced during the winter months. We would play these tunes in between the traditional folk melodies. Usually, the crowd was delighted!

■ ■ ■ ■

Uncle Nazar stopped speaking, scratched his head, and stared into space, remembering. He had thick hair which was beginning to grey and thin on top. I sat impatiently.

After a few moments, he said with some satisfaction, "Yes, Nephew, we were quite talented. I hope you have inherited some of these talents. If you have talent and make use of it, it's like 'having an invisible bracelet on your wrist.'"[1]

"I know, Uncle, I know!"

"You know! Pah!" he exploded, "what do you know? You don't have the slightest idea of what I'm talking about."

Even though I hadn't done anything to deserve his anger this time, I bit my tongue. I wanted to hear more.

"Don't interrupt me when I'm talking," he roared, "I lose my place, forget where I left off!"

Only years later did I realize I wasn't the object of his anger — it was that picture in his mind which drove him wild with rage, the one he didn't want to remember. It was somewhere in the deep recesses of his mind, behind a dark cloud, hidden all these years. He was avoiding the anguish. Instead, he poked around,

---

[1] This is a folk saying. It means that a talent is something no one can take from you.

spoke of small things, evading whatever it was that was so painful to relate.

■ ■ ■ ■

That particular morning, I think it was around 1885, the entire village had turned out for the festival. The picnic grounds bound us Armenians together, because this is where so many important occasions were celebrated — weddings, baptisms, anniversaries, and certain religious festivals, such as the holiday of the Mother of God in August. All these events marked the rhythm of our lives. In a sense, it was sacred ground. We Yessaians arrived proudly carried our musical instruments, bidding one and all "good morning."

We tuned up and got ready to play. Hovsep put the clarinet to his lips and pierced the morning with a sharp blast. I followed, thumping on the *dumbek*. When this oriental drum is beaten with passionate rhythms, the stretched sheepskin drumhead explodes, penetrating your heart and soul. The deep, vibrating sounds of it could be heard in the nearby hills.

Your Uncle Artin played the *oud*, a pot-bellied guitar that has twelve strings and is strummed with a feather pick. Your Uncle Mardiros could make his listeners sing or cry with his violin, depending upon his mood.

By this time several hundred people had gathered on the grounds. Our dance tunes heated the blood of the younger folks. They started a circle dance. One of the male dancers took the lead; women were not allowed to lead. The circle kept growing as more and more people joined in. A new circle was started inside the original circle. The lead dancer, with a handkerchief in his hand, led the dancers in a frenzied celebration of kicking, bending forward, then kicking to the left, then to the right, all in rhythm — very smoothly and with finesse; forward again, tilting backward slightly; the outer circle moving clockwise, the inner one counter-clockwise. What a beautiful sight to see!

The boys and I were absorbed in the music. Suddenly there were screams of women and children. People blocked our view. I looked up and could only see sabers swinging above the crowd.

We didn't understand what was happening. Then in the next second . . . in the next second. . . .

■ ■ ■ ■

Uncle Nazar paused, . . . momentarily stuck in the time warp of that day. . . . "It is too painful to describe . . . I can't. . . ."

I kept my mouth shut. In a few moments, with a fresh cigarette between his fingers, he was able to go on. . . .

■ ■ ■ ■

A *pogrom* was taking place. We were being raided by Turkish tribesmen. Some invaded the picnic grounds while others were plundering our homes. They were killing indiscriminately. Men, women, and children were hacked without pity. Babies were snatched up and tossed into the air to be caught on saber tips. Some who were missed by the swords and fell to the ground were crushed under the hooves of the horses.

Oh, Jesus! There was nothing we could do. We were caught off guard and helpless. Then, it seemed that as quickly as they had invaded our "picnic" grounds, those wretched curs rode off carrying away some of the children.

In shock, we inspected the loss. We counted the dead bodies lying in puddles of blood. Some victims were still alive, but were grievously injured.

The young men went to get weapons, and then gathered to pursue the killers, hoping to rescue some of the children. We never saw the children again. The attackers had made off with them. The Kurds and Turks wanted Armenian children to improve their blood lines. They wanted the Armenian brains.

This was a day of evil.[1] The pain inflicted by that slaughter was never forgotten. Every time it was brought up in conversa-

---

[1] Such raids on Armenian villages were not unusual. They might occur every few years. This is one of the burdens the Armenians were forced to bear in the Ottoman Empire.

tion, there would be a beating of breasts, endless wailing and crying. The villagers dressed in black; wreaths hung from doors where family members had been killed.

Regrettably, such raids were nothing new for the Armenians. These hideous *pogroms* and kidnappings were in most cases, we later learned, a part of Sultan Abdul Hamid's scheme to repress the Armenians of his empire.

When Armenians complained to Turkish government officials about the massacres, they were usually put off with excuses. Sometimes officials issued bold proclamations, promising that the guilty would be tracked down and arrested. These proclamations were just paper crumbs tossed to the Armenians to appease and deceive them. Proclamations, what a laugh! They were meaningless. Your father later learned many of these things from his loyal friend Ibrahim Pasha.

■ ■ ■ ■

Uncle Nazar had a tendency to dangle bait in front of me only to pull it away. Now he had done it again.

"Who is that, Uncle?" I ventured to ask.

"Ibrahim Pasha was a Turk who played an important role in your father's life. I will explain this later on in the story."

"Oh, Uncle," I pleaded, "tell me now."

But he had no pity on me.

"Don't interrupt. The right time will come. You will have to wait."

And so I had to wait. I was impatient with Uncle Nazar, for I wanted to hear only the exciting parts of the story; the political stuff didn't interest me. Uncle's long drawn-out views and history lessons fell flat on my young ears.

CHAPTER TWO
Farewell to Efkereh

The blinding sun penetrated the window in the loft, draping my small sleeping quarters with sheets of daylight. Fully awake now, I made a mad dash to Uncle Nazar's bedroom and pounded loudly and irreverently on his door.

"Come on, Uncle! It's Sunday! Wake up! You promised to tell me some more stories. You promised not to go to the coffee house today. You promised!"

Uncle Nazar and Dad's favorite hangout was an Armenian coffee house where they spent hours chatting with friends and acquaintances, playing *tavlu* [backgammon] and drinking Turkish coffee. Between pulls on the *nerguila* [a water pipe for smoking], the men would talk chiefly about the past, the sad days in the homeland, and how fortunate they were to have made their escape to America.

If I was lucky, Dad would take me along. He began to do that when I was only seven. Oh, how I loved it! The exotic smells, the thick patches of tobacco smoke, all swirling around the room to the musical accompaniment of gurgling water pipes . . . the snap and click of the dice . . . the *tavlu* players' cries of *shesh! besh!* [five! six!]. I can close my eyes now, and at once I'm there. I can hear them still, as they spoke of the Turkish atrocities, choking with tears as the bitter memories came flooding back. I was very young, and found their gory tales exciting — however, I understood, too, that the experiences they recounted had been indeed terrible, a heavy cross to bear.

But not today. Today Uncle Nazar would stay home . . . and feed my growing addiction to his storytelling.

"All right, all right! I'll be out in a minute. Go put the coffee on, make yourself useful . . . make the toast, something, anything! You've been fooling around too much lately, young man!" The severity in his voice was my punishment for having awakened him so early.

He finally trundled into the kitchen in his bathrobe, grumbling as he tried to remove the cigarette stuck to his lower lip, his fingers stained yellow and teeth light brown from nicotine. Uncle Nazar was a handsome man, with thick salt-and-pepper hair, giving him a distinguished appearance. He resembled Frank Morgan, the old character actor who played the wizard in *The Wizard of Oz*. At the time, Uncle Nazar was in his early seventies; he didn't know his birth date — he only knew that he was seventeen years older than my father.

"Where is the coffee?!" he demanded sternly as he sat down. It was there in front of him, of course. So, eager to please, I merely picked it up and put it down again. He took a hearty sip and frowned. Ahh, sweet relief; that frown meant the coffee was good. ***Now*** I could speak.

"Uncle, please go on with the story!"

"Don't rush me." He lit another Lucky Strike, called it a rotten weed, said it had cost him his health and wasted his money, and told me for the thousandth time how he hated being enslaved by such a filthy habit.

"Please, Uncle Nazar," I pleaded, "tell me about your cigarette habit some other time."

He threw up his hands in surrender. "Okay, okay, where was I?"

■ ■ ■ ■

Several years had passed since the nightmare of that picnic day but it preyed constantly on my mind. I was worried about our continuing to live in our isolated village. No one knew when another pogrom would take place.

It seemed possible to me, after thinking it over, that Smyrna might be a safe haven for Armenians because the Turks would be less likely to commit atrocities in a large cosmopolitan city filled with foreigners.

Things got really bad between 1894 and 1896. The Sultan wanted to keep the Armenians in their place. He encouraged the Kurdish and Turkish tribes and brigands in the hillsides to plunder and murder defenseless Armenians and snatch away their children.

During those times, we thought that we were being attacked by Moslems because they hated Christians. It was more than that. It was political and economic. The Armenians were too progressive for the Turks. Too European in their outlook. Too-well educated and industrious. It was the Turkish leaders who turned the gullible masses against the Armenians to keep the Armenians "in their place."

Our family had lived in Efkereh for hundreds of years and had no trouble with our Turkish neighbors. We four older brothers grew up in our ancestral home. When we married, we brought our wives to live there, too, just as our forefathers had done.

The house was a large stone structure, three stories high. Each of the eight bedrooms had its own little stove for warmth. The living room alone measured over two thousand square feet! Along the two walls were built-in benches running the length of the room. The oriental rug on the floor was enormous — it took your great-grandparents eight winters to weave it!

The toilet was outside. It was difficult to get to it during the winter months because the snow sometimes was as much as two or three feet deep, so we used chamber pots that had to be emptied.

Near the house there was an entrance to a cave. The whole mountainside was sculpted by natural caves. While the entrance to our cave was small, the cave expanded and contracted as it wound through passageways and caverns for what seemed to be miles — at least as far as I can remember it. It is said that it extended all the way to St. John the Forerunner's monastery. The caves were used for a number of things. We sheltered our livestock there in the winter. Next door, was another entrance to the cave. It was large and accessible. That was where the Armenians had a church from early times, St. Kevork [St. Gregory], where your great-grandfather held services. The free-standing St. Stepanos [St. Stephen], Nephew, was not built until the end of the 19th century. It was built over one of the entrances to the cavern. There were many cave churches in nearby Cappadocia.

There were musical instruments all around our house, it seemed in every room. Your great-grandfather — who couldn't read a single note of music — amused himself while a youngster by playing the organ standing in the main living room. Eventually he began composing songs.

His father marveled at the boy's natural ear for music, but he wasn't happy about the dance tunes.

"Son, you mustn't play this kind of music. We come from a long line of priests and you must play melodies that are pleasing to God's ear. You must play only *sharagans*, religious hymns."

But the boy was rebellious. Every time his father went away, the boy would call his friends over, sit down at the organ, and play dance music late into the night.

On one of these occasions, his father walked in on the scene. He chased the boys out, went over to the organ, and slammed it shut. He then grabbed your great-grandfather by the ear.

"I believe this is the ear the devil whispered into, is it not?" he shouted. "I have the perfect solution, believe me! We can cut it off right now, can't we?" He grabbed a butcher knife and made a small cut on the boy's ear, just enough to scare the living daylights out of him. From that day on, any music played on the organ had to be church music, and nothing else.

The church in the cavern next to our house was big enough to hold several hundred people. Regional authorities discouraged the practice of Christianity, but the Turks living in our village looked the other way. We had no problem with our local Turks. It was live and let live.

In another part of the cave were the graves of our ancestors. When we were kids, we would take lanterns and go deep inside and discover all kinds of relics, such as bows, arrows, copper bracelets, and bones, both human and animal. Playing there was one of our favorite childhood pastimes.

Your father, Donik, was a tough kid. Many times he came home with a bloody nose, a scratched face, or a bleeding scalp.

As I told you before, the best-loved Turk living in our area was Dr. Oskan. Everyone respected him. He had a pure white Arabian horse he called *Ateş Parçasi* [Piece of Fire]. Not only did Dr. Oskan usually ride this magnificent animal when making house-calls, sometimes he would run him in races. He let Donik race his horse. Donik rode *Ateş* in eight races, losing only once, and that was by a nose. The doctor loved Donik and would say to Mama Yessaian, "He's my Armenian son."

Your father designed a new style horseshoe and received permission from the doctor to shoe *Ateş* with them. Dr. Oskan said they made a big difference; *Ateş* could run longer distances without faltering. The doctor was very pleased. Since Donik would not accept any money, the doctor gave the boy a pair of binoculars as a gift. Your father could hardly believe his good fortune. Never had he received anything he prized as much. He even took them to bed with him!

When he was fifteen, in 1895, Donik began driving us crazy with arguments in favor of the family moving to Smyrna. From the day *Ateş* had proven the value of Donik's horseshoe design, the boy continually nagged us to go to Smyrna and start a horseshoe business. He insisted that all the horse owners would give us their business. I wasn't so sure. Your dad was impatient with my lack of vision.

"You know that I love you, Nazar," he said, "and that I have great respect for you as my older brother; sometimes I even look upon you as a father — but, *Effendi*,[1] you don't have any imagination and faith in our talents."

"Look, little brother, what would we use for money to get started?"

"Leave that to me; I will find a way."

"Donik, you're bragging again! Where would you find the money? You don't even know anyone in Smyrna."

"No, but you will see. Trust me." he said simply.

I shook my head. However, I had to admit that his ideas sounded promising. Maybe he was right. Just how much money would it take to back a venture of this kind?

We older boys finally made the decision to leave Efkereh, but we didn't tell Donik immediately. We didn't want him badgering us about taking him on the initial journey. If Donik had suspected we were considering moving to the big city, he would have been

[1] A Turkish title of respect, equivalent of "Sir."

the first to pack his bags, driving us all mad with his babbling and his impatience.

Most important, though, he was much too young to risk taking on such a dangerous journey. I had no intention of putting my little brother's life in jeopardy. Besides, we had other plans for Donik — someone had to stay with the women.

When we finally told him that we were going to Smyrna and would send for him after we were settled, the boy was outraged. He fumed and spat at us, roaring like a wounded lion.

"How dare you! This whole scheme was ***my*** idea . . . from the beginning to the end. I've tasted it, dreamed it, morning, noon and night. Now, because you are older than I, you think you have the authority to stop me from reaching my destiny! I will never let this happen. Never! Never!

"I'll be behind you somewhere, behind a bush, a rock, something. And when you get to my cherished city, you're going to find me standing on some high place waiting to welcome you. Besides, you are going to need me to clear away all the obstacles that may lie in our paths!"

We didn't know what to do with him. There was no reasoning with him. He wouldn't shut up about it.

Mother finally intervened. "Take him with you — it was his idea from the beginning. We women can manage things here."

Frankly, I don't think she really wanted to let him go; it was just that he had completely worn her down with his shouting and screaming and she couldn't take it anymore.

And so it was decided. Donik would come with us, but only on condition that he work — no kid stuff, no fooling around. This was serious business. If he wanted to be treated like a man, he had to act like a man.

On the eve of our departure, we readied five horses for us to ride and four jackasses to carry our supplies and our tent.

Mother packed us some marinated lamb for shish kebab, *bulgur* [cracked wheat], and chicken broth. We took *yogurt* [cultured milk] in a sheepskin, *basterma* [dried beef] and several jars of *raki*, a potent drink similar to Greek *ouzo*.

Next, we packed the tools of our trade: hammers, anvils, chisels, vises and bellows. The bellows would be used to flame the coals for the white-hot heat that allowed us to fashion iron into different forms. Last but not least, we loaded our musical instruments on your father's pet donkey, Ju-juke, who was too young to carry heavier loads.

My head was in a whirl — here we were uprooting ourselves, leaving our wives and children, all because of the enthusiastic and persuasive words of a fifteen-year-old.

Donik drove us mad, infuriating us with his boasting and bragging and going on and on about how he was the only one who had any sense, how he had a gold mine in his head, and that it was time to tap the mother lode. He was going to make us all rich, and yak, yak, yak until I was ready to beat him up.

Of course, the true reason for all the anxiety on my part was that I was beginning to have second thoughts about the whole venture. It was so *risky*! It meant changing our whole lives and starting over. Besides, it would be a really dangerous journey from the moment we left the confines of our small town.

Young girls never ventured out of our village alone. The boys were another story. Every now and then a couple would get bold and wander down the road. I remember when I was a boy, two of my friends went off to explore. They were attacked, beaten, and raped by brigands. The boys were in a state of shock, almost dead. Their shame was unbearable, so their parents sent them to live with relatives in another village beyond the mountains. We never saw them again. The villagers, however, talked about it for years. It was a warning to everyone.

This tragic event had burned deep crevices in my mind. And here we were, thinking of playing games with our lives. Of course, your father wasn't concerned. He was much too young to know fear. I was the one who was tormented with anxiety. I dropped to my knees and prayed, asking our Lord to watch over us during our journey.

Donik was the first one up the next morning, full of piss and vinegar, ready to conquer the world. He ran around the house yelling, "Wake up and live! There are adventures and new opportunities waiting for us!"

Oh, how I ached to clobber him. "Shut up, you crazy kid!" I said. "I'll kick your ass if you don't stop being so damned cocky!"

When we got outside, we saw that many of our friends and neighbors had gathered to see us off. Before we could stop him, Donik climbed up on a tree stump and motioned for the people to gather around and listen to what he had to say.

"Today, my brothers and I," he bragged, "will open up the trail to Smyrna. We will reveal the hiding places of the Turkish and Kurdish bandits. We will draw maps and record the time spent to get from one place to another. Then, my brothers and sisters, we will conquer the city of Smyrna with our wit and charm."

We other brothers had already mounted up. I moaned and beseeched the heavens to give me the patience to deal with this impetuous brat. "No Yessaian ever bragged as much as you do," I yelled at him. "God only knows whose genes you carry — some Hittite with a big mouth, I'll bet!"

I ordered him to get on his horse. The little show-off was done with his speech anyway, so he cartwheeled off the tree stump right onto his waiting mount. The four of us just looked at each other and couldn't help but shake our heads and laugh.

We were soon surrounded by friends and neighbors stuffing coins and sweetmeats into our pockets, cheering us on. We felt like new recruits being sent off to fight a heroic battle. Donik had won their hearts.

Now we had enough to eat to last the duration of our trip. No time need be wasted to hunt for or buy food. We also had enough money to last us for some time in Smyrna. I winked at my brothers, warning them not to say anything about his tree-stump act. No need to swell his head any more than it was already.

We again turned the animals toward the road and started out. I instructed the boys never to wander any farther than forty or fifty feet apart, and always to make sure that each of us was within sight of the others.

I told them that every half-hour or so one of us would backtrack to see if we were being followed. We must keep a sharp eye out as we go along to make sure no one surprises us.

Donik immediately raced ahead. This angered me, so I pulled out my revolver and squeezed off a few rounds into the air. He came charging back, wanting to know if anything was wrong.

"Yes, something is wrong! You're already breaking the rules! Going off alone, you will endanger our lives as well as your own if you act this way. Stay put or stay home! Which is it going to be?"

Donik asked forgiveness and promised it wouldn't happen again.

I made my voice as tough as possible, I wanted to impress them with the importance of my words. "Boys, the only way to get to Smyrna is with caution, awareness, praying to Our Lord, and looking out for one another. When we arrive, God willing, let us learn the manners of the city and not act like men from the back country."

It was a beautiful morning, we were full of excitement and anticipation. Donik wouldn't sit still in his saddle. Every now and then he would stand up in the stirrups, put his binoculars to his eyes and look in every direction, pointing out different sights along the trail. All that, and we hadn't even gone a mile yet.

"You better watch it, Donik! Those highwaymen might just be looking for you!"

"Let the bastards come, I'm ready for them!"

CHAPTER THREE
Bound for Smyrna

The first four days went smoothly. It seemed too good to be true. I must admit we got overconfident. We had covered about a hundred miles and were still enjoying our adventure. We had seen wild boars, snakes, and wolves. But what we were really looking for was two-legged animals who rode fast horses and had ammunition belts strapped across their chests.

On the fifth evening, we unloaded our animals, fed and watered them, settled down to have our evening meal, and poured a few glasses of *raki* to celebrate our historic journey. We were going to baptize your father with his first alcoholic drink — this was the way young Armenian males were inducted into manhood. I ordered Donik and Artin to gather some firewood.

"Artin, stay here and rest, I can do it alone," Donik said confidently. "I'll be right back."

We were about to make our first toast when Donik's screams suddenly rang out. I called to Artin to grab his rifle and follow me, and I told the others to stay put and guard the camp.

Artin and I ran into the woods, guided by Donik's frantic cries. We found him surrounded by five snarling wolves, their fangs flashing like sabers. They were circling Donik, ready to tear him apart.

I whispered to Artin to stay calm. We had to shoot carefully, to make sure our bullets found their mark. Otherwise, the wolves might attack. We chose our targets. We fired two shots and two wolves went down. At the sound of the gunfire, the other three dashed away through the brush.

Donik's face was as white as a bowl of yogurt. I instructed him to piss in a jar, and then I made him drink his urine. Donik nearly gagged, but he followed instructions. We all understood it was a folk remedy to prevent shock. The four of us grimaced as the boy downed the odious liquid, but I have to admit it also gave us great pleasure to see the big mouth get his comeuppance.

It seemed to work, for he soon pulled himself together and was his normal brash self again. He jumped up on a rock, and we all groaned in agony and covered our ears as he started to speak.

"What did I tell you!" he yelled at the top of his lungs. "Don't you see? Nothing can stop us now, not even fierce wolves!"

That close call hadn't taken him down a peg at all. Didn't ***anything*** affect that little runt?

"Get down from there, *deli bok*! [you crazy shit!]. We don't have time for your crazy speeches. Let's eat and get to bed early tonight. God only knows what tomorrow will bring."

The next morning, we woke up refreshed and got an early start. Donik's binoculars always dangled from his neck. He would bring them to his eyes every now and then and comment on the beauty of the unusual landscape. Now and then we heard him mumbling softly to himself, "I'm going to be famous — Smyrna will recognize me as one of her great sons."

Because he was aware that we didn't want to hear any more of his bragging, he tried to keep his thoughts to himself. Still, sometimes, he would slip and carry on again. All I had to do was throw him a disgusted look and he would shut up.

As was our custom, we stopped every two or three hours to rest the animals, feed them, and rub down their muscles. We also rotated their burdens, giving all of them a turn at the heavy as well as the light loads. Your father's pet donkey carried the same load the whole time; he was still a baby and his load was the lightest.

As a joke, Donik had named him Ju-juke, which was a Turkish expression for a baby chick. Armenians used the same words in reference to a penis. While we were at rest, suddenly one of the animals was screeching in agony. Ju-juke! He had caught his leg between two large rocks while cavorting, had panicked before we could get to him, lunged forward and broke a limb. He lay on his side, panting and moaning in pain.

We spent two hours of our precious time trying to convince Donik that there was nothing we could do for his suffering pet except to destroy him. I signaled the other three boys to form a circle around Donik, blocking his vision so he couldn't see what I was doing. I took out my razor and with one quick thrust sliced through the poor beast's jugular vein. I wiped the blood from the razor to shield it from your father's eyes, hoping he hadn't seen what I had done.

In times of stress, a lie is the only comfort. "Look!" I called over to your father. "He not only managed to break his leg but he also cut himself when he fell on this jagged rock."

Little Ju-juke was becoming weaker with every dying breath, softly closing and opening his eyes until, mercifully, they stayed closed. Hoping to comfort Donik, I told him that Ju-juke's soul had gone to donkey heaven.

I looked down at the animal. There were better things we could do than to let him rot and be picked clean by the buzzards. I began to dress the carcass, ignoring Donik's cries and indignant protests. I cut some of the meat into cubes, pushed a skewer through them, added onions and hot peppers and roasted it on a fire the boys had built. We warmed up the bulgur pilaf and sat down to our evening meal. But Donik wouldn't eat. He was very sullen and depressed.

After our meal, I salted the rest of the meat and loaded it on one of the jackasses. We set off again. An hour later, the air had turned decidedly colder. The road had taken an upward turn, and we had been climbing for some time. Since we'd left Efkereh, we had suffered many changes of temperature as the road rose and dropped, sometimes experiencing extremes of heat or cold in the space of a few hours. The nights were always cold as we passed through barren wasteland and high plateaus. The days were hot or cold depending on our altitude.

As the gray evening clouds grew darker, we stopped for the night. Our thoughts turned to our families and homes. I wish I were home now, I mused, touching my wife here and there, hearing her whisper, "Don't, don't, the family might be watching us," all the while leading me to our room, locking the door behind us. I missed the sights and joyful sounds of our children. I wondered if we would ever see them again.

For some unexplained reason, we didn't think to put anyone on watch that night.

The next morning, on the sixth day, I couldn't sit up in bed. The ceiling of the tent was resting on my chest. The canvas was ice cold. We were buried under snow!

We got out of the tent, ate a quick meal, and reorganized ourselves. As we set out, Donik was silent. He was still mourning his pet donkey. Although we tried to cheer up Donik, we couldn't penetrate the barrier.

A few hours later, we had left the cold behind us and now the sun hammered on us as we rode along. The only sounds to be heard were the clip-clopping of the animals over the sun-baked ground, and the banging of pots and pans swinging from their backs.

Suddenly the silence was broken. "You cannibals!" Donik shouted, choking with anger and looking straight at me. "You acted like the wild wolves about to tear my flesh! There's no difference between the wolves and what you barbarians did! YOU ATE MY JU-JUKE!"

Our first reaction was to laugh; Mardiros giggled so wildly, that he almost fell out of his saddle. "If we ate your precious jewel," he managed to gasp, "what did you use to piss with this morning?"

Donik got the joke, but held his laughter by biting his tongue. Donik was really angry — it was the first time he had ever shown disrespect for his elders.

I had had enough of his childish behavior. "My dear little boy, what did you want from us? Was it our fault that your pet was trying to screw all the females in our caravan? Come on, now, you speak out like a man yet think like a child.

"You keep saying you're our leader. How can you be a leader if you let your emotions take control of you? A good leader has to be tough and take on whatever comes without letting his heart get in the way of his head."

The next fifteen miles were traveled in absolute silence. Then Donik turned to each of us and apologized for the way he had behaved. He began giggling at what Mardiros had said about his "Ju-juke," and before long, we were all laughing and joking. After a while, we began to talk enthusiastically about our future.

Without warning, Donik stood up in his stirrups, threw his hands to the heavens and shouted, "I'm going to wrap up the city of Smyrna and put it in my back pocket!"

Oh, my God, I thought, what have I done? Which was worse? Letting him mourn his pet or hearing him brag again?

■ ■ ■ ■

Uncle Nazar looked around to see if my father was within hearing range. "I don't want him to know that I was speaking of him. He might start bragging about his heroic adventures again, and I couldn't stand it at my age. I already have one foot in the grave and don't need a push to meet my Maker."

I started giggling madly when he said this. Father heard the commotion and came in. "What's so funny?"

"Oh, nothing, Dad. Uncle Nazar was just telling me about his very fat girlfriend and how he had to push her up the stairs because she was all out of breath and couldn't make it to the top floor." Uncle Nazar gazed at me in open admiration of my quick thinking.

"Well, that's enough for tonight, Artin,"[1] Dad said. "It's almost two in the morning, I think it's time we all went to bed."

I went over and kissed them both goodnight.

As I lay in bed, I replayed the stories in my head and imagined myself with them on the road.

---

[1] Artin is a diminutive of Harutiun [Paschal], which is Harry's Armenian name.

CHAPTER FOUR
A Flirtation with Allah

Morning came not a minute too soon for me. I jumped out of bed, wide awake and eager to hear more tales about my father's youthful adventures. I roused Uncle Nazar from a sound sleep.

It seemed to take him forever to get up, pull on his robe, and step into his slippers. Soon after drinking a cup of mother's strong Turkish coffee, his eyes clicked wide open, and I could see the cobwebs washing away from his brain. He sucked in the smoke of his first Lucky Strike of the day, leaned back in his favorite lounge chair, rested his head on the cushion, and narrowed his eyes as he searched his mind to pick up his story where he'd left off.

■ ■ ■ ■

The next three days went smoothly. We stopped to feed the beasts and our own groaning stomachs. Of course, we always made sure the animals were fed and watered properly before we took care of our own needs.

The boys started a fire and we reheated the meat on skewers with onions, peppers, and cloves of garlic and some olive oil. As flames licked at the skewers, the air became filled with the delicious smell of roasted meat and vegetables. We also had some *pita* [flat bread] which we warmed over the fire and cut into small pieces, to use for scooping up the pilaf and tossing it into our mouths. There in the wild, we had no authority looking over our shoulders. We were enjoying our freedom — a small freedom, but freedom nevertheless.

We figured that it wouldn't be long before we reached the outskirts of Smyrna. Donik kept wiping his binoculars clean and looking eagerly in the direction of the city. As we reached a prominent hilltop we finally heard him shout, "Hey, fellows, hey! Look!" He bounced excitedly up and down in his saddle. "I can see the ships in the harbor!"

We all took turns looking through the glasses at the magnificent sight. I couldn't believe it. We had reached Smyrna without any trouble. What good luck! We were within a day's journey.

We decided to stop for the night. We did our chores and then sat around the fire to relax. We toasted each other several times for our good fortune. Then we unwrapped our musical instruments and played several Armenian and Turkish dance tunes, including the Turkish warrior's saber dance. Afterward, we switched to slow, sentimental ballads, which reminded us of the loved ones we had left behind.

The trip had taken its toll. We were very tired. I told the boys to put away their instruments and get some sleep. Our final day on the road would be a long haul and we needed to be well-rested. Because of our excitement and fatigue, we again neglected to put someone on watch for the night.

The following morning, I could hear the boys moaning and groaning when I woke up. I figured that maybe they'd had too much *raki* the night before and were paying for it with hangovers. Suddenly, the ugly snout of a rifle barrel was shoved through the tent flap. I couldn't see who was at the other end of the gun, but a loud voice bellowed in Turkish: "*Çikin, gâvurlar!* [Come outside, you infidels!] First throw out all your weapons and come out one by one with your hands in the air. We'd just as soon shoot you dogs, so don't give us an excuse to do it! What are you fuckin' *gâvurlar* doing on this road anyway?"

My heart sank as Donik said sarcastically, "We are traveling in a *free* country, aren't we?"

As frightened as I was, I had to bite my tongue to keep from laughing at your father's remark. I heard Artin snicker.

It's a miracle they didn't kill Donik on the spot. Instead, the Turk fixed him with a murderous stare and spat out, "Shut your goddamned mouth, you fuckin' Armenian dog! Get on your knees, you sons of bitches! Let's see if we can put the fear of

Allah into your hearts! Recite the creed, "There is no god, but God; and Mohammed is his prophet."[1]

Donik was the only one still standing. I was just wondering what foolish thing he would say next when he opened his mouth.

"I have my own God who rules all the people of the world, all the four-legged animals, and even the two-legged animals such as you!"

The silence was deafening. My knees started to shake. I waited for a shot to ring out. The Turk's rifle was aimed at Donik's head, the hammer cocked, his finger on the trigger, ready to squeeze!

I jumped up and pushed the gun aside. In the same instant it fired. I quickly grabbed Donik by the neck and shoved him down on his knees.

The ugly Turk had his saber in hand now, touching Donik's scalp with its sharp edge. Your father, I'm proud to say, didn't flinch. "You would be just another of the many infidel[2] dogs I've put into the ground. So don't antagonize me, *gâvur!*" He deftly sliced a small gash in Donik's head. Dark red blood came gushing out and streamed down his face. I grabbed the man's arm. "I beg forgiveness, Sir, please overlook the actions of my immature brother. He will now do as you ask, Effendi!"

The brute erupted with a stream of obscenities and blasphemies. "You're lucky, infidel! Your brother has persuaded me. I was about to cut your balls off. Anyway, we're taking all your animals and possessions! By rights we should kill you for having

---

[1] The God of the Muslims is in fact the same God as that of the Christians [Al'läh=El'ōhim, also called Yahweh], although many uneducated Muslims and Christians did not understand this. The major difference between the two religions is that the Muslims believe that Mohammed was the greatest and the last prophet, supplanting the revelations of Jesus. It was for this reason that Christians and Jews were "protected" by the Muslims, if they submitted, as "Peoples of the Book" [the Bible], and not considered pagans.

[2] An infidel, is one who does not accept Mohammed. A pagan is one who does not believe in the true God. Untutored people, of course, did not understand this distinction.

guns." He turned to his men and made a gesture for them to take our things.

"You are lucky, we leave you with your heads intact and your tent. As for all that iron, you can shove it up your asses. We have no use for it."

And with that, he called to his men and they rode off into the woods, leading away our precious horses and jackasses with all our money and supplies.

I immediately turned to take care of the gash in Donik's head, applying tobacco and clay to it, and binding it so that the bleeding stopped.

"Oh my God! What do we do now?" Mardiros wanted to know.

"What's there to do but go home," Hovsep replied. "We don't have one copper coin among us, nor animals to carry what little was left by those bastards."

"Let's not rush to a decision; let's think this over without getting emotional," I said.

Donik jumped up and shouted, "WE CAN'T QUIT NOW! WE'VE COME THIS FAR AND I'M NOT GOING BACK!"

Mardiros, Hovsep, and Artin yelled at Donik to keep quiet. They said that our misfortune was all his fault and that we had no business leaving Efkereh and going to Smyrna in the first place. I grew angry with them. "Listen you fellows, shut up; fault-finding is not going to get us anywhere!"

Deaf to the grumbling of his brothers, Donik went to where he'd hidden his binoculars the night before and pulled them out. He carefully wiped the lenses clean, put them to his eyes, and searched the horizon. "Hey, Nazar! There's a house over in that direction."

He paused to make sure he had our attention before going on. "Why don't we wrap all our remaining possessions in the tent so the five of us can drag them toward the house. Maybe we can get help there."

There was really nothing else to do, and so for the next hour we dragged the canvas filled with our stuff over the washboard surface of the trail. We had to stop several times to catch our breath.

When we got within a half mile of the house, Donik and I left the boys and went to try our luck. We prayed the people would be Armenians.

At our knock, an elderly gentleman cracked the door open a few inches. He could tell we were Armenians and we could tell that he was a Turk. Turks can identify an Armenian from among a hundred Turks, and an Armenian can do the same with a Turk.

"Peace be with you, Effendi," Donik said with disarming cordiality. "My brothers and I ran into trouble on the trail. We were on our way to Smyrna to convert to Islam. As you know, Effendi, some of us Armenians love this land and want to be a full part of it. Well, Sir, we were attacked by a band of *gâvurlar.* They were Armenian bandits." I almost choked when I heard what he said.

"*The robbers were Armenians?*" The Turk was skeptical.

"Yes, Effendi. They took our money and stole our beasts of burden. The men were so brazen they even let us know their names: the big bearded one was called Mesrob, and the other one — he had only one eye — was Minas. Perhaps you have heard of these scoundrels?"

No, he said, he hadn't. But the old Turk, intrigued by our little brother's tale, opened the door wider. "Come in! Come in! Please make yourselves at home." He startled us when he shouted out. *"Dudük Hanim! Gel buraya orospu!"* [Lady Dudük! Come here, you whore!]. A woman in her early thirties, obviously his wife, came running into the room.

She had been listening through the door and had seen through Donik's lies at once. She walked in, took one look at us, and hated us on sight. We knew, however, that she wouldn't dare express her feeling; it would be an insult to her husband's authority. The husband was the ruler in a Turkish home. The wife's place was in the kitchen and the bedroom.

Dudük Hanim's penetrating black eyes were focused on the two of us as she gently touched her husband's arm and said, "What is your pleasure, Effendi?"

Without looking at her, he barked, "Bring food and drink for our young guests!"

She ran off to the kitchen without a word.

"I am known as Arabagee [Wagon Man] around here," the old Turk went on. "My business is renting horses and wagons to farmers who want to haul their goods to market in Smyrna. That's been my livelihood for the past sixty years . . . I am nearing my seventy-seventh year on this earth. Allah must have heard your prayers and sent you to me. Well, then," said Arabagee with a gleam in his eye, "what happened between yourselves and the Armenian bandits?"

Donik took a deep breath and went on with his tale. "Well, Sir, they took all eight of our beasts, all our money, all our food, and even carried off some of my brothers' shoes. We were fortunate that they didn't kill us. If we were blessed with a few horses and enough food to reach Smyrna, we would be assured that Allah was holding out his protective arms to us."

I gazed at my brother in wonder. Where did he ever learn to tell tall tales like that?

The old Turk looked pleased. He came over and kissed each of us on the forehead. "My sons, ask for your needs and they will be given to you." He handed us glasses of *raki* which he poured from a bottle. "A toast to your new religion, the true faith. When you accept the true Prophet and submit to God's will, your lives will be made easy."

I became very nervous. I didn't want to drink to that toast. During all this time, Dudük Hanim was standing behind her husband cursing the two of us in silence, her mouth twisting open and shut in fury.

The old Turk turned to her and asked for a basket of food and a bottle of *raki* for us to take to our three waiting brothers. "Yes, Effendi," she replied softly, "this minute."

Arabagee turned back to us. "Now, then, what can I do for you, Effendis?"

"We would like to borrow three wagons, Sir?" Donik ventured.

"Can you make do with two?"

Before Donik could say anything, I quickly accepted. "Effendi, that will be fine, you are kind. We will be very careful with your animals."

"I trust that once you have changed your religion and gained employment, you will return my wagons to me."

We nodded our heads in agreement. I couldn't believe our good luck.

Dudük Hanim came back with a basket of food. The Turk took one look at the half-filled basket and slapped his wife across the face. "We're not feeding children," the old Turk shouted, "these are grown men! Don't be so goddamn stingy with ***my*** guests, you tramp. Take this basket back and fill it up like it should be." She obediently went back to fill the basket. Arabagee followed his wife into the kitchen cursing all the while.

Donik started complaining to me. "If you had let me ask for four wagons, we would have ended up with three."

"Two wagons are fine," I said, "stop bitching. Don't be so greedy." The boy couldn't help it. It was simply his nature to want to make a good deal.

Donik started to laugh over the success of his lie. "I don't feel we have done anything wrong. It was a matter of life and death for us. We, ourselves, have helped many Turks out of difficulties. So what is wrong with one of them helping us?" In reality, the only person who got hurt was Dudük Hanim, and she was a stingy bitch.

Donik thought it was all good clean fun. "A Turk likes to punch his wife once or twice a week. The wives expect it. Some even like it. They nag their husbands until they feel the back of their hands. Pity the Turk who has four wives. Hey, brother, would you like to have four wives?"

I gave Donik a dirty look and his snicker turned to a scowl. By this time, Dudük Hanim returned with the basket of food and Arabagee invited us to follow him to the stable to get the horses. He picked out four horses and hitched them to two wagons for the trip.

The old man came over to us, kissed us on both cheeks, and said, "Go with God, He will protect you."

We thanked him over and over, expressing our deepest appreciation.

I was feeling guilty, but Donik had the silliest grin on his face when he hugged the old Turk.

We loaded the wagons, climbed up, said our farewells, and headed out to the trail. I kept thinking of the food Dudük Hanim had prepared. Suppose she had poisoned it?

It was a short ride to where the boys were waiting. When they saw us returning with two wagons, they greeted us with waving arms and shouts of joy.

When they heard of the game Donik had played with Arabagee, they ruffled Donik's hair and slapped him playfully on the butt. They heaped him with praise and congratulated each other for having such a clever brother.

Donik was in his glory; once again he was the man of the hour.

CHAPTER FIVE
Our Good Samaritan

Puffing heartily on a Lucky Strike, Uncle Nazar complained that he wished he could kick his dreadful habit and stop smoking. He shook a yellow-stained finger at me and said, "Boy, don't ever start smoking this shit; it will stunt your growth and eventually kill you." Then he took a big gulp of *raki* and pointed at the glass. "This, on the other hand, is good for you, if you don't overdo it."

I made sure to agree with everything he said, since I was eager for him to return to the story of the Yessaian brothers without prolonged side-trip lectures. "Yes, Uncle, you are right. Now can we get on with your story?"

His response was a yawn, actually more of a bellow that would make a camel jealous.

"These are the most fascinating stories I've ever heard, Uncle. Can't we get on with it?"

He must have been feeling mellow; instead of roaring at me not to interrupt, he gave me a kindly smile, leaned over and patted my face, and then gave my nose a tweak.

■ ■ ■ ■

We had traveled some twenty miles and were now seeing sights alien to our eyes. The beautiful blue-green Aegean Sea, the crowded harbor, the distinct outline of the city itself were all before us. Realizing that we would be in Smyrna within the hour, our hearts beat faster.

How were the cosmopolitan citizens of this great city going to react to five Armenian hicks from a village? How could we get money for food and shelter? How would we raise the capital for our little business? How long would it take for our enterprise to make enough money to support the five of us? When would we be able to send for our families?

These questions gnawed at me, spinning around in my brain like wooden horses on a merry-go-round. Only Artin shared my concerns. Mardiros and Hovsep were in a state of ecstasy, with Donik as their self-confident leader.

We entered the fabulous city. We found a caravanserai to shelter the horses and store the wagons. Donik told the innkeeper to water and feed the animals and bed them down for the night. He said that we would take care of the bill at the end of the week.

Donik laid his hands on the man's shoulders, looked him straight in the eyes, and said with assurance, "If you take good care of our animals, we will give you all of our business in the future." He was putting on airs again, like some patrician, and the innkeeper swallowed every morsel.

When we got outside, I cautioned Donik. "This is not Efkereh. Here they skin you alive and throw your ass in jail when you fail to pay your bills."

He just shrugged. "Don't worry about a thing, I'll take care of it. Trust me."

I figured either this kid had a magic wand or he was absolutely crazy and belonged in a nut house. I gave up worrying and decided to join the others for sightseeing.

We walked along the esplanade bordering the harbor. The flags of many nations flew over the ships at anchor. We had never seen a real ship before. We were impressed.

And the sidewalk cafés! They were all along the esplanade, each with its own mixture of exotic aromas and sounds. Middle Eastern music drifted from the cafés.

Sailors of all nations walked arm in arm with local "girls." Donik couldn't keep his eyes off those painted women. To be fair, none of us could. They looked gorgeous to us.

The girls wore tight-fitting skirts and silk stockings with the seams traveling down the sensuous curves of their legs and disappearing into their high-heeled shoes.

"I sure would like to have one of those girls hanging on my arm," Donik said wistfully. "Think of all the fun I could have."

That was the first time I had ever heard Donik make even a slight reference to sex. I gave him a severe look. "You are not going to play around with these sluts. You will marry a girl back in Efkereh. You better get that straight in your head!"

"Hey, I just thought of fooling around a little," Donik responded sheepishly.

"Oh, yeah? Think of the diseases you can catch. There's one called elephantiasis. That little rash will make your balls swell up like melons and you'll have to carry your pair of beauties around in a wheelbarrow!"

Just the thought of our little brother pushing his precious cargo around the streets of Smyrna in a wheelbarrow broke us up in laughter.

A little later, we reached the part of town where the fashionable shops were located. We found it fascinating to do window shopping. When we peeked into the window of a lady's boutique, we snickered when we saw the flimsy women's clothing on display. We imagined how revealing these lacy things would be if draped on a woman's body.

We continued on our walk. Our stomachs began growling with hunger. At one of the sidewalk cafés, we noticed a distinguished old gentleman, obviously an Armenian, playing *tavlu* with another man. Donik kept eyeing the gentleman. I knew the wheels were whirling around in that scheming mind of his.

"You fellows wait here," he told us. "There's somebody I have to talk to."

"All right, go ahead," I yelled at him, "but don't talk yourself into something we can't get out of." Before I could say anything more to him, he was already gone.

Donik approached the gentleman, leaned over, and began talking to him. The man gestured to the empty chair beside him, and our little brother sat down, still talking a mile a minute. After not more than half an hour, the dignified gentleman stood up and shook hands with Donik. We saw the gentleman give orders to a waiter to pull up another table and some chairs. Donik turned to us and called us over.

The distinguished gentleman introduced himself and cordially shook our hands. "I'm an Armenian like yourselves. My name is Sarkis 'Aga' Kouradjian. My distinguished friends have given me the honorific title of 'Aga.' My Turkish friends call me

'Doshchi[1] Sarkis Aga.' My Armenian friends call me simply 'Sarkis Aga.'"

Sarkis Aga was tall and slim, and obviously strong of limb. His handshake was firm. His eyes were penetrating black spheres, and he had a full head of shining silver hair.

"Please, my compatriots," he said graciously, "have a seat at my table and be at ease. You are my guests."

He smiled at Donik. "Donik has told me about your family and the troubles you had on your journey to Smyrna. It took courage to make such a trip."

I put my arm around Donik's shoulders. "To tell the truth, we were persuaded by our young brother here. The credit, or blame, goes to him."

Sarkis Aga laughed pleasantly. "Yes, he is very persuasive, this young man. In fact, he has just talked me into giving all of you jobs. If you do well, then I will consider setting you up in your chosen work. Right now I will give you one week's pay in advance so that you can buy food. I will provide space in an old building where you can stay. Once you begin to earn money, you can repay me."

His generosity overwhelmed us. We couldn't believe our good fortune. "How can we thank you," we said almost choking with emotion.

Our benefactor chuckled again. "Well then, it's settled. It is now up to you to prove my faith in you. For now, let's eat, drink, and celebrate your arrival in Smyrna. *Pari Yegakh* [Welcome]."

■ ■ ■ ■

We moved into Sarkis Aga's building that evening. It wasn't much, but what did we country boys care. We had a roof over

---

[1] *Dosh* in Turkish means "rock." A literal translation would be "The man of rock." He was called that because he supplied the city with stones from his quarry for monuments, roads, and buildings. *Aga* is a title of respect superior to that of Effendi.

our heads. The robbers had left us with our sleeping gear so we had bedding for the night. Mardiros, Hovsep, Artin and I still couldn't believe our good fortune. We were so happy. We were convinced that the Lord had sent Sarkis Aga as our "Good Samaritan."

■ ■ ■ ■

We started working for Sarkis Aga and were finally earning money. A week after our arrival, we decided it was time to return Arabagee's wagons. Donik and I harnessed up the horses and took the rigs back to the old Turk with our deepest thanks and a small sum of money.

Arabagee was overjoyed to see us. His confidence had not been misplaced. He showed us warm hospitality. Donik, of course, carried on the charade by brashly informing him that we had become Moslems as we kissed his hand. The old man's eyes twinkled.

Dudük Hanim was surprised to see us. I don't think she believed we would ever return the horses and wagons. She was as sullen as before, but behaved with circumspection.

We left the old man with the traditional kiss on both sides of his face. I think a bond had developed between us.

■ ■ ■ ■

We learned later that Sarkis Aga helped lots of Armenians who migrated from the interior to Smyrna. He wanted our people to succeed. Sarkis Aga also helped local Turks and Greeks. He was well-known for his generosity. He was a good man.

To Donik, Sarkis Aga's help was nothing out of the ordinary, just a simple business deal between two businessmen.

Sarkis Aga was a religious man. He and his wife — a very devout, caring person — supported both the Armenian and the Greek churches by donating time and large sums of money to them. Sarkis Aga was certainly an astute businessman, yet he knew doing good helped him to do well.

Several months later we had proven ourselves as hard workers and also had managed to save a little money. Sarkis Aga then did as he had promised. He provided us with a small shop in the section where the artisans worked. The store was quite suitable. When Sarkis Aga handed the keys to Donik, he said, "Remember the rent is due on the first day of the month. May God bless your endeavor."

We organized the shop and immediately went to work making all those things we had made in Efkereh as well as decorative wrought iron gates, fences, and decorative window bars, which were popular in Smyrna.

We also made a few horseshoes according to Donik's design. A few days later, Sarkis Aga came to visit. He was impressed by our progress. We also showed him the special horseshoes Donik had designed. Sarkis Aga took several sets with him to try on his stable of Arabian racing horses. Donik was real excited by the Aga's interest.

When Sarkis Aga left, the boys gathered around our creative little brother praising him to high heaven.

God forgive them, I said to myself, for they know not what mouth they have unlatched.

There were no tree stumps in the store, so Donik stood on a chair and repeated his blow-by-blow description of how he had managed to persuade Sarkis Aga to aid us. I tuned out, and fell asleep in the middle of it, a thousand questions whirling around in my mind.

My worries were for nothing, it seems. The next week Sarkis Aga came back to our shop and said he had tried out the horseshoes and liked them. He had also demonstrated their advantage for the horses to several of his close friends. All were eager to buy. "Now then," he said, "what will you charge?"

I named a modest sum. He shook his head, no, and indicated it was too low. "You have overhead now: rent, charcoal, coal oil, iron, and entertainment for your best customers. That is expected here in Smyrna.

"You must take them to lunch or dinner, or to the bathhouses. I own five Turkish bathhouses where you can treat them to a bath and massage. Tell the manager to put it on your bill, and I will give you a discount when you pay.

"You must add all these expenses to the price of your goods. Otherwise, you will go broke." He told us to charge two English pounds. We accepted his advice. Now, I thought, we were really on our way to success.

■ ■ ■ ■

Our little business flourished almost immediately. It was a gold mine. The money started to roll in. Donik got cockier by the day. He figured it was all his doing and, in a sense, it was. He never let us forget that we wanted to leave him at home to mind the women and children. "What would you have done without me?" he would tease.

As money went into the cash box, Donik would smile and go, "Tch, tch, tch," and then laugh wildly. I loved my baby brother, but his behavior was grating my nerves. I must admit, though, that he had taken hold of our fortunes and had done a fine job so far. Everything was going our way; the future looked bright.

Sarkis Aga sent his wealthy friends to our shop to order custom-made wrought iron fences and decorative ornaments for their homes. This was a large and profitable part of our business. Many of them wanted to buy our special horseshoes and the orders were piling up. We could hardly keep up with them. Donik was bursting with pride. He painted a few of the horseshoes gold and nailed them to the wall. Then he placed a sign underneath that read: "WHAT EVERY HORSE YEARNS FOR." There was no restraining him now.

We were working seven days a week and up to ten or twelve hours a day. It was hard on all of us, but we stuck to it. We wanted to succeed.

We could make anything — horseshoes, kitchen utensils, fences, ornaments — it didn't matter. We had become quite skilled. Donik would heat the metal in the furnace, cut and shape it in crude form, then pass it to us for finishing. The rest of us performed particular operations, keeping the metal hot as it was passed from one to the other. This "production line" helped us to make things more efficiently.

One day, Sarkis Aga came in to inform us that the Smyrna mounted police department, the *zaptiye*, was willing to sign a contract with us to supply them with horseshoes. Sarkis Aga asked for a five percent commission for his sale. The contract would be lucrative, and his commission substantial. Sarkis Aga instructed us to send his share of the money as a gift to the Armenian and Greek churches, in our own names. He was teaching us charity.

■ ■ ■ ■

Our business kept growing and growing. We were being swamped with orders and were making money hand over fist. The shop was too crowded now. Too small for our needs. We needed a whole building and went ahead and rented one from Sarkis Aga. Still, we couldn't keep up with our orders. Something had to be done.

Besides, Donik complained constantly that all he did was work, work, work. He had no time to play. So what did our little brother do? He decided to make a metal-cutting apparatus to speed up production.

He worked at it for months, and kept at it during the wee hours after closing time. One morning we found him standing in cold water to stop his feet from swelling. He had been on his feet for more than eleven hours straight, in the same spot! We told him he would kill himself if he didn't slow down.

"Look, I want the money, but I don't want to work hard forever. I want to play six months and work six months. If the good Lord gives you a brain, then you should use it to make life better for yourself and those around you."

Finally, the machine was finished. It was gigantic and impressive. The details of the contraption are somewhat fuzzy in my mind . . . . Oh, yes, I remember now . . . he had rigged up a horizontal blade that moved up and down between two sturdy vertical supports. The hardened steel blade had weights on top of it to make it come down fast and hard. He arranged pulleys with chains to raise the heavy blade up to its home base. When it reached the top, a spring-loaded pin would snap in to hold it in place. When he pushed down on a floor pedal, the motion would release the head and it would come down with a heavy thud into a parallel slot cut into a large anvil-type base, cutting anything placed over the slot.

He honed the blade in such a way that it had a shearing effect rather than a chopping one. Now we could cut metal to size, without heat, in an instant, saving forty percent of our cutting time. We were also able to cut iron into uniform pieces, without any guesswork or waste, saving us almost twenty percent in raw materials. What a feat our little genius had accomplished! Now he wanted his reward.

We agreed that for about eighteen to twenty days of the month, Donik would supply us with cut metal for wrought iron fences, horseshoes, door knockers, mailboxes, kitchen utensils, fireplace ornaments, garden tools, and wagon hitches and the rest of our product line. The remaining days of the month would belong to him to do with as he pleased.

Our cocky inventor walked around with a grin on his face from ear to ear; his pockets jingled with gold pieces. One day, he decided to look the part of a wealthy young manufacturer and marched to the best tailor in town to get fitted for a couple of suits.

The tailor made suits out of fabric imported from London, fashioning them into what the city's elites were wearing about town and in the exclusive cafés. The tailor was an expert fitter. His customers, some of them foreign merchants, came from as far away as Egypt, Persia, and Russia. Clients could wait up to three weeks just for a fitting, and another four weeks for the suit to be finished.

When Donik walked into the shop, the clerks looked him up and down and refused to wait on him. They laughed when he explained he wanted to be fitted for two suits. He still wore his village garb — pantaloons that ballooned out on the sides all the way down to his ankles where they were wrapped tightly with ribbon-like bindings, sandals with no socks, and an oversized cotton jacket with sleeves rolled back. He looked like a backwoods hick.

"*Burdan siktir ol, pezevenk*!" [Get the fuck out of here, you pimp!], they said with derision.

"*Senin gibi eşeklerin kafalari bokunan dolu*" [Jackasses such as you are loaded with shit in the head], Donik replied haughtily. He then turned around and stalked out.

Our front door banged open and Donik came in as mad as all hell. "Those idiots took one look at me and thought I was a hick. They wouldn't even wait on me. They told me to get the fuck out of there." Then he began cursing all of humanity — Turks, Greeks, Armenians, whatever. He shouted that it was all God's fault, that He had made men such dunderheads, such narrow, selfish beings. "If God created man, He should have done a better job of it. Most men are just plain bastards. What kind of world is this where people can't be decent to one another?"

"Listen, Donik, you're just mad because you didn't get your suits. It's no big deal. Stop ranting and raving and just go to Sarkis Aga. With just a snap of his fingers, he'll get them for you."

Sarkis Aga was outraged when he heard what had happened to Donik. This man was Sarkis Aga's own tailor. Then he looked at Donik and laughed. "Well, my boy, you can hardly blame them. Just look at you. What kind of businessman are you? You look like a bumpkin from the provinces! You are still wearing pantaloons, no socks, and your feet are filthy. On top of that, you haven't even washed your hands or face this morning. You are a sorrowful sight and you smell like a goat. Get yourself cleaned up and meet me in front of the tailor shop this afternoon."

Donik went to the bathhouse and gave himself a good scrubbing. He came out looking clean and combed. He dressed and went off to meet Sarkis Aga.

When Sarkis Aga walked into the tailor shop with Donik, the clerks got a bit nervous. Sarkis Aga demanded to see their father, the *usta* [expert]. When the master tailor came out, he smiled and shook Sarkis Aga's hand warmly. When the *usta* was informed of Donik's unpleasant experience in the shop that morning, he begged the Aga's pardon. "My jackass sons are stupid. Please let me wait on your young friend myself."

The *usta* gave his sons a look that could kill. "My young Effendi," he fawned over Donik, "why didn't you tell my worthless sons that you were a friend of the most highly respected man in all Smyrna? Come, let us see what we can do to please you."

Donik smiled to himself. Just a few hours ago these Turks treated him as if he were garbage. Now this famous tailor was bowing and scraping, treating him like a prince.

Donik went wild spending money. He ordered two suits, six tailor-made shirts, twelve pairs of socks, a pair of men's garters, twelve sets of undergarments, a pair of shoes, a pair of riding boots, and a *fez*.[1]

After five weeks, Donik's agonizing wait for his suits was over. The *usta* himself came to our shop, followed by his assistant carrying several boxes. "It is not my regular practice to deliver, but I wanted to meet your brothers and to tell them that your family is always welcome in my store. Here are your clothes, wear them in good health."

Donik wore his fez tilted to the side, unlike most Turks who wore theirs squarely on top of the head. He must have been imitating the way American sailors wore their jaunty caps. He admired the Americans, and dreamed of going to America someday, if for no other reason than "to buy a Ford."

■ ■ ■ ■

Uncle Nazar paused and lit up yet another Lucky Strike, then he sipped from yet another cup of Turkish coffee.

"I really shouldn't keep referring to your father as our 'little' brother. He wasn't little anymore. He had grown taller than the

---

[1] A brimless, cone-shaped, flat-crowned hat made of red felt, with a tassel. Favored in this period by "modern" Muslims who did not want to wear the traditional turban.

rest of us, nearly six feet tall . . . and he sported a fine moustache, too. He was a handsome man."

"I love these stories," I said enraptured, "they are like the movies, Uncle."

"The movies are fake," he shot back, "these stories are real. You must remember them and pass them on to your children. Children should know their roots — a tree stands taller when it knows its roots."

■ ■ ■ ■

It was now 1897, and your father, decked out in his new clothes, was ready to take on the world. He was full of self-confidence. Donik now seemed to think of himself as a big shot and wanted to mix with the elite of the city who frequented the popular clubs.

One evening, Donik dressed himself in his new clothes. I must admit he cut quite a figure. He went down to the harbor and sought out one of the better cafés frequented by the rich and powerful Turks. The café was dimly lit. Waiters buzzed about filling orders, replenishing drinks, and serving *meze* [hors d'oeuvre]. The patrons looked at ease and self-satisfied. Some sipped Turkish coffee, smoked cigarettes, and carried on conversations. Others played *tavlu*. Some of the men were smoking water pipes loaded with hashish; the aroma of the opiate was everywhere.

As Donik walked in, the *maître d'* greeted him and showed him to a small table. He looked around at the crowd and noticed, in particular, a large table near the dance floor where a dozen or so young Turkish men were enjoying themselves. It was obvious by their self-assured demeanor that they were well-off and well connected. The waiters were giving them special attention, particularly to the striking young gentleman who appeared to be the leader of the group. Donik noticed that most of the young men wore star-and-crescent pins on their jackets: in his naïveté, he assumed he was looking at a table of "Young Turks."[1]

To put it mildly, Donik didn't lack for self esteem. He yearned to associate with successful young people and imagined himself seated at the table having a good time with these spirited young Turkish men. To tell you the truth, Nephew, your dad was just an energetic young man who wanted to have fun; and while he was a good Armenian, he didn't care about nationality, class, or religion.

After a while, the striking young gentleman turned and fixed his eyes on Donik, realizing that he was Armenian. Armenians generally frequented their own cafés and rarely ventured into a Turkish club alone. Donik stared back at him.

A few minutes later, a waiter brought Donik a decanter of *raki* and some dishes of *meze*.

"Effendi, Ibrahim Pasha would consider it an honor if you would accept these delicacies in the spirit of fraternity." As he set down the dishes, the waiter smiled contemptuously: he recognized Donik as an Armenian.

Donik suspected that this was only a game. The Turk undoubtedly wanted to find out what business an Armenian had being there. An insult could be waiting behind the gesture. If he accepted Ibrahim Pasha's gift, he might be falling into some sort of trap.

"Please thank the gentleman for his generosity. I feel honored that he offers me a drink. However, I only accept gifts from those whom I know. Since I don't know him or any of his friends, I must decline his kind offer. Please take the food and drink away."

The waiter was visibly shaken. "Do you know what you're saying, Effendi? Ibrahim Pasha is the son of an important man in our country. He, himself, is an important man in our city, the

---

[1] The "Young Turks," were members of a Turkish nationalist secret society called the Committee of Union and Progress. The society was organized in 1896, and a faction of the Young Turks finally overthrew Sultan Abdul Hamid II in 1908. Their emblem was the grey wolf, not the star and crescent. These men were probably just young government officials.

Deputy Commissioner of Police. They are aristocrats, related to the Sultan's family. I must warn you, Effendi, you are playing with fire if you refuse his hospitality. It would be an insult."

Donik became angry. "Evidently you are either deaf or you don't understand Turkish. Let me tell you once again in Armenian."

The waiter blanched white. "*Af edersin,*" he pleaded. "*Yok, yok.*" [I beg your pardon. No, no.] That language is not appropriate here, Sir! . . ."

Donik cut him short. "Then do as you're told! Return this tray of food and drink to the gentleman who sent it. Tell him I said 'I thank you but I cannot accept your gift.'"

The waiter snatched up the tray, turned on his heels, and returned it to the table where the young Turks sat. Donik sat back in his chair and waited for the reaction.

The distinguished-looking gentleman got up and walked over to Donik's table. The Turk's face was ashen. He had been offended by Donik's rejection of hospitality, a studied insult in those circles, but was trying to maintain his calm and dignity. He didn't explode as most men would have, rather he wanted answers from this little bastard who had humiliated him. "*Oğlum, ismin nedir?*" [My young man, what is your name?]

"My name is Donik."

The Turk could now be sure, because of his Christian name, that this young upstart was Armenian. "*Nerden geldin?*" [Where are you from?]

"I'm from the village of Efkereh, four hundred and fifty miles east of here, near Kayseri.[1] Why do you ask?"

"You are Armenian."

"Yes, I am!" Donik answered proudly."

"Are you looking for someone here?"

"Yes, I am looking for friends. Is there anything wrong with that?"

[1] Called Caesarea among the Armenians and Kayseri by the Turks.

The Turk ignored his question. "I am Turkish. My name is Ibrahim Pasha. I'm prominent in this city. No one refuses my hospitality."

"I mean no offense, but I refuse to accept gifts from strangers."

Ibrahim Pasha himself had fallen into a trap. If he bloodied this upstart's nose, it wouldn't be much of a victory, for the kid was just a pup, wet behind the ears. Ibrahim Pasha couldn't go back to his table empty-handed either. He needed some sort of victory — after all, his buddies were watching to see what would happen. He didn't let his anger show, he kept his composure.

"What friends are you looking for? Are they Armenians?"

That question opened the floodgates. "My friends are Armenians, Greeks, Turks, Arabs, and Kurds. They are real men, men of character; men who know right from wrong; men who will stand on the side of justice; men who will use their strength to help their fellow men, not to hurt them. That's what my friends are like!" Donik seemed as surprised by his own outburst as the man standing before him.

The two stared at each other for a moment. Then Ibrahim Pasha burst into laughter. The tension was broken.

"Come, my young lion, let us do the *zeybek* together."[1]

Donik was overwhelmed. This important young Turk wanted to befriend him.

■ ■ ■ ■

"Why *did* the Turk go to all that trouble, Uncle?" I interrupted recklessly. "Why did he send my dad drinks? Why did he go over to Dad's table? Why did he let Dad get away with talking back?"

"First of all, Turks were always on guard when an Armenian entered one of their cafés. It was unusual. They wanted to know what he was up to.

---

[1] In old Turkish culture, when one man asks another to honor him by dancing the traditional *zeybek*, he is tying a knot of friendship.

"While most Armenians stayed out of politics, Nephew, and minded their own business, the Armenians had two important political action groups: the *Dashnaks,* fervent Armenian nationalists, some of whom at this time were trying to work with the Turkish reformers; and the *Hunchaks,* also nationalists, who occasionally assassinated unjust Turkish officials. These Hunchaks were feared by the Turks.

"Ibrahim Pasha was feeling out your father, trying to find out what he was up to, whether he were dangerous or not. After Ibrahim Pasha had spoken with Donik, the Turk concluded that the Armenian lad was spirited but harmless. That is why he called Donik *'aslan,'* a 'young lion.'

"And then, too, he liked the boy at once. Donik had — and still has — a way about him, something that drew people to him, something that made them want to know him. I guess they call it charisma.

"Your dad easily wins people over. There is something innocent about him. He can converse with complete strangers as if he has known them all their lives. Even when being obstinate, he is attractive to people — he was even more like that when he was a young man.

"That's why Ibrahim Pasha stood at Donik's table, took his rude behavior, and continued to feel him out. He was fascinated with Donik. He saw at once that the boy was proud, but was no threat to the Turks. For all of your dad's bluster, he was quite charming — a bit different. Ibrahim Pasha liked that."

■ ■ ■ ■

Ibrahim Pasha ordered the musicians to play a *zeybek*. Both men went to the middle of the floor and began to dance. They held their hands high, fingers snapping sharply to the beat of the music as they stepped to the rhythm. Donik and Ibrahim Pasha were very good dancers, and each made sure to impress this fact on the other. Their movements were extremely graceful. Every now and then one of them would dip, touch the floor with a knee, bring it up again, slap it with his hand, and then continue the rhythmical steps. One of the other men came forward with drinks for the dancers, as is the custom. Donik and Ibrahim Pasha linked arms and tossed down the drinks. Thus, their friendship was sealed.

Donik was invited to Ibrahim's Pasha's table and introduced to the young men there — all greeted him politely with the exception of one who was called Keskin Oglu because of his sharp tongue [*Keskin* means "sharp," *Oğlu* means "son of"]. This guy hated anyone who wasn't a Turk. His chief desire in life was to rid Turkey of its minorities, especially the Armenians.

"*Nerden geldin, puşt pezevenk?*" [Where are you from, you disgusting pimp?]

In a flash Donik's hot head took over and he leaped to his feet and smashed a dish of *homus* [mashed chick peas] into Keskin's face. Shaking with rage, Donik turned to Ibrahim Pasha and muttered, "I'm sorry, Effendi, but I can't swallow such an insult! I cannot eat or drink with this man here at the table." He pointed toward the seething Keskin Oglu. "He should be tied outside with the animals!"

Keskin Oglu jumped up in a rage. His sophisticated veneer vanished. Hatred twisted his face. He rushed at Donik, grabbed his beautifully tailored coat and shirt by the collars and ripped them off his back. Ibrahim Pasha sprang at Keskin Oglu to pull him away from Donik. They grappled and Keskin Oglu grabbed a knife from the table. Ibrahim Pasha swung with all his might and caught Keskin Oglu squarely on the chin. The young man fell to the side and landed on the blade, which sliced through his coat and pierced his side. Blood flowed from the wound, running out on the floor.

The wound didn't seem serious, but two of the men drove a ranting and raving Keskin Oglu to the nearest hospital. The other men at the café waited while sipping drinks and talking quietly. Finally the two young men came back and reported that Keskin Oglu's wound was only a surface cut and that the doctor had bound it and sent the cursing Keskin away. Once Donik learned that Keskin Oglu was all right, he excused himself and came home to tell us about his adventure.

Donik was a tattered mess, his clothes ripped to shreds. When we saw his condition, we knew someone had attacked him. We grabbed iron bars and bolted for the door with blood in our eyes. "Hold on," Donik ordered firmly, "first let me tell you what happened."

He told us the whole story, and we wondered what he wanted to do with a bunch of Turks. "This relationship can lead to no good," I warned. "These guys will get you into trouble. Armenians don't socialize with Turks in the cafés." Donik ignored the comment. All he could think about was the aggravation he had endured and the money he had spent to get his new suit! Now Keskin Oglu had ruined the suit and destroyed Donik's new image in a split second.

The suit, as you can imagine, was irreparably damaged. So Donik returned to the tailor and reordered the same suit with the same material. Since his fitting patterns were on file, the job took less than a week.

One evening, a few days later, Donik dressed himself in his new suit and strode off to the café. He walked in, sat at the same table where he had sat the first time, and prepared to order. He looked out of the corner of his eye and saw that Ibrahim Pasha was seated at his usual table with his friends. The same insulting little waiter came over.

"Effendi! You have a lot of nerve showing your ugly Armenian face here, after the commotion you caused a few weeks ago. I don't know why Ibrahim Pasha let you get away with it." The waiter spoke loudly, drawing the attention of the other patrons.

Donik's pride was at stake. He motioned the waiter closer. As the man bent toward him, Donik grabbed his ear. "Why don't you learn some manners. Why can't you act like a gentleman? What do they teach you Turks at home?" As he spoke, Donik twisted the waiter's ear pushing him down until finally the waiter was on his knees, writhing in pain.

The *maître d'* came over to ask if there was anything wrong. "No," Donik answered, "I dropped the tip as I handed it to him, and he's looking for it."

"Effendi," the *maître d'* said, "I have a message from Ibrahim Pasha. He invites you to dine with him at his table."

Donik got up and slowly strolled over to Ibrahim Pasha's table. As he walked, he looked and saw that it was the same group of young Turks as before, except for Keskin Oglu. Donik went up to Ibrahim Pasha and apologized for the incident the last time they had met, but Ibrahim Pasha politely interrupted him. "Donik, my young friend, don't concern yourself. Keskin Oglu was a ruffian, not fit for polite company. We will not allow him back with us until he learns how to behave like a gentleman. Please sit down next to me. Tell us more about yourself and your brothers."

The waiters set the table with highly polished silverware and beautifully decorated china. After the *meze* were served with decanters of *raki*, a roasted lamb was placed in the center of the table, accompanied by steaming bowls of rice pilaf and platters of vegetables that had been roasted on an open fire. There was rich creamy yogurt, laced with garlic to use as a sauce. For dessert there was *baklava*, made of flaky layers of filo dough filled with nuts and soaked with honey; *locum*,[1] the softest confection; and rich ice cream topped with cherries and walnuts.

After a few mouthfuls of food, Donik stood up, automatically looking for something to stand on. Then he thought better of it and stood behind his chair instead.

"Gentlemen, I would like to believe that my friends like me for what I am as a man — for my intelligence, industry, and character — not because I am a Turk or an Armenian, or a Christian or a Moslem. My nationality and religion should have nothing to do with what people think of me. A man is a man and that is that. We are all of value in God's eyes."

Ibrahim Pasha looked at Donik with approval. "You seem to have been a diplomat in one of your previous lives. You speak well." This caused everyone to laugh, Donik included. When the laughter faded, Donik became serious again.

He stared into the eyes of each of the men seated around the table, one by one. Then he turned to Ibrahim Pasha and said, "It's ironic you should suggest that. Yes, I have had many reincarnations and have lived on several planets."

His words kindled their curiosity. What would this guy say next?

---

[1] Sometimes called "Turkish Delight."

"This is, in fact, my fourth life on earth. God created the earth and placed people on it. But rather than doing good, people did evil. The Lord personally punished them many times, but they would not repent of their sinning. The Lord became tired of dealing with immoral men himself and so he sent a great flood to punish them. After the flood, the people behaved for a while, but returned to sinning as soon as they conveniently could.

"Then the Lord sent the prophets. The prophets were either ignored or killed. And so, about two thousand years ago, the Lord sent his only begotten son. Again, the people didn't repent and instead nailed the Lord's son on a cross.

"The Lord then decided to send another great Prophet, Mohammed, may his name be blessed, as you believe. But even this great Prophet could not get people to behave properly. People honored this Prophet more by talking about him than by following him. Many crimes have been committed in his name. He would be ashamed of his followers.

"Well, the Lord became desperate. He looked around for another messenger. Who could he send? Since the great men had failed, he decided to try a sinner. He called on the Devil. 'I'm looking for a man with courage. He doesn't have to be perfect, I'm not looking for a saint. He doesn't have to be too bright, either. I want a mild sinner who will do as I tell him.'"

By this time many people had crowded around the table to listen to Donik. They had never heard anyone talk like this.

"The Devil replied, 'I think I have just the right guy, not too smart but with a lot of courage, a good heart too. But he likes to get into mischief and he is not above telling tall tales. If you remember, it was you who sent him down here.'

"Well, my friends, I was that man. The Lord decided to use me. He sent me to medieval Spain during the Inquisition. I was supposed to talk sense into the Grand Inquisitor who was killing people of the wrong faith. Well, it didn't work, the Inquisitor didn't listen. I was burned at the stake and my ashes scattered to the four winds. This was my second worthless life.

"After a while, the Lord decided to try once more, of course again at my expense. He sent me to revolutionary France to talk sense into the revolutionaries who were killing people left and right for their wrong ideas. Well, it didn't work. No one wanted to listen to me. I was sent to the guillotine myself and lost my head. This was my third useless life.

"After another couple of centuries, the Lord called me aside and said he had another job for me. 'Well, I didn't do too well on the last two, so why send me again?'

"'This is an important job,' the Lord said. 'I just have to do something. I don't want to see my creatures suffer, and things are getting bad in Asia Minor and Anatolia. I want you to go down there and instill some virtue in the ruffian Turks and bring peace between them and the Armenians. Be careful though, the Turks are nice people but they are awfully bullheaded. They may listen or they may just cut you up into little pieces and scatter your body parts around the landscape. You will just have to go and do your best. Maybe it will work this time.'

"Well, gentlemen, here I am again! What will happen, I don't know. Perhaps I can succeed this time, perhaps I will fail again."

Roars of laughter echoed through the café. People nodded their heads in agreement and started to talk to one another about Donik's story.

Ibrahim Pasha smiled at Donik and said, "That is a charming story. Perhaps people like me can help you, although I am not sure what can be done."

After much toasting to brotherhood, the young men settled in to have fun. The music started and the young Turks pulled Donik to the center of the floor. Then they began to do a circle dance around him. Donik was inspired to do a solo in their midst. Their arms and legs moved gracefully to the rhythms as Donik, according to tradition, danced around, moving first to one part of the circle and then another.

When the dance finished, they all returned breathless to their table for more drinks. The show was about to begin; the musicians started to play Middle Eastern belly-dance music. The clinking of finger-cymbals could be heard as a line of belly dancers entered from the side. They took to the floor in a flurry of laughter. From the other side, a lovely, exotic creature appeared. Her ravishing, sinuous body was draped with flimsy silk. Her face was covered with a veil except for her flashing eyes; above them, a string of gold coins was strung across her forehead. Small cups covered her heavenly twins, and on her dainty feet she wore silver bells.

The other girls stopped dancing and began clinking their miniature cymbals to the music. The belly dancer snaked her way toward the table where the lone gentile sat among the Turks. She wriggled erotically before him, making him nervous. Eventually, Donik realized that this was all for his benefit. Ibrahim Pasha and the others had arranged it.

The girl took Donik's hand and in a flash was atop the table, dancing with wild abandon. As the veils dropped from her body, she draped them around Donik's neck. Never had he experienced anything like this. He broke out in a sweat and felt himself becoming aroused.

When the music stopped, the girl held his hand to step down, but this time she didn't let go. "*Gel, yavrum, biraz keyf edelim.*" [Come, my baby, let us make joy for a while.] Too embarrassed to get up by himself, Donik was lifted to his feet by the men who then pushed him up the stairs behind the dancer, to her room, to the cool silk covering her bed, to paradise.

She shut the door gently, dropping the latch in place to lock out the rest of the world. She took a lemon from the window sill, bit into it to make a hole and squeezed the juice into her palms. Then she tenderly caressed Donik's face with her soft hands while whispering sweetness into his ears.

It was his first time. Everything whirled in slow motion. Enchantment overtook his entire being, just as it had the first time he saw Smyrna's beauty through his binoculars. For him, this woman had become Smyrna, and he was about to enter her once more. Her nimble fingers moved slowly, gently liberating his body. While her fingers did their work, her lips were busy whispering songs of ecstasy and kissing his exposed flesh. She was a beauty all right, her curves were sculpted mounds of creamy skin. Donik had never seen the naked body of the opposite sex. She took that naïve virgin boy and introduced him to the elevated heights of carnal pleasure.

A little later, our young brother had come down to earth again. Ibrahim Pasha was the first to spot Donik coming down the stairs.

His clothes were ruffled, as was his hair. Fixing his cravat as he left the last step, Donik touched the ground floor with both feet. He looked around to see if anyone was watching him. Were they aware of what wonderful thing had happened to him during the last hour?

He had a silly grin on his face as he made his way through the crowd and found his chair beside Ibrahim Pasha, who whispered, "*Maşallah, bugün adam oldun*!" [Thanks to Allah, today you have become a man!] The aristocrat patted Donik softly on the back. "Your memory of this evening will live with you until your dying day."

The Turks gathered around as Ibrahim Pasha announced, "We have decided to give you the honorary name, 'Haji Bey.' A *haji* is one who has made the pilgrimage to the Holy City. *Bey* is a high title of respect, just below a *pasha*. It's a name to be proud of. You are worthy of it because of your courage, ideas, and wit."

Suddenly there was an explosion of light as the café's photographer recorded the event in a group portrait. The men around the table applauded and refilled their glasses, celebrating long into the night.

From that night on Donik was a changed man. He was now "Haji Bey," and would answer to no other name. His young Turkish friends had put him on a pedestal, and he moved about the city with the self-assurance of an aristocrat.

Your father spent more and more time with his new Turkish friends, making the rounds of the cafés and casinos night after night. He was burning the candle at both ends, and he couldn't wake up for work in the morning. His friends had made a man of him before his time. He was only seventeen. We were concerned. Your father was drifting further and further away from our Armenian Christian way of life. Something had to be done.

We followed him one night and were shocked at what went on in the café. We had never seen anything like it. We could not believe it as we watched Donik reveling in his wild ways, drinking excessively, fooling around with the girls, and living it up. There was no way we could control this prodigal brother of ours anymore. We had to let Mother know what was going on and get her to stop it.

We communicated with our family back in Efkereh once a month, sending a letter and a little money. Mail service was primitive and not reliable. Sometimes we sent our packets with friends going east, sometimes we would pay a Turkish messenger to carry a packet for us. So it took a while before we could raise the alarm with Mother.

When Mother got our letter, she reacted as most mothers of a wayward 17-year-old boy would — she exploded in anger! Her first reaction was to have him brought home immediately. Later, she had second thoughts. She realized that this young man had to be handled with velvet gloves, so she devised a plan and wrote a letter.

Early one morning, after a night of carousing, Donik stumbled into the shop with his tail dragging. He was totally hung over. We sat him down and told him we had a letter from Mother. She misses you very much, we said.

"Of course, of course," His Highness responded cockily, "I'm her favorite."

We had to bite our tongues to keep from laughing.

"She wants to see you. She wants you to come home to visit."

Donik woke up immediately. He smelled a trap. "Doesn't she understand I can't go home right now? Doesn't she realize I'm needed here. You can't get along without me."

Donik moped around for the next couple of weeks and thought of every excuse to put off the inevitable trip. Finally, a second letter arrived from Mother. She wanted Donik back immediately! Mother's word was our command, so Donik accepted his fate and finally began to make preparations for the journey. We offered to go with him, but he said he could make it alone.

Meanwhile, Donik had been eyeing one of Sarkis Aga's horses. The horse was black with an ivory mane and tail, and sleek as a panther. Donik went to Sarkis Aga and begged the Aga to sell him the horse. Sarkis Aga liked Donik and said he could buy the stallion on the condition that he promise to take good care of him. Then Donik went shopping for a fine buggy that we could all share.

Donik went to the fashionable shops and bought perfume, face powder, and fine soaps and other gifts for all his sisters-in-law. He bought toys for his nephews, and then he bought Mother an overcoat and a purse. He loaded his pockets with gold and silver coins.

We were still worried about letting Donik go back alone, but he reassured us. He would be fine.

"I have plenty of protection," Donik said, pointing to a box. "You see this box? It contains dynamite."

I looked inside and counted a dozen sticks of explosive! I couldn't believe my eyes. "Where did you get these from? You could be hanged for having dynamite."

"I got it from Sarkis Aga. He told me that if I were caught, not to worry, he would fix it."

We just stared at Donik in amazement. He was completely out of control. He just did whatever he wanted. We were truly glad we were sending him home. In the morning, we gathered to see him off.

Donik hid the box of dynamite under the buggy seat along with a rifle. He also concealed a pistol under his jacket. He had packed enough food for ten days, most of it *lavash* [crisp, thin bread], dried beef, cheese, and olives. Then His Highness made one of his speeches.

"Boys, I won't be gone too long, so don't worry. I'll spend only a few days at home and be right back. Do the best you can without me."

We were relieved to finally see him off. We couldn't help roaring with laughter. Little did he know he was in for the surprise of his life.

CHAPTER SIX
Adventures of the Road

Donik's intention was to stop at the end of the first day and visit with Arabagee, the old Turk who had helped us after we had been robbed on the road.

Donik was in luck. Arabagee was at home. His wife had gone to visit her mother for a few days, and her absence made Donik feel at ease. Dudük Hanim had left a servant to take care of her husband. The kindly gentleman invited Donik to spend the night, and the offer was accepted with appreciation.

Over supper, your father continued with his lie to Arabagee, telling him that he, Donik, had become a Moslem and that his teachers had given him a new name, "Haji Bey." The new name, at least, was the truth.

Donik later admitted to me that he had actually felt ashamed of himself for lying to the old man. Arabagee, your father finally realized, would have helped us anyway, despite our being Armenian Christians. The old man was a good person.

They went to bed early. In the morning, they got up with the sun and ate breakfast. After breakfast, Arabagee presented Donik with a large basket of food for his long journey back to Efkereh. Donik didn't need the food since he had brought a sufficient supply for the ten-day trip, yet he had to accept to be polite. It would have been rude to refuse the old man's gift.

As Donik prepared to leave, the old Turk cautioned him to be on the lookout for the Armenian bandits. "If they attack you, don't let them know that you're now a Moslem. It will be the worse for you. I'm sure God won't mind if you tell a white lie to save your life." He winked at Donik and smiled.

Donik blushed, convinced now that the old man knew the truth. He threw his arms around Arabagee and hugged him, then kissed his arthritic hands as a token of respect.

The old Turk's eyes filled with tears. "Have a safe journey, my son, go with God."

Haji Bey jumped up on the buggy, cracked the whip, and took off at a gallop. A couple of miles down the road, he spied a woman with a heavy load riding on a donkey. As she came closer, he realized that it was Dudük Hanim, Arabagee's wife. When she recognized Donik, a deep frown creased her face.

Dudük Hanim cast her eyes aside to ignore him. Haji Bey, however, brought the horse to a stop across the road. *"Hoş geldin, Dudük Hanim"* [Welcome, Dudük Hanim], he greeted her. *"Nasilsin?"* [How are you?]

"Gâvur, buralarda ne geziyorsun?" [Infidel, what are you doing around here?] Her eyes flashed with fire. "*Git! GIT! Burdan siktir ol*!" [Go! GO! Get the fuck out of here!]

Haji Bey shot back a few verbal salvos himself. "You have no cause to cackle like a brainless chicken, to get all hysterical! Shut up for a moment and let me speak. I have done no harm to you or your husband. Right now I'm on my way back to my village to visit my mother and my family. I stopped to pay my respects to Arabagee. He is a wonderful man and I look upon him as my own kin!

"Sure, I admit I told your husband a lie, but he understood all along that I was only trying to save our necks. He is a good and charitable man. I respect you, too, Hanim. We are all God's creatures, trying to make it from day to day. So wash out your foul mouth with soap and show better manners.

"I want nothing from you and intend you no harm, in fact I'd gladly be of service to *you* if you happen to need anything."

The woman searched your father's face for a moment to measure the sincerity of his words. Then Dudük Hanim laughed and said, "You may be right, Infidel. You have a certain way of reaching people with your words. Perhaps you are not so bad after all. We shall see." Then she urged her donkey on toward her home. "May God be with you, my boy," she called back over her shoulder."

Though her back was turned and he knew she couldn't see him, Haji Bey waved goodbye. He was feeling good inside.

The next twenty miles passed quickly because Donik had Arabagee and his wife on his mind. The day was hot and the horse was tired, so Donik brought him to a stop beside a running brook. It was a good place to rest, water and feed the horse, and have a bite to eat. The stream sang a tranquil song as it rippled over the smooth stones. How tempting the cool water seemed!

Haji Bey took off his shoes and went wading. As he stood staring dreamily into the water, he slowly became aware of a shadow on the surface alongside his own reflection. He jumped back in alarm.

"Please, Effendi," came a frail and frightened voice, "do you have something to eat? I haven't had a bite in four days and I'm hungry."

Haji Bey whirled around. Gazing at him with large sunken eyes was a Turkish child of about eight or nine. The boy was emaciated. The skin on his face stretched tight across his high cheekbones. He looked as if he were about to collapse.

"I've walked all the way from my village in the hills, Effendi. We barely made a living up there. A few weeks ago, my parents died of consumption. Our neighbors forced me to leave because they thought I was infected and might spread the disease to them. I am very hungry; please, do you have anything to eat?"

The child's body was filthy and his scalp crawling with lice. Immediately, Haji Bey's heart went out to him. He handed the boy some soap and told him to wash up in the stream. Then he went to the buggy and took out a jar of *raki*.

"You'd better be telling the truth, kid, because you're about to get your head washed with a very precious elixir. This stuff is usually drunk, and fills your head with happiness. But let's see if it'll drive the lice out of your filthy hair."

Donik bent the boy over the brook, and gently poured the *raki* over the boy's head and rubbed it with his hands. The lice fell like rain on the water. Minnows came hurrying to the surface to eat them as they landed. The boy washed in the stream and then Donik scrubbed the boy's body with the remaining *raki*. As he did so, the youngster cried out that it was burning his skin. Still, it felt good.

After the boy was clean, Donik asked him his name.

"I am Hashim Oglu, Effendi."

"Well, come on then, Hashim, sit down and let's eat. Just don't stuff yourself. Your stomach has shrunk and you'll get sick if you eat too quickly. Eat all you want, but only a little at a time."

A strange thought crept into Donik's mind as he watched the little boy devouring the food. Could this be an act of Providence? Had God inspired Arabagee to insist that Donik take more food? Maybe God has a plan in all this. Then Haji Bey made one of his snap decisions.

"Kid, I've decided. I am taking you with me."

The little boy's eyes widened in surprise, he was hardly able to believe his ears. Donik smiled at him. "That's right, kid, I'm taking you with me!"

How that pitiful thin face lit up with joy and relief. He had a friend who cared for him.

Hashim helped Haji Bey as best he could as they hitched up the horse. He then hurried to climb into the buggy, as if he were afraid Donik would change his mind. They liked each other at once, those two.

As they bounced along the road, Donik told the youngster all about himself — why he was called Haji Bey, of the good times he had with his new friends in Smyrna, and how for some stupid reason his mother wanted him back home.

"Women," Mr. Experience said knowingly, "they're so damn hard to understand. Don't ever try to figure out a woman, Hashim, you can end up in the *khentahnotes* [crazy house]. They can mush up what little brains the Lord has put into your head."

The young boy hung on Haji Bey's words as if they were Gospel. Of course, he couldn't possibly have understood everything your father was blabbing about, yet it didn't matter, either. What he knew for sure was that this wonderful man had appeared out of nowhere with a snorting black steed, had cleaned and fed him, and was now taking him away with him to . . . where? He didn't even know. He didn't care. He had been saved.

"I've got big plans for you, kid. You're going to be my true brother, even if you are a Turk. You can keep your religion and the name your parents gave you. I'm going to take you back to

Smyrna and send you to school. You can work for a few hours every day in our shop, too. We will teach you the business.

"But right now, we're heading for Efkereh, that's my hometown. Here, take the reins while I keep watch behind to make sure we're not being followed."

The miles and days rolled by. They were making good time along the rough trail. They killed the time by talking. "Hashim," Haji Bey said one afternoon out of a clear blue sky, "if you can come up with a proper name, you can have the honor of naming my horse."

The boy was overjoyed. "Effendi, you read my mind. I already have a name for him! I didn't mention it because I was afraid you wouldn't like it."

"What's the name you were thinking of?"

"*Siyah Yildiz!*" he said with delight. "He's so shiny, Effendi, he sparkles in the moonlight!"

Haji Bey rolled the name over his tongue. "'Black Star.' I love it. It's a perfect name for such a grand creature."

They pulled the buggy off the trail and watered the horse, pouring some of the water over his head as a baptism. Both stroked the beautiful creature and said, "From this day forward, you will be known as 'Black Star'."

As if he understood, the majestic stallion snorted and shook his mane proudly. His behavior was aristocratic in every sense of the word.

With Hashim at the reins, they took to the road again. Haji Bey put the binoculars to his eyes and turned to take a look behind them. His pulse quickened. In the distance a cloud of dust rose above the trail, rapidly getting larger. Horsemen!

His heart seemed about to jump out of his chest. To avoid frightening little Hashim, he forced himself to act calm.

"Hashim, reach under the seat and get me a couple of cigars and some matches."

The child quickly did as he was told. He could sense something was wrong.

"Now light one of them and hand it to me. Don't puff on it too long," Haji Bey chuckled nervously. "We don't want to teach you bad habits just yet."

Hashim lit the cigar and handed it to Donik, then he urged the black devil to a full gallop.

"Slow down, Hashim! Slow down! I want to get a better look and I don't want to kill the horse." Donik peered through the binoculars, trying to hold them steady. Although he didn't say anything out loud, thoughts were rushing through his mind: Oh, Lord, they're coming on fast! Oh, shit! They have to be bandits!

Haji Bey pulled a stick of dynamite out of the box. Slowly he put the burning tip of the cigar to the fuse and dropped the stick of dynamite onto the trail. With one part of his mind he listened to Hashim urging Black Star to an even faster pace. With the other, he counted out five seconds, lit and dropped another stick of dynamite. Muttering a prayer, he stuck the cigar in his mouth, crossed himself with one hand, and held the binoculars to his eyes with the other.

Maybe another stick wouldn't hurt, he thought. He waited ten seconds this time and dropped a third stick with another prayer. Oh Lord, don't forsake me today.

The first stick of dynamite exploded, stopping the bandits in their tracks. But only for a moment. They reoriented themselves and took up the chase again. Five seconds later the second explosion went off, again halting them momentarily. Once more, the horsemen regrouped and came charging.

At that point Donik didn't give a damn if he killed one of them or not. He knew he was fighting for their lives. He pulled out his sidearm, aimed and squeezed off a shot. One of the horsemen screamed in pain and fell off his horse. In the same instant, the third explosion went off. Two horses took a spill, throwing their riders into the dust. This time they gave up.

"I think we won this round," he shouted to Hashim. Then Haji Bey laughed with nervous relief.

They slowed the horse to a gait. There was no camping out that night, they just kept going at a slow pace. They made a good thirty to thirty-five miles that day and night, stopping periodically only to rest the horse and have a bite to eat. They didn't even stop to relieve their bladders, they just pissed over the side of the buggy as it bumped along.

As the morning sun broke, the two boys were exhausted and hungry for breakfast. In the distance, Haji Bey saw a house they hadn't noticed on their way to Smyrna — the house was off the road in a valley, half hidden behind a clump of trees. Donik decided to take a chance. He turned the horse off the road on to the trail leading to the valley. As they drew closer to the clump of trees, they saw five or six other houses.

"Hashim, let's see who lives here."

About twenty yards from the house, a giant of a man sporting a white handlebar moustache and holding a long rifle in his hands stepped out on the trail. "*Ne istiyorsun, Effendi?*" [What do you want, Sir?]

"We are tired, Sir, and need a safe place to camp. Perhaps you can help us."

At that moment, a beautiful woman with large black eyes and light olive skin stepped out of the house. She walked up to the man, took hold of his arm, and whispered in a soft voice. "*Asonk inch guzen, martes?*" [What do they want, my husband?]

Haji Bey's heart jumped for joy: Armenians! Before the moustached one could answer his woman, your father spoke up in Armenian. "*Yes Hai yem, Degin. Hai yem.*" [I am Armenian, Madam. I am Armenian.]

The man and his wife smiled and beckoned Donik and Hashim into the house. The woman invited the boys to sit and eat breakfast with them. That was the way it was in those days. When hungry strangers came to your door, you would offer them hospitality.

While Haji Bey and Hashim were devouring the food, the moustached one began to ask questions. "What are your names and where are you from? What are you two youngsters doing in this area all alone? Don't you realize you're in one of the most dangerous regions of the country? These hills are filled with bandits."

"Effendi, my name is Haji Bey, even though I am an Armenian. I was born Donagan, or "Donik" as I was called. I am from Efkereh, not far from Caesarea. This frail boy here is called Hashim Oglu, and he is from a village a couple of days journey from Smyrna. He is my newly adopted little brother. We are traveling from Smyrna to Efkereh to visit my mother."

"This boy has a strange name for an Armenian. In fact, the boy doesn't look Armenian at all."

"I was given the name "Haji Bey" by my Turkish friends; and this young lad, Hashim Oglu, *is* a Turk. I found him on the road. He was hungry and alone. His parents died and there was no one to take care of him, so I brought him along and have adopted him. I am taking him with me to Efkereh to visit my mother and other relatives. My four brothers and I left home and moved to Smyrna to start a business."

The moustached one told them that his name was Takvor [Rex] Sarkisian. His father was an Armenian, his mother a Turk. It was a marriage of passion, not arranged. "My father fell in love with a beautiful, dark-eyed maiden. The families, of course, didn't approve. The young couple ran off together and built a cabin in the *Dumanli Dagi* [Smoky Mountains]. That was where I was born.

"Our family was not treated well by either our Armenian or Turkish neighbors. That's the way things are; mixed marriages do not have it easy. So my parents decided to start a new life farther away from their place of birth. My father's brothers came with him and they established this little community here.

"Both my father and mother are now dead. My father's brothers are in the houses behind us. This woman beside me is my dear wife, Isqouhi [Verity]. Both of her parents are Armenian. We have four children. Now tell me about yourself. How did you get here without being robbed or murdered? The road is especially dangerous around these parts."

Haji Bey told them his story, beginning with when he and his brothers left Efkereh. "Now you tell me," said Donik, "are you, yourselves, not afraid of robbers?"

"No. As a matter of fact, the brigands who terrorize this region are related to my dead mother. Their leader is my distant cousin. They have a camp a day's journey from here, but they visit us about once a week. In fact, you will probably meet them tonight."

Haji Bey stopped in mid-bite. "They come by once a week? They may be coming *this* evening? I think we had better be leaving!"

"Don't worry." Takvor laughed. "You are safe here. After all, they are my distant relatives and are well-behaved here. I don't approve of their way of life, but what can I do? They are good to me, and so I am good to them."

Donik jumped up. "No, I am serious. I think we had better be on our way! Thank you for your hospitality. We appreciate it."

Takvor would have none of it. "Don't be in a hurry. Stay here a few days and rest up. When you and your horse are well-rested, you can go.

"You need not fear the bandits. They behave here. It might even be to your advantage to meet them. Regular travelers are allowed to pass with only the payment of an English pound or two. If you plan to go back and forth between Smyrna and Efkereh, it would be a good investment."

Donik could see the sense in what Takvor had said and so decided to spend the day with the Sarkisians and wait for the bandits to arrive.

Toward evening, Donik could hear the horses approaching. The bandits had finally come. Haji Bey peered cautiously from the window as their leader dismounted awkwardly. He was a giant of a man, even bigger than Takvor. He weighed every bit of three hundred pounds. The man cut an imposing figure: his fingers were covered with gold rings; he had a gun in his belt and a saber at his side; and his ammunition belts crisscrossed over his chest. His three companions looked like smaller versions of their leader.

He looked around, spied Black Star, recognized him, and lumbered over. He began stroking the majestic steed, talking to him with greedy eyes as he caressed the animal's genitals.

"Soon, very soon, you will be mine, my black beauty," he said aloud, wanting to be heard. "You and I shall roam the countryside chasing *gâvurlar*. We'll play our favorite games with them. I will skewer them one by one on my saber." He spoke loudly for your father's benefit; he suspected that he was within hearing distance.

Takvor walked out to greet his wayward relatives. "Come in,

come in, Osman, I want you to meet Haji Bey and his young brother."

"What are these pimps doing here?" The tips of his moustache twitched as he spoke. "The bastard is an Armenian, I know it. How in hell did the pimp come by an honorable Turkish name? If you think I'm going to let him out of here alive, you're crazy!"

Takvor became stern. "You son of a bitch, if you touch even a hair on the head of either of these youngsters, you're a dead man! I'll shoot you myself. These boys are relatives on my father's side, so be nice to them or go away."

The mountainous man pushed Takvor to one side and stormed into the house. The floorboards creaked and groaned under the weight of his immense frame. He lunged forward, snarling and spitting at Haji Bey. "*Gâvur!*" he roared. "*Gâvur!*"

Like puppets on a string, three of his henchmen came rushing in after him. One of them had a bloody rag wrapped around his right hand. It looked like it covered a new wound, probably a wound inflicted by Haji Bey's pistol shot during the chase the day before. Osman stood there, staring at Donik with murderous eyes, his mouth flashing uneven rows of gold teeth.

■ ■ ■ ■

Unable to hold in my excitement, I jumped up. "What happened next?"

Uncle Nazar frowned. "Don't start with your interruptions."

"Okay, Uncle, please go on then."

He stared sharply at me. "You Americans are always in a hurry. You have no patience, even with your own language, even for making love." He muttered something under his breath like: "Boom, bang, it must be over in a couple of minutes."

"What was that, Uncle?"

"Nothing!" he glared at me, "I was just thinking out loud. I'm in no hurry. Why are you in such a hurry?"

He leaned back, lit up a cigarette and dragged luxuriously on it.

■ ■ ■ ■

Well, Osman gripped his saber so tightly that his knuckles turned white against his dark skin. "*Seni keseceğim, Gâvur!*" [I'm going to cut you up, Infidel!] Slowly he drew his sword and raised it up as if he were about to lop off Donik's head. Suddenly there was a clap of gunfire. Everyone jumped in alarm. Takvor had fired off a shot at the ceiling.

"Imbecile! Half-wit!" he roared at the top of his lungs. "Didn't I warn you? Didn't I tell you! Back off, you jackass, or I'll put a bullet through that thick skull of yours."

Osman's vicious look changed into a smirk. He turned back to Haji Bey and asked, "Not to change the subject, but where the hell did you get that dynamite?"

Haji Bey was ready with his fairy tale, of course. "From the mounted police in the city of Smyrna." Osman's mouth dropped open in disbelief. Your father, of course, was just getting started. "They taught me how to use it against outlaws like you. I only threw three sticks yesterday. I could easily have killed you if I'd cared to."

"Kill me, *Gâvur?*" The brute roared with laughter. "You wouldn't dare try that!"

"Look, Osman. I want no trouble with you. I generally mind my own business. Just tell me, what will it take for you to let me and my five brothers travel back and forth on this road in peace? Takvor said I must pay you two English pounds each time I make the trip." Donik flung two coins on the table. "Here's your damn extortion money, lap it up," he said with characteristic bravado.

Osman's ugly face cracked into a wide smile of satisfaction. He scooped up the gold pieces, put them in his pocket, and pulled out five metal tokens. "Here, pimp, carry one of these with you and give one to each of your stupid brothers. This boy doesn't need one, we recognize our own. The next time you're stopped by my men, just show the token and hand over two English pounds. That's all. Understand, Infidel?"

The four brigands sat down at the table while Isqouhi served them a veritable feast. They stuffed their faces with rice pilaf and lamb stew smothered with tomatoes, okra, and onions, accompanied by a liter of *raki*. Osman and his men ate like pigs. The grease from the stew slithered down the sides of their mouths.

Osman was still angry about the sticks of dynamite. He occasionally threw murderous looks at Donik and finally stared at him and said, *"Gâvur, biliyorsun seni keseceğim birgün."* [Infidel, I want you to know I'm going to cut you to pieces one day.]

Haji Bey suddenly remembered the photograph he had in his traveling bag of himself with his Turkish friends, taken the night they had honored him with his new name. He pulled out the picture.

"*Hayvan Osman! Iyice bak, bu benim kardaşlarim.* [Osman, you animal! Take a good look, these are my brothers.] You'd better think twice before giving me any shit!" He waved the photograph in the bandits' faces. "These are men high up in the government, you ass! This gentleman," he pointed to Ibrahim Pasha, "is a big shot in the *zaptiye*, the mounted police. The others are his sharpshooters, his scouts! So take this as a warning, *hayvan*; if you have any ideas of double-crossing me, now that I've paid you your blood money, forget it!

"If I don't return from Efkereh in thirty days, my friends will come looking for me. They know you operate along this road and will know who to come after. If you value your life, be careful, and pray to God that you never have to come face to face with an angry Ibrahim Pasha."

Osman's beady eyes blazed with anger. Since Haji Bey didn't know if he would now get a reply from Osman or a swipe of his saber, he forced himself to gaze calmly at the fat face. The fat brigand continued to glare murderously at your father as he got to his feet.

"You have a big mouth, *Gâvur*; be thankful that I do not care to shut it permanently this evening." He wiped a filthy sleeve across his greasy lips. "Just make sure you and your brothers carry the metal tokens I've given you when traveling the road, otherwise you may find your head in your lap."

He broke out in a sinister laugh and strode out the door. The three puppets quickly followed. Both your father and Hashim ran to the window to make sure the bandits didn't harm Black Star or go near the buggy, where several sticks of dynamite were still under the seat. Osman and his men merely mounted their own horses and rode over through the trees to the place where they would spend the night with their little band of cutthroats.

When the bandits had disappeared, everyone in the house breathed a sigh of relief. They sat down and talked about Turkish-Armenian relations. "I have no hope," said Takvor. "People are stupid, they don't know how to live and let live." Donik, of course, gave one of his speeches.

■ ■ ■ ■

The following morning, Haji Bey and Hashim said farewell to Takvor and Isqouhi Sarkisian and resumed their journey. It would take them another three days to reach Efkereh. As they drove down the road, all thoughts of the highwaymen vanished from their minds. Their spirits were high in anticipation. Hashim was doing well, he was beginning to get color back in his face, and his youthful strength was returning. As they bumped along, Hashim suddenly gave your father the shock of his life.

"Pari luis, yegpairés, ais ardu, inchbes yes?" [Good morning, my brother, how are you this morning?]

"Hashim, you're full of surprises," your father blurted out. "I didn't know you spoke Armenian."

Hashim laughed. "I also speak a little Greek, too. People were mixed in our area. Many of my neighbors were Armenians and Greeks, and so I picked up the languages playing with the boys in my village."

Hashim was happy and began whistling Turkish tunes. Donik, always ready to enjoy himself, joined in. Suddenly the boy threw his arms around Donik and hugged him. "I love you, my brother. I'll always be loyal to you, remember that."

Haji Bey put his arm around the young kid and kissed his forehead. "You're a great boy, Hashim. I'm looking forward to seeing you grow into a fine man. I'm really happy to have my own little brother, one who respects me and accepts my decisions. A brother who doesn't argue with me and try to put me down. My older brothers have sat on me too long. They have no imagination and won't listen to me."

They had reached Caesarea and were now turning on the trail to Efkereh. The last leg of their journey was drawing to a close. The young travelers were exhausted from their long ride. At last Haji Bey spotted the outline of Sourb Garabed Monastery on the mountainside. Efkereh was just three miles from there.

Joy filled your father's heart. "We're home! We're home! In a couple of hours we'll be home!"

Donik wiped the tears of happiness from his eyes. He had left home a baby brother, just a raw kid. Now he was returning as a man, riding in a handsome black buggy pulled by a beautiful black stallion, his baggage filled with valuable gifts for his family. He gave his imagination full range and pictured himself as Vartan Sbarabed.[1] He was triumphantly approaching the gates of his village, his head held high and his chest bulging with pride. The hero had returned!

---

[1] Sbarabed=General. General Vartan Mamigonian, the Armenian military leader who fought valiantly against the Persian invaders of Armenia in 451 A.D. for the sake of Armenian religious liberty.

CHAPTER SEVEN
Haji Bey Comes Home

For the hundredth time in the last two days, Mama Yessaian shielded her eyes against the sun to scan the road leading up to Efkereh. The road came up out of the lowlands, so she could see quite a distance.

Instinctively she knew her little boy was near, she felt it. She had also been doing her arithmetic. There were so many days for her last letter to get to Smyrna, so many days to convince her hard-headed baby to leave, so many days for the road, and. . . .

Her heart quickened as she saw a ball of dust rise in the far distance. Then slowly she could make out the form of a horse and buggy. Is it my son, she wondered? She strained to see and shook her head. No, it must be some Turkish official coming from Caesarea on government business.

The buggy disappeared behind a hill. Then it reappeared and came closer and closer. My God, it's him! It's Donik! . . . My son! . . . MY BABY!

Haji Bey saw his mother, threw the reins to Hashim, leaped from the buggy, and ran the last few yards to his mother. Her tears wet his cheeks as she embraced him, planting kiss after kiss on his happy face.

She held him at arm's length to get a good look. "Good Lord, how you've changed! You're so different. What have your brothers done to you? Have they worked you too hard? My dear, dear boy!"

Mama had already put on her velvet gloves and begun her performance. Oh, a lot of it was true. He *was* changed, he was growing up, that was natural. She knew that we had all worked hard the first year-and-a-half in Smyrna. She also knew that after your father had invented the cutting machine, he'd had ten to twelve days off each month, plenty of time to carouse with his hard-drinking Turkish buddies and with the wild women of Smyrna. Next, she thought, it would be gambling. Thank God she'd gotten him back before he'd fallen into *that* sewer!

Mama looked with surprise at the frail child bringing the buggy to a stop. "And who is that?" She turned a beady eye on your father. "Didn't one of your brothers come with you?"

Haji Bey reached up, grabbed Hashim and swung him to the ground. "Yes, Mama, one did. This little boy is my adopted brother," he said proudly.

Hashim bowed his head respectfully and spoke in Armenian. "Madam, I am Hashim Oglu. I am an orphan. Your son found me hungry and wandering alone by the wayside and was kind enough to feed me and ask me to join him on his journey. I don't want to trouble you. I'll be on my way."

"You'll do no such thing, my child. You are welcome to our home. Donik, or Haji Bey, or whatever they call you, take your new brother right now and see if you can find Dr. Oskan to have a look at him."

They drove up to the Yessaian home in silence. Mother got out of the buggy and started into the house. Then, turning back, she placed her hands on her hips and shouted, "As for those fools, your *other* brothers, I'm going to fix all four of them! I'll break their necks when I see them again. Imagine their letting you travel that road by yourself!"

■ ■ ■ ■

For Donik, of course, it felt good to be home. He was happy to see his mother again and he enjoyed the company of his sisters-in-law and his little nephews. He also enjoyed visiting with old friends, telling them stories of Smyrna. And he certainly enjoyed his mother's great cooking. It was even restful being away from the hard work of the shop and the hard play in the cafés. . . .

But two days later Haji Bey was already itching to leave. . . . He missed the cafés, the gaiety, the music, the dancing, and the banter with his new Turkish friends. And God, how he missed the bedroom games with the belly dancers, their wiggling bodies, their magical fingers.

Mama knew at once that he wanted to leave and so she kept up her act.

"Your new brother Hashim must get acquainted with all his new relatives, Haji. You must take him around to meet them all, spend some time with them. And you look very tired, my son. The trip back will be rigorous, and so you must get your rest." Her voice and words were soothing to him.

"Your brothers work you too hard. Let those lazy boys do without you for a while." She was laying it on too thick, and Haji Bey was becoming suspicious.

"Mama, I need to get back. I have to start teaching Hashim a trade, I'm going to make an iron worker and businessman out of him. And I shouldn't leave my brothers for so long; they need me in the shop. I have to return to Smyrna in . . . in the morning."

Mama forgot all about her velvet gloves and lost her temper. "What's your hurry? What's itching in your pants? I forbid you to leave! Understand?"

"I'm not a little boy any more, Mother," he yelled back. "I don't need to be coddled, I don't need your nipple! I'm a grown man, so treat me as one. It's final! I'm leaving in the morning!" He was trying to act firmly, like a man, yet his boyish anger betrayed him.

Mama turned her back on your father and stalked out of the room. Haji Bey was very naïve. He thought he'd won. Hah! He forgot how tough Mama was. She wasn't defeated. She was now ready to spring her trap!

Later that afternoon, Haji Bey was sitting outside, moping, and waiting to be called for dinner. He looked up and suddenly lost his breath. Across the street, out of their neighbor's house, stepped a young girl — not just pretty, but a beauty! — with long black hair, black eyes, long shapely legs, a small waist and her heavenly twins blossoming.

Mama's voice from behind startled him. He hadn't heard her coming out. "She might be a real catch, son. Probably can cook and sew . . . Knowing her mother, I bet the girl knows how to keep an immaculate house."

"Who is that? It can't be the Chackerian girl! She was just a baby!" Your father, Nephew, remembered Siranoush as a scrawny little thing.

"She's fourteen, my boy. She'd make a very good wife."

Haji Bey's mind was whirling. My God, Mama's talking about marriage! What about Smyrna, all those good times . . . ? He needed time to think. Yet he couldn't take his eyes off the girl. He wished he could get closer to her, to talk to her, to tell her about himself, to get to know her better. . . . Oh boy, couldn't they have the time of their lives together!

"Mother, I want a better look at her. Sure, she doesn't look bad from here . . . I just want a closer look."

"You know better than that, son. You just hold your horses and let me see what I can find out about her."

Ah, our mother . . . she was a cat playing with a mouse. She already knew everything there was to know about the girl, she had chosen her weeks before Haji Bey had arrived. When Mama heard from us about her baby's carousing in Smyrna, she knew that she had to tie him down, get a female wrapped around his ankle, burden him with children. It was the only way to tame her wild son, to save him from himself.

So she went out shopping for a bride for her son. She visited many neighbors with daughters between thirteen and sixteen. During her third visit with the Chackerians, she made her decision. She inspected the girl as if buying a chicken in the market.

"Young lady, I understand you can cook some and that you do all your mother's housework?"

"I do what I can," the girl answered shyly.

"My daughter is very modest," Mrs. Chackerian interrupted. "She is constantly on the move. If she isn't washing dishes, she is dusting. If not dusting, she's preparing supper. She is our treasure."

Mrs. Chackerian was selling. Mama was buying. The girl, however, would be kept in the dark. She had no idea of the games being played by her elders. When a girl was chosen, she was asked by her parents if she were willing to marry so-and-so and she could answer either "yes" or "no." That was it.

If the girl agreed to marry, the parents would make all the arrangements with her future in-laws. If a girl lived a distance from her intended, she might know him only slightly or not at all. There was no such thing as finding your own spouse or "marrying for love." The youngsters would meet at a *khos gab*,[1] when the families visited to formalize the marriage agreement and to make arrangements for the wedding. Marriage was taken very seriously; there was no such thing as divorce. Parents prayed that they were making the right choice.

Haji Bey didn't leave Efkereh the next morning as he had planned. Smyrna wasn't on his mind at all, but the Chackerian girl was. He was actually lusting after her. He had given Mama the nod and she'd taken off like a rabbit and was across the street in a flash.

A couple of hours later, Haji Bey watched from the window as the Chackerians helped Mama across the street to our house. The girl had given her consent. The parents had drunk a few toasts in honor of the coming merger of the two families. Mother became a little giddy, from nervousness and the fact that she generally didn't touch alcohol.

Mama blinked her eyes and focused on your father. Her words were slightly slurred. "Do-nik, my naugh-ty son, you sh-hould count your blessings bee-cause you're now en-gaged to marry the jewel of Ef-ker-eh, Si-raa-noush. I'll break every bone in your body if your eyes ever stray from her. She'll make you a fine wife, a loving mother to your children." Mother was tired out from all the tension, excitement and drink. Her daughters-in-law helped her to her room and put her to bed. She'd had a hard, but profitable, day.

That night when your father retired to his own room, he imagined himself after the wedding with his young new bride. They would lie together on the bed. . . , they would make love. Then, as he lay back on his pillow, he let his mind wander back to Smyrna and to the good times that were so short and sweet. Was he doing the right thing in giving it all up?

We received a letter from our little brother. "My dear brothers," he wrote, "I'm afraid you're going to have to do

[1] A visit by the prospective groom and his family to the prospective bride and her family for the purpose of agreeing to the marriage. It was a formal occasion.

without me for a little while longer. Mother has found me a bride, the delicate 'Rose of Efkereh,' Siranoush Chackerian. She was growing up right here under my nose, and I didn't even notice her. While we were away, she blossomed into a beautiful young woman. God help me, I am already in love with her.

"I can't believe this is happening to me. Siranoush has captured my heart. I don't think I can live without her. Have I gone mad?

"I need your help. Please find us wedding rings. Buy her a couple of pairs of those French high-heeled shoes, a couple of dresses, silk stockings, underclothing, and French perfume. Go to the lady who runs the fashion shop on the esplanade near the tailor shop. I enclose Siranoush's weight and measurements given to us by her mother.

"Then go to my tailor and order a wedding suit — a white riding habit with red and gold braids running down the sides, a red fez with gold trim around the edge, a pair of white gloves, and a red sash. I already have black boots.

"When you get all these things, shut the shop down and come back home for the wedding celebration. Come as quickly as you can."

We roared with laughter when we read the letter. Mother was as good as her word, the tiger was trapped. Our worries were over, we knew he'd remain faithful to his wedding vows.

Meanwhile, in Haji Bey's absence, we had hired a new apprentice, Bedri, at the request of his father, Mahmoud Bey, an officer of the mounted police. Mahmoud Bey wanted us to teach his son a trade, show him how to do business. The boy was tall and slim, not a heavy masculine type. Quite good-looking. When I first met him, I couldn't picture a hammer in his delicate hands.

Since we did a lot of business with the police, it would be to our advantage to have the son of an officer with us. In any case, we didn't want to cross Mahmoud Bey; he was an imposing figure. If the boy didn't fit in or if the work was too much for him, he'd probably quit on his own anyway.

Most of the offspring of powerful Turks were spoiled rotten, so Bedri turned out to be a big surprise. He took to his tasks with great enthusiasm. He became like one of us. We grew to like

Bedri so much that we asked his father's permission to take him with us to Efkereh for the wedding. That way the boy could get closer to the family.

Not only did Mahmoud Bey let Bedri go with us to Efkereh, he also decided to send along two of his best men to protect us. These men were happy to do a small favor for their boss and thought it might even be fun. Mahmoud Bey, in his characteristic way, warned his men that if any harm should come to his son, he would put a bullet between their eyes.

Mahmoud Bey, unfortunately, was not satisfied with his career. He never rose beyond the middle ranks. Maybe that's why he sent his son to work for us; he didn't have the pull to get the boy a good job with the police.

Mahmoud Bey did not come from a prominent family and had no one to push him ahead. What advancement he got, he earned the hard way. He was constantly looking for ways to enhance his reputation.

One day the ambitious Turk came across a sea captain who wanted to sell Gatling guns, something the police did not have but which would give the police great power if they worked well. Mahmoud, without the permission of his superiors, purchased two of the machine guns to test them out. If the weapons worked well, Mahmoud Bey would gain the attention and hopefully the admiration of the higher-ups.

The sea captain really didn't give a damn what Mahmoud Bey wanted the guns for, or even if he had gotten permission to purchase them; the captain got his price and that was all that mattered to him.

Mahmoud Bey mounted one of the Gatling guns on the back end of a wagon. "I don't, at any time, want the gun to be seen," Mahmoud Bey told his men. "It is to be kept covered with canvas. You will guard it with your lives. No one should know what is hidden under the canvas unless you are attacked by brigands. Then it won't matter. We will show our power. Furthermore, I don't want the bandits to think you're police. You will not dress in uniform so as to preserve the element of surprise if you are attacked. Let them get within firing range, then open fire and wipe them out!"

So Mahmoud Bey wanted to achieve two goals. First, he wanted the bandits to attack so the gun could be tested under field conditions; and second, he wanted to secure the safety of his son.

Mahmoud Bey also gave his men several belts of ammunition and a dozen sticks of dynamite.

The boys and I closed the shop, locked an iron gate across the entrance, and placed a sign in the front window:

HAVE GONE TO A WEDDING
GOD WILLING, WE WILL
RETURN THE END OF JUNE
PLEASE BE PATIENT

CHAPTER EIGHT
Death in the Woods

On the following day, we loaded the wagon with wedding presents and food for the journey back to Efkereh. We hitched the horses and soon were on our way. Since Armenians could not legally carry firearms, and we were traveling with Turkish policemen, we decided to leave ours behind and hid them in the shop. The two men from the *zaptiye* had their weapons, of course.

As we started out, we Armenians crossed ourselves and said a little prayer for a safe journey. Once underway, we began to play lively Turkish dance music. We broke open several bottles of *raki* and began drinking and dancing on the wagon. With the rough road, the jerking of the wagon, the large amount of alcohol consumed, and the dancing, it was a miracle that none of us fell over the side. As we passed Arabagee's place, we noticed the old gent was out watering his stock. We hollered to him and waved.

Every evening at nightfall, we pitched our tent, fed and watered our horses, and entered our tent to sleep. Halim and Mohamet, the two policemen stayed on the wagon, one on watch while the other slept. The Gatling gun was never uncovered.

On the twelfth day, we spotted the outline of our village in the distance. For the hundredth time, Halim said, "What happened to those fucking highway bandits? Why didn't they attack?" And for the hundredth time, Mohamet answered, "Don't worry, you'll get your chance."

Well, Nephew, we finally arrived in the village and the entire Yessaian clan and our friends came out to greet us. Haji Bey came running, his arms open wide, and hugged and kissed us one by one. We were so happy!

When we reached our house, we got out our musical instruments and started to play for the crowd of well-wishers who had gathered to celebrate our return. Neighbors brought platters of food, and happy-jugs were passed around. We were so caught up in the festivities that we didn't even have time to be alone with our wives and children. Coal-oil lamps were strung out all over the compound. The party went on into the wee hours of the morning. Our two Turkish escorts joined in and had a good time, too. In fact, after a while, those two Turks were thinking that Armenians weren't such a bad lot after all.

The following morning, we all woke up with hangovers. I looked over at the wagon and could see that Mohamet and Halim were still a little woozy, too. I couldn't hear what they were talking about, but I saw them hitch the horses and drive off. One of them saw me at the window and yelled over his shoulder, contemptuously, "Don't worry about us, *Gâvur,* we'll be back in a couple of hours."

An hour and a half later, we were all startled by the sound of loud gunfire going off in rapid bursts, a kind of gunfire we'd never heard before. Suddenly, there were explosions like dynamite, two, maybe three, tremendous ones. The village went berserk. Women and children went running through the streets screaming. Everyone assumed that we were being attacked by brigands again.

The noise stopped and we calmed everyone down. Artin and I went off to look for Halim and Mohamet. After searching around for a while, we finally caught sight of the wagon lying on its side; the whole back end where the gun had been mounted was completely blown apart. The gun itself had been thrown about fifteen feet away.

We heard groans coming from some bushes. It was Mohamet, holding on to what was left of one leg. It had been severed just above the knee and hung there fastened by only a piece of skin. I quickly cut the flap of skin away and tied a tourniquet with my belt to stop the blood from gushing out. He had wounds all over his body and was covered with blood.

"Get me to Bedri, right away!" he managed to gasp; his eyes wide with shock.

I didn't bother to ask why. We got him onto our wagon as carefully as possible. When I asked him where Halim had gone, he looked at me with a faraway blank expression and whispered, "To God."

We found Halim not too far off. Oh, what a gruesome sight. Half his head was blown away. We laid the body on the wagon alongside Mohamet, and I used my shirt to cover the horrible sight. Artin took his shirt off, too, and placed it over Mohamet's shattered leg. We swung the wagon around and headed for the village.

All the way back, Mohamet kept moaning, "Get me to Bedri . . . fast . . . hurry, I won't last much longer . . . hurry, get me to Bedri or your lives won't be worth a copper penny!"

When Bedri saw us, he came running. Half the village was crowded into our compound, gawking at our bloody cargo. Mohamet managed to raise himself to a sitting position. He beckoned for the boy to bend close.

"Tell your father . . . what happened was our own doing . . . We were just having a little target practice . . . Trying out a new type of gun. Halim and I died at our own hands . . . no one else is responsible . . . and tell him his fucking gun isn't worth pig shit." With that, he gave a fitful cough and died.

Some of the boys began making coffins. I went back to the scene of the accident and found a tree that had been cut down. A close look at the place where the tree had been severed showed that it had been chopped in half by the rapid rounds of the Gatling's powerful shells. The gun had ripped itself apart and was nothing but a twisted heap. Pieces of dynamite were scattered all around the area.

I figured out what had happened. Some of the white-hot pieces of shrapnel from the gun's barrel must have landed in the box of dynamite, causing the sticks to explode. That was the noise we'd heard after the gunfire.

We placed the Turkish policemen in temporary graves; and as we lowered Mohamet into the ground, I gave special thanks to him for having so gallantly made sure we Yessaians wouldn't be blamed for their deaths.

We got a letter off to Mahmoud Bey explaining the details of the tragedy and informing him that we'd put his men in temporary graves, awaiting his further instructions. We offered him our deepest sympathy for the tragic incident.

Two weeks later an angry response from Mahmoud Bey arrived, accusing us of murder. His letter was insulting, blaming us for what had happened. We thought he'd sent the gun merely for our protection, but he was really up to something else, trying to make a name for himself. His scheme backfired. He was in trouble. To save his own hide, Mahmoud Bey would have to find a scapegoat to take the blame for what had happened. We were it.

Your father then sent a letter to Ibrahim Pasha, telling him what had happened, and that Mahmoud's own son, Bedri, was here to testify that none of us were anywhere near the wagon when the gun blew up.

About two weeks later, Ibrahim Pasha and several of his men pulled up in a large wagon to the front of our house. Your father recognized his young Turkish friend immediately and rushed out to greet him. They embraced warmly. Donik brought him over and introduced him to us.

It was actually the first time that we had met, and been introduced to, Ibrahim Pasha. We found the handsome young Turk to be a refined man, soft-spoken, pleasant, highly intelligent, with all the qualities of a gentleman.

The ladies of the house quickly brought out coffee and sweets for the guests. After a respectable length of time talking pleasantries, Ibrahim Pasha turned to business. After all, he had come here not to visit but to investigate the untimely death of two Turkish policemen and to prove, if at all possible, the innocence of his Armenian friend and his brothers.

He sat down at a table and began to interrogate witnesses. First, he questioned Artin and me, to get our version of the story and to take a deposition.

Then he called Bedri over for questioning. Ibrahim Pasha interrogated Bedri and took down his testimony. After hearing the boy out, the esteemed Ibrahim Pasha was satisfied.

"Yes, it seems to have been a terrible accident, as you related in your letter to me, and you Yessaians are not responsible for it. You are innocent of wrongdoing." Then, to finish his report, Ibrahim Pasha wanted to visit the site of the deaths and to draw diagrams.

He turned to his men and said, "Let's now go to the spot where those two men were shooting and collect the remains of the gun for evidence. Then I want to find out who bought the damn gun, who was responsible for placing it on the wagon, and why higher authorities were not informed. One does not deal with new weapons without approval from high places.

"I have my suspicions about who is responsible. I think I know the culprit, but I cannot prosecute without proof. In any case, two brave men have died needlessly and someone is going to pay for it."

Ibrahim Pasha gave orders for the bodies to be readied for their final journey home.

Then Ibrahim Pasha turned and smiled at Donik. "I hear everyone calling you 'Haji Bey.' Apparently your family has accepted your new name."

"Yes, Ibrahim Pasha, they have accepted it, even my mother. The dear woman generally lets me have my way — except when it comes to choosing a wife." Everyone laughed. "That's her domain," Donik declared, "and we have learned to trust her good judgment."

As we started to stroll back to the house, Haji Bey's thoughts turned to his wedding. He grew serious, faced his friend, and said, "Ibrahim Pasha, it would be an honor if you would remain here for my wedding. I think of you as family. It would be good if you, and perhaps your men too, stayed to share my happiness. Perhaps you can remain a full week so that you can enjoy the whole celebration. After that, we could all return to Smyrna together," Donik suggested.

Ibrahim Pasha accepted the invitation with pleasure. He said that his men, however, had to return to Smyrna in the morning. He gave them instructions to stop at nearby Caesarea and give a copy of his investigative report, in which he exonerated the Yessaian boys, to Kiprit Bey, the captain of the police. The report certified that Halim and Mohamet had died accidentally. Their deaths could be attributed to the faulty gun. One of the shells got jammed in the chamber, and so the next time the chamber was rotated, another shell slammed into the jammed one and exploded in the barrel. The responsibility, accordingly, lay with the man who had purchased the gun and sent it with these men.

The business being settled, we all sat down to enjoy some *meze* and *raki*. Haji Bey swelled with pride at the presence of his important friend in our home.

"Tomorrow, after the wedding ceremony, and before I can retire with my bride, I must go from house to house on horseback, visiting all our neighbors and having a drink with the man of each house," Haji Bey explained. "The idea is to test the groom's manliness, to see how many drinks he can take before falling off his horse. It's a tradition in our village."

We continued eating and talking. Evening came on and the boys pulled out their musical instruments and began playing. We were in a happy mood and danced until exhausted.

We awoke the next morning a little worse for wear but in excellent spirits. Everything was ready for the wedding ceremony, and we were all eager for it to begin. We men went to the church to await the bride. As the eldest brother, it was my place to be the "godfather" for my youngest brother. A "godfather" at an Armenian wedding is something like what you would call the "best man" today.

Haji Bey was in one of his moods. He turned to Ibrahim Pasha and said, "My dear friend Ibrahim Pasha, I would like you to be a godfather also." Then Donik decided that he wasn't satisfied with two godfathers. He looked at the rest of his brothers, including Hashim, and asked them to be godfathers as well! Your father wanted all of his brothers and two Turks to stand at the altar during an Armenian wedding!

Grandfather, who was officiating at the ceremony, grew angry and stared at your father with hard, cold eyes that could pierce steel.

"What do you think you're doing, young man? You can't have more than one godfather. This is all foolishness."

Haji Bey smiled innocently. "Why not, Grandfather? I don't see why a person can't have as many godfathers as he wants. I love all my brothers equally."

Grandfather shook his head with determination and said, "You may love whom you please. The Church, however, recognizes only one godfather. The others can stand up front with your eldest brother if you like. It will do no harm." Grandfather didn't want to make an issue of it with his unpredictable grandson. He called the rest of us over. "All right, my sons, stand in line next to Nazar in front of the altar."

At the appointed hour, the guests arrived at the church. Grandfather turned to mother and said, "Bring the bride. Let's begin the ceremony."

Siranoush's father escorted her. Behind them followed her godmother (the matron of honor), her mother, and several young girls carrying flowers. Then the rest of her family. Siranoush wasn't supposed to look at her intended, and she kept her eyes cast down.

She was excited and her young mind was filled with questions. She knew her betrothed was called by a Turkish name. That seemed strange. She knew that he was handsome and that his family idolized him. She had been told that he was charming. Was it all true? She would have to wait until after the wedding to find out.

Haji Bey cut quite a figure. He wore his newly made white riding habit trimmed with red and gold braid, and his black boots with golden spurs. A pair of smart white gloves covered his strong young hands. He carried a red fez with gold trim under his arm. His high collar flared open framing his face with its flashing black eyes and handlebar moustache. He looked like a young prince.

The bride was also beautiful. Her father led her to the altar and she took her place next to her bridegroom. The flowers in her nervous hands trembled.

Grandfather began the ceremony. At the proper time, he placed crowns on their heads, for they were king and queen of the day. He then asked the couple to put their foreheads together and I was told to hold a cross over their heads. Siranoush never raised her eyes. Haji Bey, on the other hand, kept stealing glimpses of her bodice. Grandfather tapped his Bible on your father's head a bit hard a couple of times during the "blessings" to make him behave. The rest of us smiled at your dad's conduct, but Grandfather only scowled all the more at our irreverence.

After he asked the bride and groom if they accepted each other as man and wife, Grandfather had them drink from a single chalice. He then announced, "Today you have become man and wife. As you are the king and queen of this day, please be seated on your thrones." The "thrones" were two Yessaian chairs that had been placed behind Haji Bey and Siranoush. Grandfather then circled the seated couple four or five times, holding high the Holy Bible and chanting marital prayers. Then he blessed the congregation and said, "Go in peace." The wedding was finished. The families embraced since they were now *khenami* [family in-laws].

Hashim went to bring Black Star to your father's side. Although Haji Bey was married now, he had not yet exchanged a word with his new bride. They had made their vows to the priest, not to each other. Your father mounted the beautiful stallion and then moved the black demon slowly through the wedding crowd.

Black Star was well groomed, his ivory tail and mane combed out. We had fitted him with a black saddle and painted the stirrups gold. He was phantom-like, black as coal, as he glittered in the sunlight. He cantered slowly sideways, his head held high, his tail lifted. He raised his front legs so high one would think he was trained to do it. He was putting on a show and he knew it. It was natural for him to behave that way. He was a proud creature.

Can you just imagine, Nephew, how your father must have felt, sitting up there on this black demon, prancing around in his white wedding suit trimmed in red-and-gold braid? I'll tell you, he was quite a splendid sight!

Haji Bey rode through the wedding crowd as the guests kissed him on both cheeks and wished him and the new bride a healthy and long life together, "on one pillow," as they say. He saluted one and all and rode off to call on the first house. He was not to leave his saddle until he either fell off his horse or finished drinking with all the neighbors along the street. Actually, the latter was well nigh impossible. The strong *raki* could kill you if you drank too much. Between gulps of the liquor, the housewives stuffed food down his mouth. Black olives, cheese, calf brains, fish "eggs," hot pickles, spicy dried beef stuffed into pita bread, baklava, and lamb's feet soup were always ready for the honored guest.

Each housewife had her own specialty food spread out on a table in her front yard. When you glanced down the street, it looked like an extravagant open-air buffet. The food was a matter of pride among the housewives, for each wanted the groom to linger longest at her table.

I was keeping track of your father's stops, wondering how many more drinks it would take to bring him down from his saddle. He had managed to visit seventeen homes and was swaying dangerously. Suddenly he began to snap his fingers and flung his arms high over his head. Then he stood up in his stirrups, while Black Star was in a medium trot, and tried to climb up on the saddle to dance on the horse's back. I figured it was time to bring him back to earth before he toppled off and broke his neck. I chased him down, took the reins of the horse, and led him home.

Haji Bey tried to look sober, even forced a smile. Of course, I knew what he was experiencing because I'd gone through the same routine myself. This test of one's manhood, I now see, is pretty dumb. It was for kids. Thank God Donik didn't actually fall off his horse, otherwise he would have been teased about it for the rest of his life.

Your dad was completely drunk. His insides were churning like a volcano; he didn't know at which end the eruption would take place first. I led him to the bridal suite, which was next to my room.

The new bride was waiting. Her first words to Haji Bey were, "Oh, my poor husband, let me help you." She gently laid your father back on the bed, took off his riding boots, loosened his collar, and pressed cold towels to his face and neck. I bid them good night and returned to the festivities. My kid brother was in fine hands. It wasn't until the next morning, Haji Bey told me later, that he was able to consummate the marriage.

Music, dancing, eating, and drinking had reached a feverish pitch. A line of dancers stretched from one end of the street to the other. Guests picked up food and drink as they passed from one table to the next in front of each house. By the time the line reached the end of the street, some of the dancers would have dropped out from either too much drink or food, or both; the others turned around to continue their circle dance moving in the opposite direction.

Dancers were all over the street. Many did solos, dancing with wild abandon. Mother sat in front of our house smiling like a queen, receiving the congratulations of the merry makers. She had won. Haji Bey was trapped. She had saved her son. To tell the truth, it was a great party.

The next morning, the housewives went back outside and replaced the previous night's food with breakfast: goat cheese, black olives, hard-boiled eggs, bread rolls, and hot Turkish coffee. This went on for three days and three nights while the bride and groom stayed in their room. They did not come out until the celebrating was over. As godfather, I looked after their needs, such as food and drink, as they requested. Otherwise, we left them alone together.

Your father was pleased with his young bride, he was very proud of her. He never failed to let her know it, even in public. Although open display of affection between a man and a woman was considered *amot* [shameful] in the eyes of others, these lovebirds couldn't have cared less. Yes, Nephew, they were two children very much in love.

CHAPTER NINE
Justice on the Trail

Haji Bey didn't want to leave his child-bride and return to Smyrna. He insisted we go without him. He would come later on. We tried to convince him that he must come with us now. After all, we also felt the agony of leaving our loved ones behind, yet we had a business that required our attention. We had been away much too long as it was.

Ibrahim Pasha was also anxious to be on his way. The men he'd sent home, and who had been ordered to stop in Caesarea and report to Captain Kiprit Bey, had also been instructed to have the captain send a wagon to Efkereh to carry Ibrahim Pasha back home.

Captain Kiprit Bey was efficient. Five days after the wedding, a long wagon pulled up in front of our house. Ibrahim Pasha planned to leave the following day. He wanted all of us to travel together. We brothers were ready to depart, and so were Bedri and Hashim. Your father resisted, however, so we asked Ibrahim Pasha to talk some sense into him.

"My friend, you must come with us, for your own safety. You know how dangerous the trails can be."

"There won't be any trouble. The only real problem is that filthy animal Osman and his band of thieves. But, we have the metal tokens now for safe passage."

Ibrahim Pasha kept trying to reason with your father. Finally, reluctantly, Haji Bey gave in.

Hashim began to jump up and down in anticipation. He certainly was having a lot of adventure in his still young life. He had five new brothers to look after him, and he had served as godfather at the wedding of one of them. He had been chased by bandits. Now he was traveling to the beautiful city he had heard so much about. He was going to see the glorious sea and Smyrna's famous harbor filled with ships from all over the world. The boy constantly hovered at our sides, and when we asked him to help load our wagon, which he and Bedri were to drive, he ran back and forth working like a beaver. His eyes streamed with tears of happiness as he hugged and kissed us.

"You're a very fortunate boy, Hashim," Ibrahim Pasha observed, "you're in good hands. Listen to your brothers, and you will prosper under the umbrella of their wisdom."

Your father's thoughts, however, were on his new wife — how he hated to leave her. He was so happy with his child-bride, and so very much in love with her, that he felt his heart would burst. Mother had made an excellent choice.

As we got ready to depart, your father took out the metal tokens he had been given by the highwayman Osman and distributed one to each of us.

Ibrahim Pasha saw what he was doing and walked over. "Haji Bey, my friend, please turn those tokens over to me! If we are stopped by those thieving beasts, I'll show you what to do." While your father was somewhat puzzled, he reluctantly handed over the five pieces of metal.

The following morning, Haji Bey hid his face as we bid our loved ones goodbye. I hadn't seen him cry since he was eight. He was locked in an embrace with his new wife and she wouldn't let him go. We allowed them a few more minutes together and then gently separated them. Your father joined the rest of us in Ibrahim Pasha's wagon and we were on our way.

The twelve miles to Caesarea passed uneventfully. When we arrived, Captain Kiprit Bey came out to greet Ibrahim Pasha.

"Greetings, Commissioner! Are you all right?"

After Ibrahim Pasha assured him that all had gone well on the trip and everything was under control, Captain Kiprit Bey offered his condolences for the deaths of Halim and Mohamet. Ibrahim Pasha shook his head grimly.

"Unfortunately, Captain, those men were playing games with a faulty Gatling gun. And what happened? Poof! Two good men gone."

Captain Kiprit Bey was hospitable and invited us to join him for lunch. During the meal, he asked us about our work. When he learned we were the exclusive suppliers of lightweight horseshoes to Smyrna's mounted police, the captain showed an interest. We told him if he would bring the hoofprints of the horses he wanted fitted on his next visit to Smyrna, we would be happy to serve him.

I turned to Ibrahim Pasha and told him I hadn't realized he was the Commissioner of Police in Smyrna. "I am not the Commissioner, I am only the Deputy Commissioner."

Captain Kiprit Bey laughed. "Your friend is a very modest man. He has many talents and is highly respected throughout the Empire. He even has, I am told, family ties with the Sultan."

"That will be enough, Captain," our Turkish friend said good-naturedly, with a wave of his hand.

After the meal, we rested for an hour or so while they watered and fed our horses. When we were ready to resume our journey, Captain Kiprit Bey sent two armed escorts to accompany Ibrahim Pasha.

On the sixth day of travel, your father was scanning the horizon with his binoculars when he suddenly stood straight up in his seat and announced, "I think we have company, coming fast!"

We all turned and saw a ball of dust rising in the distance.

"Let them come!" Ibrahim Pasha seemed to relish the thought. "Don't speed up, let's see what those animals look like. It is beyond me why my government doesn't allow us to clean these murderous scum off the earth once and for all!"

My brothers and I all swung our heads around to stare in surprise at our Turkish friend. How could he not know — or was he pretending not to know — the reason for his government's lack of action on this matter?

■ ■ ■ ■

"Isn't that rather strange, Nephew? Does it seem possible that someone of his position didn't understand that highwaymen were purposely allowed to roam free along the trails to keep Armenians from entering the large cities? Other brigands were encouraged by the government to commit periodic atrocities. That was supposed to keep the Armenians in their place."

I began to squirm in anguish. Uncle Nazar was going off on *another* political tangent. How could he. How could he, RIGHT NOW?

"Many Turks wanted to overthrow Sultan Abdul Hamid's corrupt regime. Instead of bringing reform to the Empire, Abdul Hamid tried to rule by repression. Not only did the Bloody Sultan frequently have Armenians massacred, he also persecuted progressive Turks. The Young Turks, a Turkish revolutionary party, and the party of Turkish Liberals, had new ideas. Some of these men, like Ibrahim Pasha, wanted to reestablish the constitution of 1876, establish a secular state, and make all citizens equal. But others wanted to get rid of the Armenians and other minorities and make 'Turkey for the Turks.'"

"Oh, please, Uncle," I cried, "pleeeease, no politics. Not now, with Osman coming down the road!"

Uncle Nazar paid me no attention. He calmly lit a Lucky Strike, pulled off the piece of paper stuck to his lip, and sipped his coffee with a loud slurp.

"UNCLE!"

"Oh, all right, all right. You have to learn patience, Nephew, patience."

■ ■ ■ ■

The highwaymen were closing in fast, shrieking and screaming. Ibrahim Pasha gave Hashim orders to slow down a bit to "give our 'friends' a chance to catch up." As they drew nearer, your father recognized the dog-faced Osman and three of his companions.

"Look," he yelled to Hashim, "he's got the same leeches with him as the night he came to the Sarkisian's when we were there."

When our pursuers finally overtook us, they ordered us to stop.

Ibrahim Pasha was first to speak. "*Ne istiyon itler?*" [What do you filthy dogs want?], he said with obvious disdain.

Osman was so taken with surprise at Ibrahim Pasha's words that he could hardly speak. Slowly it dawned on him that the man calling him a dog was a Turk, probably an official; he saw the star and crescent on his cap.

"Osman, you stupid, filthy beast," your father piped up, "your ass is in real trouble now! This is the Commissioner of Police of Smyrna, himself, whose picture I showed you when we last met."

Osman's face turned white. He backed off, waiting grimly for the Commissioner's next words. "I hear your name is Osman, what a pity such a venerable name is wasted on a Turk such as you!"[1]

Ibrahim Pasha ordered Osman and his men to dismount. Then he told Bedri and Hashim to build a fire. He called over Osman's three lieutenants and ordered them to place three of the metal tokens in a tin cup and heat them over the fire, all the while continuing to curse the bandits and their ancestors.

"Move, move," he screamed at the shaking bandits, "we haven't got all day. It is time for me to teach you a lesson you'll never forget."

With a gesture of his hand, he motioned the henchmen to take hold of Osman. "Lay him face down on the ground. Face down, I say! Come on, hurry, move your worthless carcasses! And you, Osman, pull down your pants and bare that filthy ass of yours! We're going to return your metal tokens to you; and you, in return for them, are going to sing for us. I want to hear some music!"

"Put your ugly face to the ground, you worthless dog! Now, then, you two spread his legs apart and hold him down — do as I say or you'll be next!" We had never seen Ibrahim Pasha so angry or heard him use such foul language.

The tokens were about the size of an American quarter. Osman was beginning to get the picture. He kept raising his head from the ground and screaming, "*Be daha yapmam! Allahini seversen, ayağini öpeyim!*" [I won't do it again! If you love God, please let me kiss your feet instead!]

But it was too late. Ibrahim Pasha had made up his mind. He spit at the brigands. "You, chicken-brains," he said, "I will burn this day into your memories, especially your worthless leader's. And you, animal," he turned to the one chosen to do the honors.

"Now, you, imbecile, take the cup and remove just one token at a time. Don't drop it. If you do, you'll just have to reheat it.

---

[1] Osman was the founder of the Ottoman Empire and was revered by the Turks. They called themselves *Osmanli* [Ottomans]. The word "Turk" was a term of derision in those days.

Place the token on his ass and push it up his asshole with your finger. Go ahead! Do it! I command you! Push it all the way up, where it belongs. God knows, nobody here wants it.

"From now on, every time your leader tries to take a crap, his asshole will remind him of this day. I'm doing this for his own good, and yours. I don't want his memory to fail him. If you rob and kill again on this trail, and I hear about it, it will be the end for you all. And you, Osman, give us a song."

The Turk who was to do the honors was trembling. "My fingers will burn, they will get shit all over them," he protested.

"Why should that bother you," Ibrahim Pasha scoffed, "when it's only your fingers? Your whole body, from head to toe, is full of shit. The blisters on your fingers will be a good reminder for a long time. Get on with it . . . or would you rather have a bullet between your eyes?"

Steam began to rise from Osman's butt as the first token was pushed in, and he let out a terrifying scream. "That's it, that's it, sing for us," Ibrahim Pasha shouted in fury. Then Ibrahim Pasha had the other two lieutenants repeat the operation. By the third token, Osman had fainted from the pain. At first, I thought all this was sadistic . . . until I remembered all the innocent people, mostly Armenians, whom this beast had robbed, tortured, and murdered on this very road. It was good for him, proper retribution.

Ibrahim Pasha turned to the other bandits. "We had no use for these tokens; and since they belonged to your leader, we thought it only right that he should get them back." He threw the remaining tokens down on the ground. "When he regains consciousness, you tell him that if anything should happen to my friends here, on this trail or anywhere else in this region, I will hunt you down like the wild dogs you are and skin you alive. Understand?"

The bandits, by now, were shaking like leaves. They got on their knees and began crying, "*Af edersin, Efendi, bir defa daha olmaz.*" [I beg your pardon, Sir, this will not happen again.] The one with burnt fingers kept sucking on them in his mouth, trying to cool them off, until he realized where they had been so recently. Then the three of them began kicking and cursing their unconscious leader. We didn't dare laugh; Ibrahim Pasha was in a foul mood. He was disgusted with his own people.

"When will these Turks ever become civilized?" he grumbled to the heavens.

We left the band of thieves groveling in the dust. They had been taught a good lesson by Professor Ibrahim Pasha.

We continued our journey. Haji Bey and I sat up several nights after the others had turned in, talking about the wedding, the folks back home, and his friend Ibrahim Pasha. I had become very impressed with the man, chiefly because he didn't behave like any other Turk I'd ever known. Come to think of it, Ibrahim Pasha didn't think of himself as a Turk, he thought of himself as an Ottoman, one of the ruling class.

"That Ottoman *hemşeri* [citizen] is a genuine friend," I told your father. "Without the wisdom and support of the Ibrahim Pashas of Turkey, I'm afraid the Armenian question is going to be settled in an ugly way."

Haji Bey listened in silent surprise, then smiled and hugged me. "God, Nazar! I'm pleased to hear that you finally understand what's happening to this country. There are other good people in Turkey like Ibrahim Pasha, but I am afraid that the ignorant majority would be happy if we Armenians were destroyed."

Yes, it seems your father had already thought about getting us out of Turkey. He was heartened by my words because he felt he now had an ally with whose help he could convince our other brothers to go along.

We arrived in Smyrna without further incident. We drove directly to our shop. As Ibrahim Pasha prepared to take leave, he said, "Gentlemen, please don't let the Gatling gun tragedy back in Efkereh bother you any longer. I consider you innocent and so will my office. The case is closed. Just concentrate on your work and enjoy good lives." He kissed each of us on both cheeks and told us his men would return the horses we had leased for the trip to Efkereh and take care of our bill.

He turned to your father for a final goodbye. He smiled gently and clapped a friendly arm around his shoulders. "Now that you're an old married man, Haji Bey, I know we won't be seeing you around the cafés any more. I realize that your faith and customs place a high value on fidelity. You will no longer be able to run around."

"Yes, my friend," your father replied, "I fear you are right, I can't run around. There is no rule, on the other hand, that says I can't have a simple drink with my Turkish friends once in a while."

Ibrahim Pasha laughed. "Of course, you can. But we must be careful not lead you into temptation."

Ibrahim Pasha waved farewell as he climbed up on his wagon, snapped the whip, and drove down the cobblestone street. The wagon disappeared from sight as it rounded the corner.

CHAPTER TEN
A Question of Honor

More than a month's worth of musty air filled our shop when we returned to Smyrna. We opened the windows to let the breeze flow through. Not surprisingly, our drop box overflowed with orders for new work, and we were soon at our stations trying to keep up with the avalanche of business.

As the months slipped by and more orders came in, we had to expand the shop again. Our landlord, Sarkis Aga, agreed to knock out a wall to give us more space next door. Naturally, the rent was increased, but only a little.

"I will give you a deal, yet I have to make it all look legitimate when my sons examine the books," our distinguished landlord explained. "I don't want them to think I'm getting soft on my tenants."

We loved the old boy as if he were our father. He seemed to take great delight in seeing our operation expand and did everything he could to help us along. Once or twice a week, he would drop by our shop carrying a basket of pita bread filled with shish kebab and salad. We'd all sit down and eat while listening to him tell stories about the beginnings of his many business ventures, hanging on his every word, trying to learn lessons from the master.

Yes, Nephew, life was very good to us during that time, except when we received letters from home. There was war in the Balkans, and although many of our men fought bravely on the side of the Ottoman Empire, some of our people were being arrested for phony reasons, like spitting on the street or evading taxes. We often questioned Sarkis Aga about these incidents and he would say, in irritation, "Those Armenians probably deserved their fate. They were undoubtedly troublemakers."

Sarkis Aga grew up among the Turks and thought of them as his good friends. He couldn't see what all the fuss was about. Of course not. Because of his success in business, he was respected all over Turkey. He personally never experienced discrimination.

If any of his Armenian acquaintances got into trouble with the law, he would get them off with *bakshish*,[1] sometimes paying it out of his own pocket.

"You see!" he would say, "Turks are easy to get along with."

Heaven help those Armenians, however, who didn't have a Sarkis Aga for a friend or money in their pockets!

■ ■ ■ ■

Meanwhile, the Gatling gun incident had caused Mahmoud Bey many sleepless nights. Since the tragic deaths of his two men in Efkereh, he had become an object of ridicule within his own office. Worse yet, his entire department became the butt of many jokes within the city. Mahmoud's humiliation was complete. His son, Bedri, was very much concerned.

"Two nights ago, my father left the house and hasn't been home since." The boy began weeping.

We tried to console our apprentice by telling him that his father would probably show up soon.

Bedri just shook his head. "No, you don't understand our ways. If a man is asked by his superiors to sacrifice himself to save the face of the department, he must comply. I am afraid that this is what has happened to my father."

As we talked about his father's plight, the front door burst open and in stalked Mahmoud Bey. Bedri rushed up and embraced him. "Father! Are you all right? I have been worried about you."

When Mahmoud Bey saw the concern in his son's eyes, he hesitated and then said, "Yes, yes, of course. Nothing for you to worry about. Nothing to worry about."

Mahmoud Bey, however, cast a murderous glare at the rest of us, as if we were responsible for his downfall. Then he gave Bedri a lingering embrace and said, "Well, son, I must say goodbye, I have to go."

---

[1] The payment of *bakshish*, or giving small "gifts," was typical in underdeveloped countries where petty bureaucrats were underpaid and susceptible to bribes.

With that, he gently pushed his son aside, went out, and slammed the door.

That evening Mahmoud Bey took his usual walk to his favorite café and sat down at his regular table. He ordered a drink and *meze*, and picked at the food until the belly dancers came out. This night, one of the girls he had found especially attractive, but who had refused his attention, began to play up to him. She danced at his table, her body swaying with the wild abandon of leaves being blown by a summer storm. She stared into his eyes and wrapped her veils around his neck.

"Aren't you going to buy me a drink, Effendi?" she whispered.

"Of course, of course, my beauty!" Mahmoud Bey forgot his troubles as his pulse quickened and his blood began to heat up. "Come, sit here with me and I'll order champagne." He ordered two bottles of the best in the house and told the waiter to leave one on the table and to take the other to the dancer's room upstairs. Then he lit her cigarette for her, not noticing that her fingers trembled nervously as she dragged on the weed.

As they drank the champagne, she leaned close and stroked his hair as she whispered: "Come, my strong one, let's see what kind of lover you are tonight."

Mahmoud Bey was elated. He grabbed the bottle from the table and led the girl up to her room.

They undressed as soon as he had closed the door behind them. Mahmoud Bey was all aroused as the girl pulled him down on top of her for the final act of their bedroom drama.

Suddenly, unseen by the lovers, two gendarmes lunged from behind the long dark drapes, their knives only a glint in the candlelight. The blades found their home in Mahmoud Bey's heaving bare back. After the gendarmes pulled their daggers out of his quivering flesh, one of the men performed the *coup de grace* by making a deep hacking swipe across Mahmoud Bey's neck.

The deed was done. The orders had been carried out. No more humiliation for Mahmoud Bey and his department, just the long, peaceful sleep of the dead.

The belly dancer shoved his bloody body off of her with a look of disgust. It flopped to the floor with a thud. A smile of satisfaction slowly covered her face. Why shouldn't she smile?

She had done her job well. The gendarmes paid her the blood money and walked out.

No one asked questions downstairs. Such cafés were places of clandestine rendezvous and intrigue. It was only weeks later that a drunken gendarme whispered the ugly story to his companions. In Smyrna, such news spreads quickly.

A few weeks after Mahmoud Bey disappeared, Ibrahim Pasha came looking for your father, explaining to us that he would be leaving for London where he was to serve in the Turkish embassy. Of course, we were happy for him, although I had some concerns in my mind. To whom were we going to turn for help if the Turks began to persecute us?

Ibrahim Pasha gave them an address. "I can receive letters through this address as soon as I am situated in London. Keep the address to yourself. It is that of some Armenian friends of mine who relocated to England twenty years ago. No one else should know about it."

Ibrahim Pasha feared that the Young Turk government would get his country into another war. "We Turks are fighters, and we have done this magnificently. We have conquered many countries and created the Ottoman Empire. I'm afraid our time was then. Today, economic power is the base of political power. We lack economic power, so now our military power is slipping away. We must look to our own welfare and try to keep our country from falling apart. We do not need another war." For the first time he looked helpless in front of us, his shoulders drooping.

He walked over and embraced your father, then came over to me and did the same. He made a quick about-face and left the shop.

Your father's eyes overflowed with tears, and I wasn't doing much better. We intuitively feared that this might be the last time we would see this good and sensitive man.

CHAPTER ELEVEN
A Time for Decision

The years passed quickly. Our business expanded and we prospered. We could now send more money to our families and make periodic visits. We and our families were relatively happy. As happy as was possible, given our physical separation, and the unstable political climate in Turkey.

We brothers had learned to deal as best we could with growing discrimination in Smyrna and the random harassment of Armenians. We kept our complaints to ourselves — except for your father, who was always shooting off his mouth.

The idea of leaving our homeland was always with us. It grew stronger with each passing month. Haji Bey was always lecturing us about it. As he grew older, he managed to do without a stump or a table to climb on when he was about to give a speech. He never let a day go by, however, without haranguing us about moving to America. He wanted to go in the worst way.

It had been years since your father's marriage to Siranoush and, sadly, they hadn't been blessed with a child. I'm sure it really bothered him, especially whenever he made the long trek back to Efkereh, usually twice a year. Nephews abounded, yet he had no son or daughter of his own to come running to greet him.

The journey to our hometown had become almost routine and usually uneventful. But one time, a few years after Haji Bey was married, he and I were on the road to Efkereh when we were approached by that bloody bastard Osman and his band of highwaymen. Although we hadn't seen the pig for some time, he hadn't changed a bit. Actually, I was surprised he was still alive — the kind of operation Dr. Ibrahim Pasha had performed on him would have killed an ox.

Your father didn't mince words. "Have you forgotten you were ordered by my good friend Ibrahim Pasha to stay away from us? Certainly you must be reminded of that day every time you take a crap. If you're looking for trouble, Osman, we can supply you with plenty of it!"

The bandit shifted in the saddle until most of his back end was hanging over one side of his poor horse. Osman didn't look as ferocious as he had a few years before.

"*Gâvur,*" he blustered, "don't get too smart with me. Your days are numbered. I've been keeping my eye on you boys. Each time you make this trip, your loads are heavier, your clothes are finer in quality. Tell me something, *gâvurlar*, what gives you the right to steal our wealth from us?"

He made a move toward his saber, but my gun spoke first, shooting the fez right off his head. Osman's face went white.

"*Pezevenk*! [Pimp!]," I shouted in my anger, "the next round will find the spot between your eyes! There is nothing stopping you from getting a job and making your own money. Even after your lesson, you still haven't learned right from wrong. Now get the fuck out of my sight before I change my mind and put a bullet through your crazy head."

It was plain from the surprise on Osman's face that he hadn't expected such a tough reply, even from us.

"Your day of reckoning will come soon, Armenians!" he snarled. "Our Turkish blades thirst for Armenian blood! Someday, they will be satisfied."

He gestured to his men and they simply swung their mounts around and slowly rode off. We were relieved to see the bastards back off. I'm sure Osman's meeting with Ibrahim Pasha had stayed fresh in his mind. He must have felt the pain in his rear end every single day. We never saw those brigands again. They may have changed their ways. In any case, they certainly never bothered us again.

As Haji Bey and I continued our journey homeward, I could not put out of my mind what that murdering bastard Osman had said about Turkish blades thirsting for Armenian blood. In my heart I knew he was right. Our days *were* numbered.

■ ■ ■ ■

The years passed quickly. It was 1909. On one of our trips back home, we arrived to see all the neighborhood women gathered at our house. As soon as we entered, the women began to giggle.

"All right, what is it?" I demanded. "Are my pants on backwards?"

The women then roared with laughter. "No!" they all yelled, "Haji Bey's going to be a father!"

Haji Bey couldn't believe his ears. He had been married twelve years! We all slapped him on the back. The smile on Siranoush's face and her tears of joy told us it was true. Everyone began to celebrate. Haji Bey danced with wild abandon for more than two hours. He was almost out of his head with joy.

From that day on, your father was adamant. He was going to leave Turkey. He wasn't going to take the chance of anything happening to his family. His child was going to grow up in America!

His in-laws, the Chackerians, joined us for breakfast the next morning. Their seven-month-old son, Kourken, was with them. Haji Bey took the baby in his arms, cuddled him tenderly, and bounced him on his knee. Of course, inside, he was thinking of his own child who would soon be born.

Haji Bey cleared his throat. "My dear ones, there is something important that I want to share with you. I beg you to hear me out. I plan on going to America and, after I am settled, sending for my wife and child. I am not doing this lightly, I've given it years of thought. Our people are no longer secure here, if ever we really were. Please understand and give us your blessings. We must begin a new life in a new land."

Mama Yessaian was totally shocked. "I thought we weren't going to talk about that anymore, she said with exasperation. "Why are you spoiling our breakfast with our in-laws and neighbors?"

"Mother, we must do it." Your father stared into the baby's innocent eyes for a moment, then looked up with a sad expression on his face. "There are so many bad omens. Something evil is going to happen. Reality won't change just because you ignore it."

Mama Yessaian pursed her lips tightly. It was obvious what she was thinking: *You'll leave over my dead body!* She was a stubborn woman.

Your father shook his head, shrugged, handed the baby to his mother-in-law, Mrs. Chackerian, and went back to his breakfast. It was obvious what he was thinking: *It might take a year, maybe two, but I'm going to America.* He was a stubborn man. By this time he was nearing his twenty-ninth year and had grown into a man. After a visit of ten days, we left Efkereh.

The trip was uneventful. As we neared Smyrna, we decided to visit Arabagee and his wife, something we had done many times over the years. Dudük Hanim came out to meet us, which struck us as unusual. It was the custom for the man of the house to come out and greet friends or strangers. Something was wrong. As soon as we realized she was dressed in black, we knew. Her eyes were red from crying. She burst into tears once more and sobbed that Arabagee had passed away five days earlier.

We were all saddened by the news. She invited us in and made strong Turkish coffee. As we talked, she told us that the government was trying to take away her property. She showed us the repossession notice.

"If there was one thing my husband was particular about, it was making sure the taxes were paid on time. I know he paid them, but I have no proof. I can't find a receipt."

"He never talked with me about finances," she continued. "He always said it wasn't a woman's place to be concerned with such matters."

She insisted that we stay for lunch, and filled the table to overflowing with food. She set a place for herself in the back room, as was the custom among the old-fashioned Turks. At that time, family women weren't allowed to eat in the same room with the men. We begged her to sit and eat with us. We refused to touch the food until she sat down. Finally convinced, she sat down. Sitting with men was a new idea for her, and it took a while before she felt comfortable. Soon, she forgot her troubles and began to enjoy herself. The conversation turned to our first visit.

"I was ready to kill you," she confessed to us, "the day you were here blabbing about changing your religion. You sure fooled Arabagee, but I was on to you. The very idea, borrowing his wagons so that you could go to Smyrna and embrace Islam. What a laugh! Hah! What chance did I have to interfere. Do you remember how my husband slapped me around?"

We smiled. As we were ready to leave, we all thanked her. Your father gave Dudük Hanim a hug. "Let me have that repossession notice; I'll see what I can do for you." He promised to send word to her within the week.

When we got back to Smyrna, we found Sarkis Aga at our shop, sharing lunch with our brothers. Haji Bey had Dudük Hanim's tax notice sticking out of his shirt pocket, knowing full well that the old man would notice the official government seal and become curious. Sure enough, in a few minutes the Aga played right into your father's hands and asked about the document.

"Isn't it a shame," Haji said, "that the Turkish government would try to take advantage of a poor widow who just lost her husband. And she isn't even Armenian, she's a *Turk!*"

Our old friend read the notice and when he came to the official's name on the bottom, he exclaimed, "I know the rascal who signed this notice! He's always up to mischief. He's trying to collect the taxes twice and pocket the extra money. Corrupt officials like him will try to do this when they believe the widow has no knowledge of the paid taxes. I will take care of this."

Two days later, Sarkis Aga came to us grinning from ear to ear, waving a paid tax bill in his hand. "Didn't I tell you! The Turks are easy to get along with."

I think the old boy really believed what he said, or he was pipe dreaming. In any case, he had come through for us.

Haji Bey immediately sent the document marked "PAID" to Arabagee's widow and instructed the messenger to say: "Here is your paid receipt. If there's anything else we can do, please don't hesitate to ask. We'll never forget the favor you and your husband did for us."

Dudük Hanim responded with a message: "Thank you. You boys are very good. You have taken pity on a widow. May God repay you manyfold. If all Armenians are as good as you, we

Turks should feel honored to have you living among us. I kiss your hand."

■ ■ ■ ■

Haji Bey's firstborn was a boy. They named him Garbis.[1] We were all were overjoyed, especially the proud parents. As the months went by, your father thought more and more about his wife and baby, wondering what the future held for them.

Although I know the political parts of my story bore you, Nephew, it's important that you understand that conditions for Armenians in Turkey had worsened by 1910.

Armenians and Turks had lived together in peace for hundreds of years. In the 19th century, when the Empire began to decline, the troubles started. Maybe the troubles were getting worse, or maybe the people were just getting tired of bad government. In 1894-1896, there were large-scale massacres in many cities; 300,000 Armenians were killed. Efkereh, fortunately, was spared.

Then there was the great massacre of 1909 in Adana, and that happened after the "reforming" Young Turks came to power in 1908 and reestablished the abandoned Constitution of 1876. Armenians in Adana and surrounding villages were slaughtered like animals. What was going to happen next? Where would it happen? Would we be involved the next time? Why couldn't the Turks and Armenians live in peace? Why did the Turks persecute Armenians? Haji Bey, in particular, agonized over these questions.

When your father returned to Smyrna from one of his trips to Efkereh, several months after the baby was born, he was very upset. I thought I knew what was eating at him, but I wasn't sure. I asked him, "Is there something wrong back home?"

"No. I guess . . . everything's fine . . . if you refuse to see reality and want to live in a dream world." He leaned close and grabbed my arm. "Nazar! All our loved ones are sleeping! They think that things will get better between the Armenians and the

---

[1] Diminutive of Garabed, "Forerunner," after St. John the Baptist.

Turks, but I can see clearly that they will only get worse." His eyes flashed, his voice became an angry hiss. "Even you, Nazar! And Artin, Hovsep and Mardiros! None of you sees the storm gathering over our heads!"

I pulled my arm away. "Hold on there, my young impulsive brother! That's not true. Your brothers and I have done a lot of thinking, too. It's just that I, as the head of the family, hadn't made up my mind yet about what we should do. Well, my dear brother Haji Bey, Mardiros and I are now ready to leave whenever you are. We've saved a few gold pieces and can afford the trip . . . so, let's go!" I realized that by saying this to my brother, there was no turning back.

Your father was beside himself with joy. As for me, now that I had actually said we were going to go, everything seemed easier; I became optimistic. "Once we reach American soil and get ourselves settled, we'll soon make money and send for our wives and children."

"And if we can't convince them to come, what then?"

"You leave them to me," I said.

Haji Bey and I laid out a plan by which Artin and Hovsep would stay in Smyrna and run the business with the help of Bedri and young Hashim, while Haji Bey, Mardiros, and I would go to America and try to get established. Then we wrote back home and told our families that we had decided to take our fate in our own hands and that we were going to America. We would send for them after we were settled.

The letters started flying back and forth — for weeks and weeks. The family begged us not to go. We, insisted on going. Mama furiously demanded that we give up our foolish plan. Haji Bey insisted that it was the only thing to do. Oh, Nephew, we became so overwhelmed with everyone's opinions and suggestions that Haji Bey and I just threw up our hands in frustration.

Even Sarkis Aga got into the act and tried to persuade Haji Bey to remain in Smyrna and take part in his new project to build a movie theater and show films imported from Hollywood.

There was no more time to argue with anyone. The smell of war was in the air. We figured that we had to go soon or we wouldn't be able to leave at all. We rushed to make the arrangements. We got passports, visas, and booked passage.

Then the big day arrived. Haji Bey, Mardiros, and I said goodbye to Bedri and Hashim at the shop, and embraced them with tears in our eyes. Then Artin and Hovsep took us down to the harbor in a buggy, loaded with all our personal belongings, down to the ship. The sky was blue, the sea calm, yet our hearts were heavy. We wept a storm of tears as we bid farewell to our brothers. After final embraces on the pier, we climbed the gangplank and boarded the ship. We presented our tickets to a deck officer and were assigned sleeping quarters.

An hour later, we felt the vibrations from the huge engines below. The ship shook, started to move slowly from the dock, and gradually eased out of the harbor. Haji Bey, Mardiros, and I stood at the railing, watching as the city of Smyrna receded from our sight. The city pulled at my heart. "Don't go, don't go!" it seemed to be calling. "This is where you belong. This is your land. This is where your forefathers are buried."

Haji Bey's reaction was different. "Geography is an accident," he said. "A man has to go where his body and mind are free, where his heart can sing."

His words made me feel much better. I couldn't help thinking that fate had made a mistake: I should have been the younger brother, and your father the elder.

CHAPTER TWELVE
Welcome to America, 1910

Our ship carried Mardiros, your father, and me smoothly to France where we boarded another to take us to America. It wasn't a difficult voyage at all. After our first few days aboard, we got our "sea legs," as they say. We constantly talked about what we might expect in America, what we would do, where we would go, and where we would live. We became acquainted with many of the other passengers, who were mostly emigrants like us. We settled into a routine of eating, sleeping, and talking. The days passed quickly.

Apprehension and anxiety began to build up in us as we approached New York. As we entered the harbor, everybody hung over the rails, waiting for the first glimpse of our new home. When we passed the Statue of Liberty, Nephew, you can imagine the "oohs" and "aahs" coming from every mouth. She was so beautiful, that lady. Many of us men tipped our hats to her. All of us had tears streaming down our happy faces.

After landing on Ellis Island, the immigration officers herded us into the cavernous halls of a massive building. There we were given extensive physical examinations and many injections. Finally, we were allowed through the gates and taken to the foot of Manhattan Island.

We three brothers stood on the bustling streets of New York with our belongings in our hands. Our first task was to find a place to live. We managed somehow to hail a buggy. Since we didn't know English, or anything about the city, how could we tell the driver where to go? I started to speak Turkish to the driver and then switched to Greek. What else could I do? To our amazement, he answered in broken Greek!

"When you live in New York," he explained, "it helps to know a few languages. I don't know them all well, but I manage to talk with guys like you. I'm a Jew, my parents came here from Russia, from Odessa, when I was two years old."

And how did he like living in America, I asked. He laughed, looking around at all the activity going on in the streets.

"I like my life here. I can't compare it to any other country, since I only know this one. According to my parents, this is paradise." Since we had no idea where we wanted to go, the cabby took us to Astoria, to a Greek neighborhood where everyone spoke Greek.

We rode through the crowded streets, our eyes and ears filled with the unbelievable sights and sounds of the great city. Beeping automobiles rushed past horse-drawn carriages. Clanging trolleys screeched along on steel rails. Buildings as tall as mountains seemed to reach to the clouds. Movie houses with their bold marquees, one right after the other, lined the streets. Oh, Nephew, I can't describe our happy feelings that day. Electric lights. Water faucets. Indoor toilets. All those modern miracles!

Irishmen, Englishmen, Frenchmen, Jews, Arabs, Greeks, Spaniards, Germans, Poles, Russians, Chinese, and Italians, *all* living in harmony and going about their own businesses. Synagogues and churches of all peoples stood in quiet testimony to mutual tolerance. This was surely the land of freedom, the place they called "heaven on earth." The people back home would have to see this place with their own eyes before they would believe it. We hardly believed it ourselves, and we were right there!

The cabby let us off at a Greek coffee house. The fellows there recommended a boarding house run by a Greek lady as a nice place to stay. Our ignorance of English made it difficult for us to find decent jobs. A furrier finally hired us for ten cents an hour. We stayed with him for a few weeks but soon got sick of working for nothing. Financially, we had been much better off back in Smyrna. We hadn't come to America to be poor.

We heard of an Armenian settlement in Massachusetts, in a city called Worcester. And that, Nephew, is where we decided to go to seek our fortune.

When we arrived in Worcester, we went directly to the Armenian coffeehouse. We met a nice man almost immediately, a Mr. Bagdasarian, who was a supervisor in a local shoe factory. They needed workers, he told us. Then he invited us over to his house for dinner that very evening. We left our things in an

Armenian rooming house and walked over to Mr. Bagdasarian's place.

Andranik Bagdasarian had come to the United States about fifteen years ago, after Sultan Abdul Hamid's massacres in the 1890s. "Our village was attacked the year before I left," he told us. "It was a terrible massacre. My father was killed before my very eyes, as were most of my relatives. My mother and I survived and I was determined to get out of Turkey before the next massacre began.

"I'd saved my money over the years while apprenticing in a leather shop. This money, plus what my father had left us, was just enough to get us to this beloved country. I was lucky, on shipboard I met and fell in love with an Armenian girl who was also emigrating. We were married by the ship's captain. She turned out to be a truly special lady, as you can see.

"I'll tell you one thing, boys," he went on, "if you have anyone left back there, get them out as soon as possible."

We told him that was what we intended to do.

The next day, we went to the factory where Mr. Bagdasarian was employed. He arranged for us to be hired on the spot, and we were to report to work the next morning.

Then Mr. Bagdasarian said, "You have been assigned to a department with a foreman who has a mean streak in him. That is why there are immediate openings. He likes to fire people. Do your best to get along with the bastard until I can find you openings in a better department."

Early the next morning we went to work. Mr. Bagdasarian took us to our department and turned us over to our foreman, Mr. Otto. Nephew, you should have seen this character. His large frame and powerful voice gave him the look of a wrestler. He was the spitting image of that German actor Erich von Stroheim, right down to the bald head, monocle, and cigarette holder. I swear he could have been the actor's twin brother! The employees called him "Skin Dome" behind his back.

Bagdasarian had warned us that Otto, who had immigrated to the United States from Germany ten years earlier, was hostile toward anyone who wasn't from northern Europe. Otto especially disliked anyone whose color was a little on the dark side, like the immigrants coming from the Mediterranean and Middle Eastern countries. He hated Armenians, Greeks, and Italians . . . which meant we were already on the big German's shit list even before meeting him. Of course, I prepared myself to be fired immediately because I knew your father's big mouth would surely get us into some kind of trouble.

Otto had also served as an officer in the German army and had a military bearing. His loathing for us could be felt at once. We never had a chance with him. His monocle hung on a string that was tucked into his vest pocket. Whenever he came around our work stations, he would pop it into his eye and try to find defects in our work. If he couldn't find anything wrong, he'd bellow, "You fucking giavours are gonna burn in Turkey some day!"

The first time he used the word "giavour" we were genuinely surprised. Apparently, when Otto had served in the German army, he had been stationed in Turkey for a year as a staff officer. Turkey and Germany were drawing closer after the 1890s and there were military exchanges. Why Otto left the army and came to America we never learned. Maybe he got into some kind of trouble. In any case, he had learned this expression from a Turk and seemed to enjoy using it.

It wasn't long before Haji Bey had had enough of Otto's insults and browbeating. There is no question that this guy was trying his damnedest to find an excuse to fire us. "If he doesn't cut it out, I'm going to shove that monocle up his rear and see if his brain is imbedded with the rest of his shit!"

"It isn't worth going to jail just to get even with that pimp," I told your father. I tried to keep peace because I didn't want us to lose our jobs, Nephew. We needed them badly at that time. What else could we do? We had to keep our mouths shut.

Skin Dome was an all-around rotten guy. The bastard would even take advantage of female employees, especially if they were young and pretty. He would force the girls to have sex with him in the storeroom. Although Otto's routine was well known throughout the factory, the guys in the front office looked the other way. They were only interested in production and making the stockholders happy. And the bastard really kept production and quality up. He ran his department with an iron fist. When quitting time came around, we were all so exhausted and nauseated by the stench of cowhide, we could barely make it home.

The beast's sadistic side showed when he no longer desired a particular woman. If the woman turned out a defective shoe, he would throw it on the floor, spit and stomp on it, and then stare at her with his little pig eyes and growl, "You're fired!" How he savored standing there watching his victim crying. Then he'd strut away and look for another young thing to take her place.

About the third week, Haji Bey had reached the boiling point with old Skin Dome. He kept moving us around from one job to another, hoping that we'd foul up so that he could fire us.

At this time, Otto was between women. A new girl was hired, a pretty little thing of not more than sixteen. Otto had his mark. He walked over to her and placed his arm around her waist. There he was, his bald head shimmering under the glare of the overhead lights, shouting in the girl's ear so she could hear him over the roar of the machines. We all knew what he was up to. The poor kid was as frightened as hell. She shook her head and began crying. Otto persisted. Obviously he was threatening to fire her if she didn't cooperate.

Now, with tears streaming down her face, she gave a tiny nod. Ah, Nephew, that helpless child was mortified.

Your father exploded. "Nazar! I've had it! I'm going to fix that son-of-a-bitch! Keep an eye on that door and let me know when you see him coming back. I'm going to prove to this company that we can do a better job than Otto. I'm going to get that fucking bastard."

Oh, boy, here we go again, I thought uneasily. "Come on, Haji," I pleaded. "We don't need any trouble, it's not worth it. Let's get the hell out of here! Listen," I said, trying to distract him, "I'm getting bored with this job. Let's go to Detroit and get a job at the Ford Motor Company. Old man Ford is paying five dollars a day."

Haji Bey's eyes lit up at the prospect of working in a huge car factory; however, I couldn't sway him from the plan he had in mind right then.

Your father had been making a time-and-motion study of the manufacturing process. He came up with some ideas. There were eight of us in our group, and we were paid by piece work. Haji Bey convinced everyone that he had the plant superintendent's permission to make some modifications on their machines. These changes, he said, would increase their production, and their pay, by twenty percent.

I tell you, Nephew, your father always had a good line. His favorite expression was, "trust me." Since he was usually right, Mardiros and I helped him make alterations to the machines. It took us two weeks to do it secretly. Old Skin Dome never even noticed.

Well, my boy, Haji Bey's idea was a great success. We began turning out more pairs of shoes with less effort and making more money on top of it.

One day, old Skin Dome came in horny. He marched over to the young girl and called her away from her machine. His eyes were filled with lust and so she understood what he wanted. Her face blanched white, and I thought she was going to faint. He jerked his head toward the storeroom. The pathetic kid was shaking with fear as she reluctantly followed him. She looked back helplessly at the rest of us, her eyes begging us to somehow stop what was about to happen to her. Otto pulled her into the storeroom and slammed the door.

Haji Bey was enraged and started to go after them. I grabbed his arm to hold him back. Before he could pull away from me, Mr. Bagdasarian walked in.

Apparently the front office had noticed the increase in production in our section over the past few weeks. The superintendent had asked Mr. Bagdasarian to look into it. Bagdasarian suspected who was behind the increase and why, so he felt it was better to stall a few days before checking it out.

When he walked in, he looked straight at Haji Bey and said, "Production has gone up here, and I want to know why. Has someone been monkeying around with the machines? If so, who's the genius around here?" Our entire group smiled with relief, pointed to Haji Bey, and began applauding.

Mr. Bagdasarian grabbed your father's hand and shook it. "Well done, my young friend. You could go places in this company, and. . . ."

Haji Bey interrupted. "There is something far more important to talk about right now." His face was flushed with anger. "Otto is in the storeroom taking advantage of a young girl. We have to do something right away."

Mr. Bagdasarian quickly called the superintendent and they both hurried to the storeroom. They caught Otto just as he was about to deflower that pitiful girl. They fired the bastard on the spot.

We and our coworkers decided to meet at the local bar after work on Friday to celebrate the victory over Skin Dome. We invited Mr. Bagdasarian, too. We all sat at a big table and ordered hamburgers, drinks, and snacks. The girl who had been rescued from Otto was there as well. Her face was radiant with happiness.

A little later, Skin Dome stomped in looking for Haji Bey. Otto knew it was Haji Bey who was responsible for his downfall. His bald head was red with rage as he stormed over to our table.

"Giavour," he snarled, "I'm going to fix you for this!"

Mr. Bagdasarian got up and stepped between Otto and Haji Bey. He told Otto to get the hell out of the bar, or, better yet, out of town.

"Otto," he added, "you've abused one girl too many. This girl is Irish and her brother and his friends are longshoremen in Boston. They have come up tonight to put you out of your misery. Your life isn't worth a plug nickel in this town."

Skin Dome had the wind knocked right out of him. He snarled like a cornered dog, turned on his heel, and headed for the door. No one ever saw him again.

■ ■ ■ ■

We thanked Mr. Bagdasarian for all he'd done for us and told him we were leaving for Detroit. He tried over and over to get us to stay with the company, telling us that we would get promotions, but we insisted that our minds were made up. He was a good man, that Andranik Bagdasarian, he even offered to drive us to the train station when we were ready to leave.

A couple of days later, we took him up on his offer and he drove us to the train station. He told us to keep in touch. Then he handed Haji Bey a check for a hundred dollars! That was the equivalent of six and a half paychecks! A hell of a lot of money.

"The president of the company personally has sent this check and letters of recommendation to you. He asked me to remind you that you will always be welcome back in our company."

We thanked Andranik for his kind words and the check, and climbed aboard the train carrying a basket of food that Mrs. Bagdasarian had prepared for our journey.

As we sat in our seats sharing a Mason jar of *raki*, I could see Haji Bey's juvenile cockiness beginning to take command of his good sense. He was about to make a speech. Mardiros came to the rescue by clapping a hand across Haji Bey's mouth. The Haji was silenced . . . for the moment, anyway.

Next stop for us, Detroit!

CHAPTER THIRTEEN
Early Days in Detroit

Mr. Bagdasarian had given your father the address of an Armenian coffeehouse located in downtown Detroit. When we arrived at the train station in Detroit, we hailed a horse and buggy, loaded our baggage on it, and took off for the coffeehouse. As the buggy bounced along Michigan Avenue, row upon row of trees reeled by us. Soon we were in the downtown district. We went over to Monroe Street and the driver dropped us off in front of a building. The coffeehouse was on the second floor.

We carried our bags up the stairs and entered a smoke-filled room. Practically everyone was smoking cigarettes, cigars, or Middle Eastern waterpipes, and the air was so thick you could barely make out people's faces. There was one dark-complexioned man, decked out in a fine suit, who caught our eye. He was playing cards. In his mouth was a long, black, unlit cigar that he chewed on every time he picked a new card or threw one away. He suddenly glanced our way.

"*Hoş geldiniz!*" [Happy arrival!] he said in Turkish.

"*Hoş gördük, Efendim*" [Happy to see you, our good Sir], we answered back. We knew from the way he spoke that he came from a part of Turkey where the Armenians had completely lost their mother tongue and spoke only Turkish. Even the behavior and bearing of most of these people were more Turkish than Armenian.

The stranger tossed in his cards and turned his attention to us. "What are your names? What town are you from? When did you boys arrive in the promised land?"

Haji Bey gave him a brief rundown of our history, saying that our families were still back in Efkereh.

"I don't know too much about that part of Turkey," the man said, "but if I were you, I'd get them out of there as soon as you can."

He told us his name was Aram Bedrosian and that he was from Yozgat. "I'm sure you gentlemen have heard that story by now. Every now and then the Turkish irregulars would raid our village and leave behind the butchered bodies of men, raped women, and bloodied children. I finally managed to put together a few gold coins and made my escape to this precious land." He reached down and scooped up his poker winnings. "Why don't you boys come along with me? We'll go to my house for a bite to eat. You must be exhausted from the long train ride."

When we got to Aram's place, your father showed him the letter of recommendation Mr. Bagdasarian had delivered to us. Aram read it and said with a smile, "You boys must have made a big impression back in Worcester. This letter will surely get you a job at the Ford plant."

Haji Bey told him that we were worried because we couldn't speak English yet. There was no way we could fill out a job application.

"I'll take you there myself," Aram assured us. "In the meantime, make yourselves at home here for a few days. That'll give us time to get to know each other."

"Won't your wife mind?" asked Haji Bey.

"No she won't. I don't have a wife yet. Not that I don't want one. It can get pretty damn lonely living all by yourself. There just aren't any Armenian girls available in Detroit.

"Someday I hope to go back home, under the protection of my United States passport, and find myself a bride to bring back here." He paused for a moment, then smiled sheepishly. "Actually, boys, there's more to it than that. I get tongue-tied whenever I come near a woman. I'm very bashful when it comes to dealing with the opposite sex."

Oh, God, there it was, Nephew, just the kind of thing your father loved to hear so he could open his big mouth and take charge.

"My dear friend," he began, "my brothers and I are planning on returning home in a year or two and I'll bring back a bride for you." Your Uncle Mardiros and I cringed as we heard that familiar tone. "She'll be a queen, you can bet your life on that."

Aram flushed happily. "Thank you, thank you, my friend, that would be wonderful." His face darkened. "But surely you won't be waiting so long to bring your families over, the situation is worsening daily in Turkey. War is in the air."

"What can we do?" Your father was philosophical. "Our womenfolk fought our coming. We wanted to come earlier, but they wouldn't listen to reason. Once we have earned some money and have a decent place to live, we will have to go back and drag them here."

Over the following months, unmarried men began to seek out your father, placing orders for Armenian brides. Aram had been talking. Haji Bey would listen patiently to these men, write down their "preferences" in his little notebook — this height, that weight and age — and, after they left, he would crumple up the list and toss it out. "They'll be more than happy with my choices," he would say.

Mardiros and I would look at each other, then to the heavens. He sounded exactly like Mama Yessaian!

We spent several days at Aram Bedrosian's; he was a gracious host. He took us on several pleasure trips around Detroit in his new four-door touring sedan — naturally, a Ford. Everyone in Michigan was in love with old Henry. After all, he was paying five dollars a day. This provided his own employees an opportunity to buy the cars they were making.

We found a six-room furnished flat about a mile from the Ford plant and got settled in quickly. Then we were ready to tackle the automobile industry.

At least two hundred men were standing in a long line outside the Ford plant the next morning. Everybody wanted a job there.

"Don't bother waiting in line," Aram said, "just follow me."

A guard stopped us at the gate, but hustled us through when Aram showed him the letter Mr. Bagdasarian had given to us. Of course the waiting men got angry. "Hey!" they shouted, "look at those fucking foreigners getting ahead of the line, taking our jobs! What right do they have to be here, anyway?"

We were embarrassed; Aram laughed!

"None of them is wearing feathers as far as I can see," he chortled. "The only native Americans are the Indians, and I don't see any, do you? And do any of these guys have a letter of recommendation like yours? No! So then, let's go on in."

Well, Nephew, thanks to Aram's help, we were hired on the spot and were told to report to work the next morning. What a wonderful country! We had jobs already. We couldn't get over it.

Henry Ford made everything for his cars at the Rouge Plant, starting from raw materials. The plant was entirely self-contained. We marveled at the machinery, the efficiency and speed of the production lines. Your father was particularly interested in the way they produced fasteners. You put stock in one end of a machine, and the machine would spit screws, nuts, and bolts out the other end.

"Nazar! Wouldn't it be something if we could ship a couple of these machines to Smyrna for Artin and Hovsep to use in our shop? Just look at the way it spits out those parts. God, we could make a fortune!"

■ ■ ■ ■

Nephew, we were falling in love with America. Sure, we worked hard, but we were well paid; the neighborhood was rough, but it was safe; and the city of Detroit was beautiful, trees and parks all over the place. You could go anywhere and do anything, if you had the money. We felt something we'd never felt before — *freedom.* It was as if we had been in a dark room all our lives, and then suddenly someone turned on a switch and amazingly there was light. For the first time we understood what liberty meant, that all men had inborn human dignity.

Unfortunately, as I can see now, we were so happy to be free as Armenians that we didn't take the time to explore the ways of our new country, to learn the language properly, to educate ourselves. We stayed among our own kind and hung on to our old ways. We didn't develop ourselves.

Artin my boy, while I want you to remain a good Armenian, you must be a good American, too. Study hard, go to college, get a good job. Take advantage of the opportunities of this great land.

■ ■ ■ ■

We were to be put to work on the Model T assembly line, under a foreman who we nicknamed "Sicum[1] Sam." He got a big kick out of running up and down the line cussing out the newcomers and threatening them with being fired if they didn't keep up with their work. As soon as we arrived at the line, the supervisor came over to Sicum Sam, barking loudly and pointing in our direction.

Oh, shit, I thought, here we go again, we're going to be fired before we even get started. It turned out that I was wrong . . . thank God. It was simply that Sicum Sam had fired three men on our line the day before and he was being told that we had been hired as their replacements.

Sam's breath smelled strongly of whiskey. I looked at your father. "Did you get a whiff of his breath?"

"That's nothing," Haji laughed. "I saw bottles being passed around all over the place. Good Lord, I even saw the supervisor taking a swig out of Sicum Sam's bottle."

We were talking in Armenian and didn't notice that Sam was watching us. He walked over to us.

"You Turkeys better get your asses moving or get the hell out of here. We don't talk on the line! Understand? You put out a quality product and keep your asses on the move every minute, every second."

I thought he was calling us Turks; and I tried to explain that we weren't Turks, but Armenians. He couldn't have cared less what we were.

"I don't give a fuck what you are, just move your asses and put those floorboards in right."

For a moment, I thought your father was going to take a poke at the little tyrant, right there on the production line the first day of our job. Fortunately, I managed to keep him cool.

---

[1] A play on the Turkish word *siktir*, "screw you."

Haji Bey shook his head sorrowfully, "I thought we had left Turkey behind us, Nazar. This guy is as bad as any two-bit shit we met over there."

"We did leave, little brother, we did leave! Just remember, the government is good in America. We have our freedom. We have our rights. We can quit at any time and go wherever we please. It's just that no matter where you go on this earth, you're going to find two-legged jackasses throwing their weight around. Even in America. Anyway, this guy is a squirt; he wants to act big to make up for his height."

Haji Bey went home discouraged. He was all for quitting our jobs and looking for something else. The memory of Skin Dome Otto was still fresh in his mind, and now here was this son-of-a--bitch Sam! Haji Bey was tired of taking shit. And the factory wasn't a nice place to work, either. It was noisy and smelly, and they pushed the men hard.

Of course we couldn't just up and quit our new jobs. We were short of money. Haji Bey was irresponsible when it came to handling money, and he still is. When he has it, he spends it. He's generous, but not prudent.

"We can't quit now, Haji Bey, we have to stick it out and work a few months at least. We need the money." Placing my arm around him, I tried talking to him like a father.

All the time Haji and I were talking, Sicum Sam had been watching us from his glass-enclosed office. Suddenly, he made a dash for our area, jumping between the rolling cars on the assembly line. He was enraged because we had been talking, especially since he had just told us it was against regulations. I half expected him to start swinging at us. He stood there pointing a finger at Haji Bey, cussing him out in the vilest of language.

In his finest style, calm and smooth, Haji Bey reciprocated, in Turkish of course. "You bark like a dog, look like a jackass, and act like a pig. You're nothing but a fart in a wind!"

While I couldn't help smirking, I was afraid we would surely get booted for this backtalk. Sam's face was cherry red, he bounced up and down like a grasshopper.

"Wait right here, alien! I'm bringing someone over who can understand your language. I'll find out for sure what you called me, you bastard!"

He was back almost immediately, his face still on fire with rage, his arms waving like a windmill. He had a young man with him. Sam stood face to face with Haji Bey with spit sputtering from his mouth as he cursed him out.

The young man pulled Sam back a step or two. "Please, Sam! Wait a minute! Let me talk to him and find out what he was saying."

But Sam was hot. It would take more than a few calming words to quiet him down. "What's he saying? I know what he is saying! This son-of-a-bitch was cussing me out in that goddamn Turkey language of his! I don't take that kind of shit from nobody, especially from an alien!"

"I know, Sam, I know," the young man continued calmly, "Just give me one minute, please." He turned to Haji Bey and said in Turkish, "Effendi! I understand you spoke some harsh words to our foreman, Mr. Hoffenmuller. Is that right?"

As usual, Haji Bey's response was serene on the surface, smooth and quiet, yet his words dripped with ridicule. Of course you had to understand Turkish to know what he was saying, otherwise you couldn't tell from his tone or expression.

"Effendi, you can tell that wheezing jackass that little farts like him shouldn't bother real men. Explain to him that if he can't act like a decent human being, he can take his jobs and stick 'em."

Although the young man wanted to laugh, he managed to keep his composure and smiled politely. "I'm sure Mr. Hoffenmuller will be pleased to hear that," he said in English, and turned to Sam.

"Sam! You've got it all wrong. These men were complimenting you."

"All wrong, my ass! What do you mean I got it all wrong?"

"No. No. They see how well you are running things. They are pleased that they are working for you, and they hope you will teach them to be good employees. They want to serve the Ford Motor Company and become good American citizens."

"You mean this Turkey said all that in just a few words? It's hard to believe."

"Would I lie to you, Sam? The Turkish language is that way, you use a few short expressions and you can say a lot."

Sam looked puzzled. He took the young man aside and whispered something in his ear. None of us could hear what was being said. A smile came over Sam's face and he ambled over to Haji Bey and shook his hand. Without a word, Sam turned and walked back to his office, the pint liquor bottle swaying in his hip pocket.

The young man was "Bulgarian John." He introduced himself and then told us what he'd said to Sam. "Sam bought the line and said he would be glad to help you boys learn; and, if you do a good job, he will assign you better work." We all laughed. God, we were lucky to get out of that one. The whistle blew to mark the end of our shift. We went over and invited Bulgarian John to eat with us at a nearby Greek restaurant.

Over dinner our new friend told us about himself. "I'm Bulgarian. My folks and I came to this country about twelve years ago. I finished high school, got a job here, went to college at night, majored in English, got a degree. Now I'm studying law. I hope to graduate next year.[1] My parents died a year ago." After a few more bites, John told us about how he picked up Turkish when he was a kid. The Turks had occupied Bulgaria for a couple hundred years, and many Bulgarians spoke Turkish. It was something like the Armenians in Anatolia.

Then we told John our story. He seemed sympathetic and understood why we wanted our people out of Turkey. From that

---

[1] Apparently "Bulgarian John" was John Romanoff, a Bulgarian born in the province of Macedonia. He came from a well-educated family that emigrated to America. He finished law school and became a prominent lawyer in Detroit, with offices in the Penobscot Building. He was identified with the help of Luben Christoff, a scion of a prominent Macedonian family of Dearborn, who had met Bulgarian John in the 1950s. This information was confirmed by Fr. George Nicoloff, a priest in the Macedonian church, and his wife Vera. John Romanoff attended St. Clements Ohridski Macedono-Bulgarian Orthodox Church on 25th Street in Detroit.

day on, we became the best of friends. He was a very smart and good man.

Walking back to our rooming house in south Dearborn after dinner, Haji Bey caught sight of a rather large house with a sign in front of it, not far from the Ford plant. John told him the sign said: "For Sale." Haji Bey studied every detail of the house from the outside. I could see the wheels were turning in his head again. He asked John to take down the phone number and call it when he got a chance.

I started getting nervous, wondering what *Baron*[1] Haji was dreaming up now. I poked Haji Bey's shoulder. "All right, tell me, what are you up to?"

"Nazar, if we get that large frame house, we can turn it into a boarding house and bring some of the men from back home. Not only could we give them room and board, we could find jobs for them at the Ford plant. Once they saved enough money, they could move out and send for their families. We can make a few dollars, too, and that will bring closer the day when we can go and get our own families."

Here we go again, I thought. "Haji, you must be out of your mind! How do you intend to bring Armenians here from Turkey? They don't even have the money for passage. And even if they can get here somehow, how will you find them jobs at Ford's?"

"As far as passage money is concerned, in a few months I could send it to them. If I run out of money, I can borrow more. Don't worry about the jobs either, Nazar, I've already figured that out, too."

Well, my boy, I prayed to God to give me strength, and I argued with Haji until I was blue in the face. Finally, however, I agreed to go along with the idea. Your Uncle Mardiros, bless his heart, threw up his hands in disgust, "The two of you are absolutely nuts!"

I insisted on being the one in charge of the money we would lend out. "I don't want any interference in that department," I told your father. "All three of us would go broke if we left it up to

---

[1] "Mr." in Armenian. Used here sarcastically.

you. In fact, I think we have the right to charge at least two percent interest on the loans."

I don't mean this to sound like it all came about overnight, Nephew. It took a lot of planning and organizing — probably three months to get the whole operation off the ground and several more months to get it operational. Yet it worked, by God, it worked! Haji Bey was right again!

We bought a large house with enough rooms for twelve borders and the three of us. Bulgarian John was our first boarder. We had a large kitchen, and Haji Bey became the chief cook. In his new capacity as "Lord of the Manor," Haji Bey secretly negotiated with a welder he knew to build a copper still. We didn't even know about it until we saw Haji Bey and the welder pushing it down our street in a little red wagon. Neighbors stuck their heads out of their windows and laughed at the two of them pulling this little red wagon with a funny contraption on top. Some recognized the still, probably most of them did. Having a still was illegal in Michigan if you made the hooch for sale. Of course, Haji Bey couldn't have cared less.

"I'm not going to sell any of it, I'm going to use the wonderful elixir to save lives."

"Haji, you're playing with fire. If the government agents ever get wind of the still, surely we will be deported."

Haji Bey insisted that his only motive was to save lives, not to make a profit, and so God would be watching over us. When I asked him how he was going to distribute moonshine, he put me off.

"Please, Nazar, don't bother me about the fine details. Wait until we brew some, then I'll see how this miracle is going to work."

We went to Eastern Farmers Market for our supplies: three sixty-gallon wooden barrels, twenty-five boxes of raisins, each box weighing twenty-two pounds. We divided the raisins evenly into the barrels, added chopped-up apples and oranges and, according to Mama Yessaian's recipe, gum tree sap that had been imported from Turkey. We then filled the barrels up with water and threw in a dozen or so chunks of charcoal to help purify the liquid.

We kept the barrels near a big pot-bellied stove to speed up fermentation. After twelve days, you could hear bubbles popping out of the liquid. The smell of the mash fermenting must have stunk up the area good, because neighbors began to complain. We told them to hold on, not to worry about it, they'd each get a bottle when we were finished. That seemed to satisfy them.

Finally, the mixture was ready to be distilled into that wonderful spirit we called *raki*. We brewed all three barrels and extracted fifty-five gallons of *raki* at 120 proof. It was highly potent, and we had to tell our new customers to cut the brew with water before drinking it.

Haji Bey filled ten one-pint bottles with his precious liquor and told Bulgarian John to take one to Sicum Sam.

"John, if you help us, you'll be playing an important role in saving lives. Get Sam to try some of this. If he likes it, tell him there's plenty more."

A few hours later, John was back. "Do you have more of that stuff?"

"Oh, yes . . . plenty." Your father's face broadened into a smile of satisfaction. "He liked it?"

"Did he ever! He let the supervisor and the men in personnel taste it. They went berserk over it! They want to know if you would be willing to sell them more of the stuff."

"No, it's not for sale. Tell them I would be willing to give them a bottle or two, however, for every man they hire that I send over for a job. Tell them we are afraid about what is going to happen back home in Turkey. There is war in the Balkans between the Turks and the little Christian states. There are rumors of a war in Europe. Turkey is likely to be pulled in. If the Turks get in a big war, God only knows what will happen to my people. The Ford Motor Company can play a role in saving lives if they hire my countrymen and give them the opportunity to move their families out of Turkey."

John took nine bottles of *raki* to the plant. He came back with news of a deal. "The supervisor said that he'll hire the men you send, providing you drop off eight pints of the stuff in his car every week. He will handle the distribution." John handed Haji Bey the key to the supervisor's trunk, and the deal was done.

His Highness was overjoyed. He had already sent money to a few Armenian men back home and they were on their way to America. When the immigrants arrived in Detroit, Haji would send them to the supervisors who, according to the deal, would hire them on the spot. These newcomers worshipped your father, thinking he had to be some sort of big man to carry such clout with a company as large as Ford's.

Over the next few months, we put twenty-three men to work. Some had to be housed in our neighbors' homes, though they always gathered at our place for their evening meals. After dinner they'd sit around and play cards or backgammon, and the conversation would eventually turn to their loved ones back home, and whether they would be able to get them to America before any misfortunes befell them.

Eventually, Haji Bey did what he said he would. He quit Ford's and took on the duties of chief cook and manager of the boarding house. Every week, each of the twenty-three men would contribute two or three dollars as passage money for others less fortunate. Even the men who brought their families over and moved into their own rented houses continued to donate their share of the passage fund.

Finally, the immigration just about stopped. It was 1914 and war had broken out in Europe. Turkey took the side of Germany and the Central Powers. The Allies were fighting against them. America eventually declared war on the Central Powers in April 1917, but never on Turkey. The U.S. wanted to keep diplomatic ties with Turkey so that it could help the Armenians over there.

■ ■ ■ ■

Of course, our little program did not go along without a few hitches. In particular, I recall one evening when a couple of cops knocked on the door as we were having dinner. I think they were named Monahan and Kennedy, I don't really remember. Anyway, that's what I'm going to call them. The cops said there were reports of a strong smell of alcohol wafting out of this house and that people could see a lot of men walking in and out at all hours. They suspected we might be running an illegal speakeasy and gambling den. Luckily, Bulgarian John was having dinner with us as usual. He invited the cops in and, with his finest English accent, began to explain.

"This place is a boarding house. The borders work different shifts, and so they are constantly coming and going. We run a haven for refugees escaping from the turmoil in Turkey. When the men save enough of their money to send for their families, they rent a flat and move out. That's why over a period of time you see different men."

The police seemed satisfied with John's explanation about the men, but still wanted to know what was causing the strong smell of alcohol. I told John to go ahead and tell them that we only made the *raki* for our own use, since the law allowed it, and did not sell it. The cops were doubtful of this part of the story, but couldn't do anything without evidence.

We invited the policemen to sit down and join us for dinner. Haji Bey brought over some of our potent brew and filled their glasses halfway with it. He then added water to the top, turning the liquid snow white. After a few repeats, the two cops were getting soused. Then we fed them shish kebab, pilaf, and salad. They lapped it up like sows at the trough. They asked for seconds and thirds and kept drinking *raki* by the tumbler.

John told them more about our activities. He explained that the Yessaian brothers were helping whoever wanted to get out of Turkey — Armenians, Greeks, or even Turks. More than ninety-five percent of the help, however, went to Armenians. After all, they were the people who were being persecuted.

After we finished off the third jar of the precious *raki*, I had to explain to them we were running a not-for-profit cooperative and would appreciate it if they would make a contribution toward expenses. Reluctantly, the cops threw a few coins on the table and got up and left.

■ ■ ■ ■

In time, as I told you, Nephew, our group of immigrants became larger and larger. We had to double them up in the rooms and send some of them to sleep at the houses of neighbors; others, who had been with us awhile, we had to encourage to find other housing altogether, to make room for new arrivals. Through word of mouth, the message went out among Armenians back home. Relatives of those already here would follow them to this new community. This went on right up until the war, which broke out in 1914, made immigration almost impossible.

Most of the men who had been able to get their families out moved to a section of town called Delray. It was sometimes referred to as "New Armenia." Other Armenians went to live in some of the better sections of Dearborn. Later, many who made good money moved to Highland Park. Armenians had moved into the Detroit area by the thousands.

Our lives had settled into a pattern. We always had a fresh batch of *raki* going full blast on top of the gas range. The alcohol fumes would put the men in the dining room to sleep after dinner, and their rhythmical snoring could be heard all the way up front in the living room, sometimes sounding like a concert of frogs.

One evening, as we sat in the living room waiting for dinner to cook, we felt the house starting to shake all of a sudden. At the same time a horrible noise, like a locomotive blowing off steam, came from the kitchen. We dashed in. Pots, pans, and dishes were rattling in the cupboards, and the still was huffing and puffing so hard that it was bouncing up and down on the stove.

Suddenly, there was an explosion like I'd never heard before. The top of the still shot through the air like a crazed cannonball and crashed into the ceiling. A gusher of hot, steaming raisins followed, peppering the ceiling and all four walls and then falling back to the floor. Haji Bey and I were covered from head to foot with hot mash. A couple of the men rushed into the kitchen to see what was wrong. As they came charging, they slipped and slid across the raisin-covered floor. It was funny and tragic all at the same time.

Haji Bey and I washed ourselves off with cold water. Then I saw Haji Bey get on a chair. For a moment I thought he was going to make a speech, like in the old days, but thank God I was wrong. He had taken a broom in his hand and was starting to sweep the raisins off the ceiling.

I was really pissed with him. I had warned him time and again not to overload the still with too much mash. Apparently he did it anyway. Well, this time he was dead wrong!

Then your Uncle Mardiros came into the kitchen. "What in God's name is going on in here? What's all the noise about? Don't you know there's a crowd gathering outside. They're going to call the police."

I slapped my forehead with my open palm. I realized we were now in for Big Trouble! "Get the hell down from that goddamn chair before you fall on your ass," I roared at Haji Bey. I could have killed him.

Meekly climbing down from the chair, he explained in a subdued voice, "If we don't get the raisins off the walls and ceiling, they will dry and stick. Then we'll have to scrape them off. It will be a lot of extra work."

"Never mind the goddamned raisins!" I yelled. "We'll paint over them and make the walls look fancy."

The still, obviously, had split apart. The air was thick with fumes of alcohol and that made us all lightheaded.

Then we heard the police sirens wailing. Now the men in blue, apparently, were headed for our place. I was sure the three of us would be marched in front of a firing squad.

Four cops banged at our door. One of our boarders let them in, and they came rushing into the kitchen with their guns drawn. We immediately threw up our hands in surrender. What did we know? Their leader, a pudgy, red-faced man with gold braid on his uniform and cap, began spitting out profanities in a thundering voice.

I broke in when I could. "Me no speakit Eengleese. Me no feshdey what you say. Notink vrong here."

"What do you mean 'nothing wrong,' you Turkey."

Bulgarian John came over to explain. "These guys aren't Turks, and no one is doing anything wrong. We just had a pot explode, than's all."

"I don't give a shit what you are! Who's in charge here?"

Haji Bey, Mardiros, and I stepped forward.

"Okay, you three Turkeys are under arrest! Let's go!"

Just then, the two cops we had met earlier, Monahan and his partner Kennedy, walked up behind the captain. Monahan whispered something into the captain's ear. Gold Braid yelled for the three of us to stay put and all six cops left the room. After a while, Gold Braid returned by himself. Another string of profanities came from the police captain's mouth, punctuated by finger pokes in my chest.

After he finished, Bulgarian John told us in Turkish, "Bad news, boys. The captain says you're not to make another drop of alcohol. You were lucky this time. Monahan and Kennedy talked him out of locking you up, provided you stop making the stuff. Otherwise, the captain said, he'll kick your asses all the way back to Turkey and you'll never set foot in this country again."

We told Gold Braid that we certainly wanted to abide by the laws of this country and thanked him for giving us a break. To show our appreciation, we asked them to stay for dinner.

At first the captain declined, but Monahan talked him into it. After cleaning the kitchen, we served lemon soup, pita bread, Greek cheese, shish kebab, dishes of rice pilaf, salad, and other delicacies. Officer Monahan asked for some *raki*, which we gave him, and then he persuaded old Gold Braid to sample some.

We called up a couple of belly dancers to come over from Greektown on Monroe Street in Detroit. Then we got out our musical instruments and began playing. By the time the girls arrived, the six cops were pretty well oiled. The dancers wrapped their flimsy scarfs around the cops' necks and brushed their ample bosoms against their faces. Gold Braid's hat was knocked sideways on his head. All the cops got up and tried to dance with the belly dancers and looked as silly as hell.

After a couple of hours, I told Bulgarian John to get rid of the girls. They had gone far enough. We weren't looking for trouble. So, he paid the girls off and sent them home in a cab.

John then persuaded the policemen to take a shower and try to get some sleep before returning to their station. The cops took showers and lay down to rest. About an hour later, Gold Braid and his men woke up from their naps. I saw twelve bloodshot eyes and wondered how it was going to look when they returned to the station house. John explained that old Gold Braid was in charge, so no one would dare question them. Gold Braid thanked us for the great food and wild entertainment. He said he'd never seen anything like it. Then he told John to tell us that the law is still the law and we must obey it or else we sure would be deported. With that, the cops left.

That innocent dinner invitation turned out to be one hell-raising night. I never laughed so hard in my entire life.

One of the last Armenians that we were able to place at the plant, just before the war broke out, was Missak. He'd been with us for three weeks, and we had known his family back in Efkereh. One day Missak received a letter from his father. It must have been one of the last ones to get out. The guy was all excited and came in to tell us about it.

"My father wants me to inform you boys that two official-looking Turks recently came to our village. Father didn't like the looks of them. He thinks they were up to no good.[1] You know my father, always suspicious."

"Does he say anything about our family?" I asked.

"They are fine, enjoying the best of health. Your children are growing like green beans, tall and lean. They all miss you, and want you to come home."

Our eyes became wet as we thought of our families. How we missed them, too.

Missak rambled on, telling us more of the news. "Do you remember the two orphaned Turkish brothers who lived on the south end of the village, the hot-headed ones — Mustafa and his one-eyed brother *Keor Oglu* [Blind Son]? Well they got into a real fight one day. They went at it with stones, then sticks, and finally with knives. When it was all over, Keor Oglu had lost his one good eye. Now he's completely blind. His brother Mustafa

---

[1] It is possible that these men were officials of the "Special Organization" which was formed by the Young Turk government to organize and carry out the Armenian genocide. The Special Organization had authority over the regular administration in the provinces and made special trips to give them instructions. The Young Turks did not want to leave a written record of their intention to rid Turkey of Armenians and so most of their instructions were given verbally by emissaries.

won't lift a finger to help him, so the Armenians of our town are taking care of the blind one. Other than that, everything remains quiet in Efkereh."

Missak handed Haji Bey a flat brown envelope. "Go ahead. Open it. It's a picture of your family, your mother and sisters-in-law, your wife, your son Garbis, and your kid brother-in-law Kourken, and all the others from your wife's side of the family."

Tears came to your father's eyes as he opened the envelope and stared at the picture. Four years had passed since he had seen his wife and child. Two years had passed since he had even heard from them. He shook his head and mumbled, "I've got to get home."

▪ ▪ ▪ ▪

The World War had disrupted all communication with Turkey, and mail was not dependable in any case. In 1917, America entered the war. There was no question now, the Allies would surely win.

The three of us sat down for a serious meeting. We missed our loved ones, and there was no way we could communicate with them. "Come on, boys," I began, "let's sell this place, take the money and go get our families. I think we've done our share of good for our fellow man. Let's go back for our own loved ones." We all agreed. The Allies were winning the war and we felt we could get back before long.

There were many problems to be solved before we could return to Turkey. How could we get American passports, tickets for the train to New York, find a ship going to Smyrna? Then there was the question of how and to whom we would sell our house. The process was to take a long time. It would stretch out for over a year.

One of our boarders, Simone [Simon] Simonian, wanted to buy the house. Simone, we knew, was greedy and without morals, something of a con man. He was always trying to fleece people. Simone wanted to buy our boarding house so that he could take advantage of the borders, most of whom were simple men who barely knew two words of English. I told him "no sale!" We ran a not-for-profit program to help people, and we wanted to see it continue.

Finally, after much soul searching, we decided to sell to Ardash Arakeloff, a man we called the "Good Samaritan." He was a real nice guy, and we knew he would continue our work. Ardash was from Russian Armenia. He had changed his name from Arakel*ian* to Arakel*off*, thinking the Russian ending would make it easier on him in the Russian Empire. Anyway, the boarders had great respect for him and were happy that we were going to sell to him.

By this time, we had gotten our "first papers" and could get passports. We still had to put other things in order, buy gifts, pack, make reservations on a train to New York, and book passage on a ship bound for Turkey. Our beloved Bulgarian John helped us with all this since our English was still very weak and we had no idea of how to get these things done. It took a long time and we grew more impatient with each passing month.

By now, it was 1918. Then came the news in November that an armistice had been signed and the war was over. It seemed now that nothing could stop us from going home. In May of 1919, the Greeks occupied Smyrna and moved inland. That was good news. Perhaps they would get as far as Efkereh and we could go there in safety, too. We had no idea of exactly what was happening.

With the war over, we could book passage to Smyrna. The last piece fell in place. As the time for departure neared, Haji Bey was in all his glory. He went out and bought a new Ford flivver to take back with him. After all, he was "Haji Bey," and he wanted to drive around the city of Smyrna in style. He'd be one of the few people in that city, especially among the Armenians, to own a private automobile. Ah, what a life! Just think, an Armenian driving around Turkey in his own car. Soon, Haji Bey's fantasy would come true. We sent the car by rail to New York where it was to be loaded aboard the ship.

We finished our shopping. I packed the gifts, a trunk full of women's and children's clothing and things, anything I thought would fit our loved ones back home. Your Uncle Mardiros did the same thing, as did Haji Bey. We also planned to take a half-dozen bicycles, both the children and the grownups would enjoy them.

It had been a long time since we'd laid eyes on our loved ones. We were certainly excited. I could hardly wait. I wanted to get home so badly I could taste it.

John hired a truck to carry us and our belongings to the train station down on Michigan Avenue. As we loaded the truck in front of the house, the mailman came down the street.

"I know you boys have been waiting years for a letter from back home. Well, here you are! You've got one. I hope it brings good news!"

I opened the envelope. As I read the letter, I felt the blood draining from my face.

CHAPTER FOURTEEN
A Black Day in the Village

The long letter was from Hashim, our adopted Turkish brother. It had taken over a year for it to reach us. He had someone write it for him in Turkish using the Armenian alphabet. It read as follows:

> Dear Brothers,
>
> I would rather have sent you my dead body instead of this letter. But someone had to inform you about the terrible tragedy here. This is the third time I have tried to start this letter. It is difficult for me to think straight. All I know is that someone must tell you of the horrors which took place in our beloved village of Efkereh, and your brother refuses to write. I have given this letter to a trustworthy Greek merchant who is traveling to France. He promises to mail it from there. I hope you receive it.
>
> My honorable brother, Haji Bey, it would have been better if when you found me by the stream that day many years ago, you had let me die. Then I would not have to write this letter. Now I must put down on this miserable sheet of paper the bad news. At the moment, I hate myself for being a Turk. Please forgive me for the following lines. I feel numb inside.
>
> You probably have heard by now that the Armenians were being driven out of Turkey. Most of them, it is rumored, are being killed along the roads. I feared for our family in Efkereh, but the soldiers would not let people travel without permission. So I could not go there.
>
> Then some weeks ago, I heard from a traveler the rumor that something dreadful had happened in Efkereh. I learned that people living outside the village were not allowed to enter, only the few Turkish families which lived there were allowed to come and go. I immediately told my

adopted brothers, Hovsep and Artin. Since I was Turkish, and would face the least danger, it was decided that I would go to the village to find out what had happened.

I took our buggy and quickly went out on the road. Soldiers were guarding any cutoff going north and south. As I approached Caesarea, there were bodies rotting along the wayside. I passed through Caesarea and got on the road to Efkereh. As I rode up to the town, I was stopped by a soldier. He made me get out of the buggy and jammed his rifle barrel into my chest. He demanded to know who I was and what I was doing there. I said that I was a Turk from a nearby village and was looking for our family doctor. The soldier snapped his fingers and yelled, "Papers, papers, papers!" So I showed him my Turkish papers while he eyed me suspiciously. I tried to remain calm as I repeated that I had come from Diarsiakh[1] because I needed to find Dr. Oskan who treated folks in this area.

I told the soldier that my father was dreadfully ill, that his chest hurt, he had pains running up and down his arm, and he had a hard time breathing.

The soldier growled impatiently at me, and told me to go away before I got into trouble. He said there was no doctor in town.

I told him that I was tired, and asked if he would allow me to go to the fountain and water my horse, rest an hour or so, and then continue my search for the doctor. Well, he accepted my story and let me enter.

The village was as quiet as a cemetery. The Armenian quarter was empty. Only the few Turkish families who lived there were left. This is what they told me: Turkish troops came one day to the village before the sun had risen. They searched the Armenian homes and dragged out

---

[1] Diarsiakh was a nearby Greek-speaking village with a few Turkish families. Most of the villages around Efkereh, as Nurzia Merzia, Belegasi, were Armenian speaking.

the men from age fourteen to fifty. Then they lined the men up outside their homes. Those who resisted were killed on the spot, the others were tied together in groups of four and marched outside the village where they were shot.

The soldiers then swarmed into the houses like hungry locusts and demanded that the Armenians give up all their jewelry, money, rugs, and other valuables. The women were given "government" receipts.

The soldiers then announced that the remaining Armenians, the old men, women, and children, were going to be "relocated." The next morning they were forcibly marched off down the road.

I was told that the Yessaians and Chackerians were driven out with the rest of the Armenians. My dear brothers, only God knows where they have been sent. Only God knows what has become of them. All I can say is that at this time there are no Armenians left alive in Efkereh.

I must end this letter now. My mind is numb from grief.

My dear brothers, my heart weeps for all of us. May God comfort you in your time of sorrow.

Hashim.

And so, Nephew, Haji Bey, Mardiros, and I sat down on the curb and cried helplessly like children.

The truck driver wanted to know what was going on. Bulgarian John explained to him about the bad news that we had received from home.

We didn't know what to do. We were so confused. Should we make the journey? Should we take the gifts? Corpses had no need for bicycles and new clothes! And, if somehow our loved ones had survived, how could we find them? Overcome with heartache, we just gave these things away to our neighbors who had gathered around to share our sorrow.

We decided we would go on with our journey. Perhaps our brothers in Smyrna were safe. Perhaps we could locate the survivors of the death march. We threw our personal belongings in back and got into the truck. On the way to the train station, Haji Bey was consumed with rage. First he cursed the Turks for killing the Armenians, and then he cursed Mother for being so stubborn and not listening to his warning. Now perhaps they were all dead — our wives, our children, and our friends — all dead. Haji Bey cried, shaking with sobs. We all cried. Our souls were shaken.

We got to the station and boarded the train. Most of the time we sat in silence. As the train wound its way back east we had plenty of time to think. We prayed that the old folks, the women, and the children might still be alive. Then we thought about our brothers whom we had left in Smyrna, were they all right? Had the massacres reached Smyrna yet? Were we walking into a trap? All these questions gnawed at our minds.

Without turning his head from the countryside whizzing by outside our window, Haji Bey murmured to me, "Nazar, see all those people out there, in all these villages, towns, and cities? They are all from different parts of the world and yet they are living peacefully, happily side by side. America teaches all people that they can live together in peace. God bless the founders of this great nation, and God bless our leaders today. I pray that they have the wisdom and courage to guard this great land in peace until the ages of ages." I stared directly ahead, but knew, from the tone of Haji Bey's voice, that he was crying again.

I started to weep, too. What am I doing on this train? I wondered. Why am I going to Turkey? For what? Dead, they were all dead! Oh sure, maybe Hovsep and Artin were still alive in Smyrna, but we had no way of knowing their fate. This much I *did* know: my wife, my children, my mother, all were probably dead. If Hovsep and Artin are still alive, I thought, they should have the brains to get out as soon as possible. What could we do for them over there?

The only Yessaians I knew to be alive for sure were us three on the train. With each passing hour, I became more and more convinced that there was no reason to return. If anyone survived, they could get in touch with us, as Hashim did, and we could bring them here. What sense did it make for us to go to Turkey?

By the time the train arrived at Grand Central Station in New York, my mind was made up: I announced that I would stay in the States. When Mardiros learned that I was staying, he decided to remain here with me. We were both despondent. Neither of us had any hope that our wives and children were still alive. We decided to take the next train to Detroit, get our jobs back at the Ford plant, and live as best we could.

Haji Bey, of course, would not be dissuaded. He was determined to return and find out what had happened.

We took a hotel room in the city and waited for the next day when the ship would be leaving. The following morning we went down to the dock to see Haji Bey off.

"Look," I told him, "if you find Hovsep and Artin, tell them to sell everything and get on the next ship for America. And if they can't sell, tell them to just leave it all to Hashim and Bedri and get the hell out of there."

I told Haji Bey to contact us through the Armenian coffeehouse. We did not want to go back to the boarding house, now that we had sold it, and didn't know where we would be staying.

We embraced and said our goodbyes with tears in our eyes. Mardiros and I watched as Haji Bey walked up the gangway. What was our dear brother getting himself into? Would we ever see him again?

■ ■ ■ ■

Your father sent us cablegrams from the ship in care of the Armenian coffeehouse, as we had agreed. They were rambling and filled with doubts. He said he was confused and wondered why he was even returning to Turkey. He had little hope of finding anyone left alive.

To get his mind off his worries, he once wrote, he had asked permission to go down into the ship's hold and look at his flivver. The captain would allow it on condition that the car not be started. Your dad was very pleased with his horseless carriage, it boosted his spirits. He feared that he would never be able to drive it around Smyrna.

While on shipboard, Haji Bey became acquainted with a young Polish couple on their honeymoon. The bride's sister, a good--looking girl, was traveling with them. It wasn't long before this young lady was flirting with Haji Bey. She followed him everywhere. To get her off his back he had to explain that he was in mourning — in mourning for his wife, child, mother, sisters-in--law, eight nephews, and other relatives and friends.

As the days passed, the cables reflected Haji Bey's growing mood of despair. He had lost his family, his wife, his son, and most all that was dear to him. Now, he began to lose his faith in God. Haji Bey wrote that no good God would have let the Armenians be slaughtered like animals. Either there was no God, or he was evil. We read these cables with growing concern.

■ ■ ■ ■

Haji Bey stood at the railing of the ship as it pulled into the harbor of Smyrna. From the ship, the city hardly seemed any different to him than the day he left. Of course there were naval ships in the harbor, not Turkish and German, but American, French, Italian, and Greek. As he walked down the gangway, life seemed to be going on more or less as usual. The only difference was that he saw Greek troops patrolling the docks rather than Turkish ones.

Haji Bey fussed around anxiously as his horseless carriage was being off loaded. A crowd of curious onlookers gathered to catch a look, marveling at the machine and complimenting him. It was rare to see a mechanical horse in their city, particularly an American automobile. When the car was finally ready, Haji Bey cranked it until the engine came to life, coughing and sputtering, and then settling down to a rhythmical roar. He hopped in, adjusted his goggles, put on his gloves and checkered cap, and was off, riding smartly down the cobblestone street.

His heart was beating fast in excitement as he drove to our shop. He eased the flivver up in front of our little factory. Hovsep's face appeared at the window when he heard the noise. When he saw Haji Bey, his mouth fell open. Haji Bey gave a sigh of relief. They were alive!

The Ottoman Empire and Its Neighbors on the Eve of World War I (1914)

Overview of the town of Efkereh, Turkey. Prior to 1915.

Photo courtesy of Mary Ayanian Sarajian

Photo courtesy of Nora Mazlounian.

A view of part of the town of Efkereh. Prior to 1915.

St. Stepanos Armenian Apostolic Church, exterior, Efkereh. Built ca. 1908.

Photo by Stepanian Freres. Photo from Project SAVE, courtesy of Mary Ayanian Sarajian.

St. Stepanos Armenian Apostolic Church, interior, Efkereh.

Photo by Stepanian Freres. Photo from Project SAVE, courtesy of Mary Ayanian Sarajian.

Family portrait taken in the village of Efkereh, Turkey.
Back row, standing: Siranoush, first wife of Haji Bey. *Seated*: The Chackarians, Siranoush's parents (also, Haji Bey's in-laws). *Front row, standing:* Garbis (*left*), son of Haji Bey and Siranoush; and Kourken, brother of Siranoush (also, brother-in-law of Haji Bey). 1914.

Family portrait of "Sultan Hanim" Miriam Kouradjian and her daughters in Smyrna. *Seated, center*: "Sultan Hanim". *Standing*: Zarmineh (*left*) and Vartanoush *(right)*. *Seated on floor*: Sarah. Ca. 1914.

Exterior view of the St. Stepanos Armenian Cathedral of Smyrna.
Haji Bey and Victoria (second wife of Haji Bey) Yessaian were married in cathedral; son Artin was baptized here. Prior to 1922.

Wedding portrait of Haji Bey and Victoria Yessaian. 1919.

Workmen repairing the road Smyrna-Paradisos. Possibly one of the crews who worked for Sarkis Aga Kouradjian.

Photo from *Smyrna: The City of Smyrna Before The Destruction*, NEA Synora, A.A. Livani, 1991. Photo prior to 1919.

View of Port of Smyrna and Passport Control area, near the pier from where Sultan Hanim and her family escaped in 1922.

Photo from *Smyrna: The City of Smyrna Before the Destruction*, NEA Synora, A.A. Livani, 1991. Photo prior to 1919.

Photograph of Haji Bey and Victoria Yessaian. Ten years after their arrival in America 1930.

Photograph taken in Mount Clemens, Michigan. *Left*: Haji Bey. *Center*: Uncle Nazar Yessaian (the primary narrator) and brother of Haji Bey. *Right*: Victoria Yessaian. ca. 1929.

Photograph of Sultan Hanim's son Krikor and his wife Gladys, taken on Belle Isle, Detroit, Michigan. ca. 1942.

Photograph of Garbis (later Charlie) and wife Rose (Margosian) Yessaian. ca. 1949? Garbis was Haji Bey's son from first marriage. Garbis survived the death march to Aleppo, Syria, was placed in a refugee orphanage, and later released from the orphanage at age ten.

View of St. Stepanos Armenian Apostolic Church, exterior, in deteriorating condition. 1993.

View of St. Stepanos Armenian Apostolic Church, interior, in deteriorating condition. 1993.

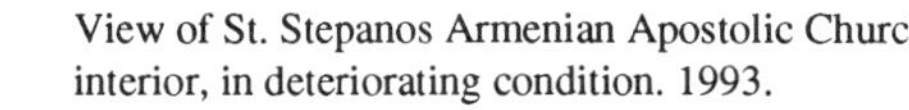

Photo courtesy of George and Rose Mooradian

Exterior view
of three homes
in Efkereh.
1993.

Courtesy of George and Rose Mooradian

The Orphans Society of Efkereh founded 1916).

From left to right. Seated: Mr. Dedeian, Minas Kaysserian, Vahram Boyajian or Dickran Choukourian, Parnak (Paroug) Paulian, Mamassian or Kalajian and Boyadjian (Mrs. Kaysserian's Brothers.) *Standing, middle row*: Vartehr Sirian, John Solakian,Garabed (Charles) Warterian, Aram Pavlian Karnig (Carl) Bahadurian, Mirijan Bahadurian and Yervant Bahadurian. *Standing, back row*: Boghos Stepanian, Parsegh Sinamian, Mike Shahbazian, Charles Shahbazian, Garabed (Charles) Kojaian and Onnig Tabibian.

Photo courtesy of Mike Kojaian. ca. 1920. (Photo identifications through the combined efforts of Marge Ossian, Queenie Hazergian, and Mike Kaysserian. *Note*: Photo identifications may not be totally accurate.)

Hashim and Hovsep came running out, shouting with joy at the sight of their brother. Embraces and excited words were exchanged as curious people poured out of nearby shops to inspect the wonderful new flivver. The marvelous mechanical horse from America drew gawkers like a magnet.

Haji Bey looked around. "Where's Artin?" he inquired.

Hovsep turned his face away, and Haji Bey could see that he had begun to cry.

Hashim sadly informed your father that Artin was dead. "As I told you in my letter, I went to Efkereh and learned about the deportation and massacres. When I returned to Smyrna, I recounted to Hovsep and Artin what I had seen and heard, more than I dared put in my letter. Artin kept asking me about details, and I had to tell him everything. Then suddenly he grabbed his chest and fell to the floor, dead. What can I say, my brother? He couldn't take the grief and his heart broke."

"And what of the deportees of Efkereh? Have you learned where they were sent? Have any of them survived?"

Hashim shook his head. "The only thing I learned is that they were forced to march toward the Syrian desert, and that most of them were murdered along the road or perished from exposure, illness, and starvation. One of the Turkish families in Efkereh, which tried to save some Armenians, gave me details of what happened. I'm sorry, but I can't relate them to you. It's too terrible."

Hashim put his arm around Haji Bey. "Don't try to go there, my brother. It's no use. It would be most dangerous and you won't find out anything about your family."

Hovsep pulled a handkerchief from his pocket and dried his eyes. "We went to the government officials here to seek an explanation, but were told only that the Armenians had been 'resettled.' We didn't press the matter any further, for we had heard terrible stories about Armenians being killed all over the interior and we feared for our own lives."

"And where's Artin buried?" Haji Bey demanded. "I must go to his grave."

■ ■ ■ ■

My Uncle Nazar's face grew pale as he related this story. His mind was being drawn back into the dark pages of yesterday. Back to things he had pushed back into the deep recesses of his mind. Things he preferred to forget. He had repressed the memory for years but finally felt it was important to share it with me. He wanted me to know about the tragedy that befell our people during the genocide of 1915-1916. I was just a kid and didn't understand the pain it caused him to speak about it.

"Uncle, there were six of you — my father, you, Uncle Artin, Hovsep, your adopted brother Hashim, and Uncle Mardiros who stayed behind with you. What happened to Uncle Mardiros? I have never seen him."

The tears now rolled freely down my uncle's creased face. "Yes, Nephew, your Uncle Mardiros stayed behind with me. Over the next two years, after Haji Bey had returned to Smyrna, Mardiros brooded over the fate of his family and became terribly depressed. He felt guilty for having left them there alone. Finally, he made up his mind to go back to Turkey. He kept mumbling about searching for the graves of his family, putting flowers on them, and saying a few prayers. He was talking out of his head."

"What graves?" I shouted at him. "Are you crazy? Where in God's name are you going to look?" I begged him to stay in America with me, not to take a chance. Unfortunately, I couldn't hold him back. He wouldn't listen. He was like a madman. He booked passage on a boat anyway.

I saw him off on a train to New York. Then I sent word to your father that Mardiros was coming. Haji Bey told me that he met every boat, but Mardiros never showed up. Never. He just vanished from the face of the earth. To this day we don't have any idea of what happened to him."

A thousand questions came to my mind, but a look at my uncle's grim, grief-stricken face stopped me cold.

"Yes, Nephew, those were the darkest days of the Armenian people. Close to a million and a half of our people perished. Yet today millions of people have never heard of the Armenian genocide by the Young Turk government. And even worse, the

Turks now deny their guilt. Their government has never made restitution for the lives and property we lost."

■ ■ ■ ■

You know, Nephew, the Allies sent the Greeks to occupy Smyrna on their behalf in the spring of 1919. The Greeks stayed for three years, until they were driven out by treachery. Haji Bey had written me that he intended to remain in Turkey so as to search for his family. He had not given up hope that he might find them. He placed advertisements in newspapers all over Turkey and Syria, where many of the survivors seemed to be located. He also enlisted the aid of his Turkish and Armenian friends.

Occasionally, he would hear something that kept his hope alive — a whisper here, a hint there. Although he knew it would be a miracle if he found his people, he remained optimistic. In his heart he believed that somewhere, somehow, at least his son had survived. This hope kept driving your father, telling him to hold on, not to let go just yet.

Haji Bey's perseverance finally paid off. A letter arrived from Hakim Bey, a man who had been part of Ibrahim Pasha's group that used to meet in the café. As Haji Bey read Hakim Bey's letter, your father jumped for joy. His son was alive! He was in an orphanage in Aleppo. And his young brother-in-law, Kourken Chackerian, was in Aleppo, too. They were both alive and well!

Hakim Bey advised Haji Bey not to come to Aleppo in person because it would be a dangerous trip for an Armenian. Hakim Bey went on to describe some of the atrocities that had taken place on the death marches. Reading the letter was like having needles piercing Haji Bey's heart. Hakim Bey concluded the letter with this:

> My dear friend, I beg forgiveness for what will go down as the most heinous atrocity in history. Please forgive us. You should not blame all Turks for these awful crimes against man and nature. Those who are responsible for these vicious murders will be brought to trial and held

> accountable for their barbarous deeds, I promise you. There are too many good Turks who feel as I do to let this crime pass unpunished. There will be justice.[1] May God protect you and guide you and your child to safety.

Haji Bey immediately sent some money to Hakim Bey to take to the orphanage to provide for the children. Over the next few days, Haji Bey read and reread the letter, thinking about its contents, trying to decide what to do next. He couldn't get the kids out of his mind. Knowing that the children would never be released to a Turk, even to an honorable man like Hakim Bey, he decided he needed the help of his old friend Sarkis Aga.

Your dad hadn't seen much of Sarkis Aga since returning to Smyrna. When Haji Bey first arrived, the old gentleman had come right away to welcome him. The boys could see Sarkis Aga as he strutted toward the shop, sporting a new walking cane with his own likeness carved into the handle. His vanity was still in full bloom, and he stood erect as he addressed your father: "Welcome, my son!"

"Good to see you, Sir," Haji Bey replied as he embraced the distinguished old man. He said it was like a miracle to see his beloved friend once again. Sarkis Aga asked Haji Bey what he thought of the New World. Your dad answered that the Aga would have to see for himself how good it really was to live in America.

"But, my boy," the old man protested, "your native land has been more than good to you; and, in any case, the Greeks are now in charge, a whole new era has opened."

"More than good?" Haji was bitter, his face twisted with anger. "My wife, my son, my entire family, all my relatives, my in-laws, and all my childhood friends are undoubtedly dead. All I have for sure is just three of my brothers." Suddenly he

---

[1] Indeed there were war-crime trials held by the Turkish government that came to power after the Ottoman Empire and the Central Powers lost World War I. Many Young Turk leaders were tried, convicted, and condemned to death by the Turkish courts-martial.

whacked the palm of one hand with the back of the other, so loudly that the old man was startled. "Are there Armenians who still remain asleep after all that has happened in this country? Do people think we are safe in Smyrna, that we can go on with our lives here as usual? They are in for a rude awakening. The Turks will come back. We Armenians will be trapped!"

Sarkis Aga answered gravely. "My son, I heard of your losses. It grieves my heart to know what took place in your village." He put his arm around Haji Bey's shoulder. "But these *pogroms*, these unpleasant incidents, happen in most countries. It is a dangerous world. In time, however, the wounds heal and the clouds once more disappear. You must give things time. In any case, we are now under a new government."

Haji Bey stared aghast for a few moments. *Time to heal? Give things time?* Sarkis Aga was blind, or a fool. Only God could awaken this old man from his trance. Haji Bey saw no use in hurting Sarkis Aga's feelings, however, so he just let the matter drop.

Although Haji Bey loved the old man like a father, after this first disagreeable encounter on his return, he found it disconcerting to talk with the old man and decided to see him as little as possible.

Now, however, he needed Sarkis Aga's help. He sent word to the old man to come by the shop. When Sarkis Aga arrived, Haji Bey wasted no time getting to the point: "My son, thank God, was somehow spared the massacre in Efkereh. He's in an orphanage in Syria. My little brother-in-law, Kourken Chackerian, is there, too. I sent some money to my friend Hakim Bey to help them out, and I will send more as long as necessary. But I now need to find a way to bring them to Smyrna. Sarkis Aga, can you be of help?"

"Let . . . let me see what I can do, my son," Sarkis Aga replied absentmindedly. The old man seemed to be preoccupied with something else. He was fidgeting. "So, umm, if I can deliver your children safely into your hands, how will you, umm, how will you care for them . . . without a wife?"

Haji Bey was suddenly on the alert, wondering what the shrewd old fox had on his mind — clearly, something was afoot.

Sarkis Aga got up, began pacing around the shop, picking up various items, casually inspecting them, and putting them back. All the while he tried to make small talk.

Haji Bey finally broke in: "Effendi, is something bothering you?"

"Well, my son," the old man said quickly, "you asked, and I will tell you. I am concerned about *you*!"

Haji Bey was surprised. "Me? Why are you concerned about me, Effendi?"

Sarkis Aga got right to the point. "You're still a young man! It wasn't meant for a man to live alone. I have a beautiful granddaughter living at my widowed daughter-in-law's house. If you get the boys back, you must have a wife to care for them . . . and you. My granddaughter, just as my daughter-in-law, is a widow. She is a beautiful woman, and she would look even more beautiful if your arms were linked together! So, I want you to join us for dinner tonight. Be there at eight o'clock, sharp!"

Haji Bey's mouth dropped open. He began to stutter, to make excuses, but the old boy was adamant and wouldn't take no for an answer. Haji Bey was to come and that was that.

That evening Haji Bey put on his best clothes. He looked like a prince. He hopped into his flivver, took off down the street, and drove to the quarter where the rich Armenians lived. When he arrived at the house, he parked his car and walked up to the front door. The door swung open before he knocked. Standing before him was Sultan Miriam Kouradjian,[1] usually called "Sultan Hanim." Sultan Hanim took one look at your father and tried to repress a giggle. He had forgotten to take off his driving goggles!

Her initial reaction, of course, left Haji Bey a bit unnerved. He wanted to escape at once, but at that moment, Sarkis Aga came out to the front hall and grabbed Haji Bey by the arm before he

---

[1] Distinguished Armenian ladies were sometimes called "Sultan." The normal Turkish feminine of "sultan" would be "sultana," but since the Armenians used the word as a name and not a title, it was Sultan. The first name was often, by Turkish custom, followed by the title of respect, "*Hanim.*" In other words, Lady Sultan.

could get away. The old man escorted Haji Bey into the drawing room, turned and said, "I'm happy you've come, my son. I want to introduce you to my daughter-in-law, Sultan Miriam Kouradjian Hanim, whose husband was my beloved son, Badrik [Patrick]. He died in 1917."

Haji Bey kissed her hand and expressed his sympathies. She smiled sweetly at him, and he liked her at once.

Sarkis Aga went on with the introductions: "And these are my wonderful granddaughters — Armenouhi, Arous, Artemis, and Vartanoush. Standing over there is Zarmineh, the youngest of the girls. These two fine lads are my grandsons Krikor [Gregory] and our very youngest, Sahag [Isaac]." Sarkis Aga turned to Artemis. "Go and get your sister Victoria," he commanded her. "Tell her she's holding up dinner. Quickly, go! Go!"

Victoria was upstairs, aware of her grandfather's matchmaking game, aggravated because she hadn't been informed in advance about the evening's guest. She heard Artemis pounding up the steps, sputtering in her excitement as she burst into the room.

"A beautiful present from grandfather!" exclaimed Artemis to her sister. "A six-foot brute . . . handsome . . . with large black eyes, a bushy moustache, lots of hair on his head . . . he's beautiful!"

"I don't want to meet any man right now, thank you! I know what Grandfather is up to. I don't want to get married. I don't want to marry ever again!"

Victoria had lost her two children and husband to cholera only two years before, and she had almost succumbed to the disease herself. She had been at death's door for two months. "Handsome, huh!" she sniffed haughtily. "Well, we'll see!"

Without even glancing in the mirror, which was her usual custom, she started down the stairs, with her head held high. She came to a stop halfway down, as her eyes moved across the room and fastened on the "handsome brute" of a man staring up at her.

When he saw her, Haji Bey actually gasped aloud. Victoria was so stunningly beautiful.

Only after Victoria was sure of her effect on the stranger did she continue to the bottom of the stairs.

"Haji Bey," Sarkis Aga said, "this is my eldest granddaughter Victoria — she was named after the Queen of England. In my payroll department, Victoria is my right hand and accompanies me every Saturday to distribute pay to my men. Altogether, I have eight grandchildren in this family; I also have four more sons and many more grandchildren from them."

The old man rattled on and on. Haji Bey had no idea what the old man was talking about and didn't care. He couldn't take his eyes off Victoria. He was captivated by the girl's beauty and graceful movements. He had already made up his mind in the first seconds of their meeting: She was going to be his bride.

Sarkis Aga continued to ramble on. Haji Bey was impatient. Would the old man never stop babbling so he could get in a word edgewise?

The old man was a wily fox. He went on and on with his small talk. He was very much aware of the couple's immediate attraction to each other. It was as if their meeting was always meant to be. Ahaaa, he thought, I've got him where I want him!

The Aga finally switched the subject to Victoria. "My dear young friend, I want you to know that my beautiful granddaughter, Victoria, lost her husband and two children to cholera. She herself would have perished if I hadn't sent for a specialist from England. She is all of twenty-three now, and we all know that life must go on. She has finished a proper period of mourning and it is now time for her to form a new family."

Victoria had sworn never to marry again. The trauma of losing a husband and two children had left deep emotional scars, of course. Now she sat thinking to herself, "Oh, please, I'm not ready yet . . . who is this man, where did he come from? Maybe later, but not now."

Time and again, her eyes were drawn to Haji Bey's. Anger rose inside her. Grandfather had meddled with her life once again and brought this stranger into their home . . . a stranger she couldn't stop looking at. Why is Grandfather doing this?

The stranger opened his mouth to speak. "I believe all of us pass through the valley of the shadow of death. I myself have suffered the loss of my beloved wife, mother, and several members of my family. I have just reached my thirty-eighth year and have had my share of pain. . . ." Haji Bey's voice trailed off. He paused for a few seconds, searching for what to say. Finally, he formed the words in his mind, turned to Sarkis Aga, and began to speak, hoping it would all come out properly and not sound too blunt or too hasty.

"Sir, you are right. Life must go on. I must form a new family to take care of my son and young brother-in-law. It would be an honor if you were to give me your granddaughter's hand in marriage." Haji Bey was totally taken with her.

There was complete silence in the room. Sarkis Aga looked questioningly at Victoria who sat with her head bowed. A few moments passed before the beauty raised her head. Instead of looking at her grandfather, she did an unorthodox thing, she locked eyes with Haji Bey, and nodded.

Dinner took over two hours. Sarkis Aga kept up his banter, going on about his successes in the business world, the people he knew, the places he had visited. Obviously, all of this was lost on the two spellbound lovebirds. Victoria's head was in a whirl as she thought to herself, "My God! An hour ago, I didn't want to get married ever again. Now I seem to be falling in love with this man I have never met before. Can I trust my heart?"

Dinner finally came to an end.

Haji Bey's eyes never left Victoria's as he spoke: "Sarkis Aga, may I have your permission to take your granddaughter for a ride in my automobile?"

Without waiting for her grandfather to speak, your mother gently replied, "Yes, of course."

As if by some signal, Haji Bey and Victoria rose from the table at the same time. He walked over to her and took her arm. And without a word to anyone, to the amazement of Sarkis Aga and Sultan Hanim, they moved toward the front door.

Vartanoush was hurriedly sent to act as chaperon. However, she soon returned: Victoria had sent her back inside!

Sultan Hanim was very unhappy. Her daughter's behavior was disgraceful! She showed her disapproval by glaring at the rest of her children. They, of course, were getting a big kick out of what was going on in their usually staid and traditional home.

As they drove along in the new American automobile, Victoria and Haji Bey were on their own cloud. Victoria's head was in a whirl as she thought about the possibility of a life more exciting than she had ever experienced. The man sitting beside her had just proposed marriage, and she had accepted. The ceremony, as customary, would take place in a few days.

Haji Bey suddenly brought the flivver to a screeching stop in the middle of the road and embraced his bride-to-be. He was so happy. People quickly gathered around, attracted not only by the rare sight of a horseless carriage, but also by the shameless embraces of the two people in the automobile. There were strict conventions about the behavior of couples in public. Haji Bey slipped the car in gear and headed for the picturesque seaside.

■ ■ ■ ■

The elegant wedding ceremony took place the following week at the beautiful Armenian Cathedral of Smyrna, St. Stepanos. The Primate, the distinguished Bishop Levon Tourian, presided. There were four priests taking part, several deacons, and a full choir. With the homilies and all, the wedding took almost two hours. People would remember it for a long time.

The wedding feast, as befitting a favorite granddaughter of Sarkis Aga, was lavish. White tents and elegant tables had been set up in the garden of Victoria's mother's grand house. Flowers bedecked the house, linen covered the tables, and the stage had been set up for the musicians. In fact, flowers were everywhere, even around the four-foot candles that were placed at strategic spots on the grounds and also around the lanterns which hung from the tent tops. The servants were formally dressed. The tables were set with fine china, silverware, and crystal.

The bride and groom arrived in a carriage with a driver and a footman. The band played a wedding march as the happy couple walked up to the head table. The guests arrived in their own carriages. The women were dressed in their finest silks and satins, and the men, of course, wore evening clothes. There were over four hundred guests. You have never seen such an opulent sight.

The food, of course, was as lavish as the decor. It continued to be served all evening. The dishes were of beef, lamb, fowl, and fish. Every kind of seafood you can imagine, including caviar from Russia. The vegetables were of a great variety, many of them having been imported from neighboring lands, including Egypt and Palestine. Fruits of all kind were piled high in decorated platters. The cuisine was Greek, Armenian, and French. Champagne and other beverages flowed in an endless river. There must have been over a hundred different types of pastries and desserts, which were prepared in Sarkis Aga's bakeries.

Long before the wedding celebration was over, Haji Bey and Victoria got up and left without so much as a glance behind them. They wanted only to be alone and to make their love complete. The merrymakers continued the party for several days, as was the custom, coming and going at their leisure.

CHAPTER FIFTEEN
The House on the Cliff

After Victoria and Haji Bey were married, they moved into the Sarkis Aga's beautiful summer house, perched on a high cliff overlooking Smyrna and surrounded by a garden. You could see the entire harbor and, beyond it, the blue gulf stretching to the sea. This beautiful home was your place of birth, Nephew. You came along just nine months after the marriage, in June of 1920.

You certainly inherited a large family for such a tiny baby. There was your grandmother Sultan Hanim, six aunts, two uncles, a great-grandfather, and dozens of cousins. Your great-grandmother, Sarkis Aga's wife, had already died. Since you were the only baby in the family at that time, you were bounced from one knee to another among all your aunts and uncles and other relatives. It was a happy time.

The way to get to the house on top of that cliff was by a very steep and difficult climb or by a hydraulic lift that could carry up to eight people. The lift had been built by a Jewish inventor and it served all the houses on the high hill. That elevator went up and down all day long, transporting all the relatives who came to see the new baby.

▪ ▪ ▪ ▪

I should tell you a few things about your mother, Artin. She was quite a lady. As a teenager, she already had many friends — Armenians, Greeks, and also a few French, Turkish, and Jewish girls. These were girls who lived in the quarter where the wealthy had their homes. Some of these families rented either land or houses from Sarkis Aga, who had built and rented out over one hundred large homes throughout Smyrna. Land was valuable and hard to come by, so some rich people were forced to lease the land for their houses from others, usually for fifty to one hundred years.

The girls enjoyed visiting each other, playing games in the garden, and going on picnics accompanied by chaperons. The families, however, rarely mixed socially.

Many of your mother's Turkish girlfriends would come to visit her regularly. They were from the best families of Smyrna, daughters of wealthy merchants, professionals, and government officials. The Moslem girls were generally required to wear modest garments. They would come to your mother and together they would go shopping to buy Western-style clothes. The Turkish girls would then bring the clothes back to your mother's house where they hid them in her closet. The girls would return on Saturday nights, dress in their smart Western clothes, and go out to house parties.

Your grandmother disapproved of her daughter being involved in this deception, so she put a stop to it. Well, soon the girls stopped coming around. They found other non-Moslem friends to help them out.

Victoria was your grandfather's favorite and he indulged her in many things. While Sarkis Aga was a stubborn old man, he was usually putty in Victoria's hands. She was the apple of his eye, the favorite among all his grandchildren. Once a month, he would come by with horse and carriage to pick her up for a shopping expedition, buying her whatever struck her fancy. It was Victoria's world, and it was the Aga's pleasure to make everything in that world possible for her.

After she grew up, for some reason he began to have her help him distribute the pay to his workers every Saturday. This was an unusual responsibility for a young Armenian girl. Sarkis Aga often broke conventions for his favorite granddaughter. Every Saturday morning, he would come by the house and pick up Victoria. He would watch her carefully, they were always attended by strong bodyguards.

Off they would go in his carriage, surrounded by Sarkis Aga's men. Their first task was to determine which café they would use for distributing the payroll. When the old man came to the harbor area, there would be a half-dozen or so café owners begging him to choose their cafés. You see, Nephew, this would mean a lot of extra business for whichever café was chosen.

There was a lot to choosing a café, of course. They had to bargain. They chose the one that gave the most free drinks and agreed to return the highest portion of the night's profit, usually around ten percent.

The café that was chosen would set up special tables and chairs for Sarkis Aga's employees. Guards would bring in the sacks of gold and silver coins and pile them on a table in front of Sarkis Aga and Victoria. The workers would form a line that would stretch out the front door and extend to the corner of the street. The Aga would then call out the amount to be paid to each man in turn and your mother would count out the money and press it into the man's palm. The men always gave Victoria a reverent bow and thanked her. Naturally, this attention caused your mother's head to swell. She was very proud, Nephew, and, oh, so very beautiful.

Sarkis Aga, of course, was familiar with the work habits of all his men and paid them what they were worth. As a result of this fair treatment, the men were extremely loyal to him and treated him with the utmost respect.

The music would start as the money was being handed out. The café owner wanted to entice the workers to stay and spend their money. Of course, most of the bachelors did. The married men varied, according to their relations with their wives. Some stayed, most didn't. Belly dancers, along with the food and drink, were a part of the enticement. They would take to the floor early.

The next morning, the restaurant owner would bring Sarkis Aga his share of the profits. Sarkis Aga would donate the money to the Armenian and Greek churches, equally, in memory of his late wife.

■ ■ ■ ■

Yes, your grandmother had many girlfriends of all nationalities. She was very popular. Many of her friends were Jews, with whom — in addition to the Armenian girls — she got along very well. Several of Sarkis Aga's mansions were leased to Jewish families. Most of the far-off ancestors of these girls had immigrated to the Ottoman Empire around the time of the Spanish Inquisition. Of course, they faced discrimination here like the other non-Moslem minorities. Many of these Jews grew wealthy in businesses that had little or no competition.

One of these businesses was cleaning out human wastes from the outhouses. It was actually a good business because the customer always had to pay, and pay on time. If a customer didn't pay his bill, the workmen would not empty the septic tank. It wouldn't be long before the homeowner would send over the payment and ask for a worker to come out. No one wanted to put up with the shit.

As the Jews prospered, they could afford to send their children to boarding schools and colleges in England, France, Germany, and even America, just as the other successful minorities did. When the students graduated, they often remained in the country where they had studied and went into businesses or professions. Many, after they were established, would send for their parents. Eventually, most of the Jews left Smyrna; most Armenians, however, stayed behind.

Gradually, the atmosphere in our city changed for the worse. Mustapha Kemal Atatürk's army was pushing the Greeks and their French "allies" out of the interior. Stories of the massacres of Armenians in the provinces, who had been repatriated after the war, were well known. This fact couldn't help but make the family and other Armenians uneasy. They were never sure if the killings would reach Smyrna.

When your grandmother Sultan Hanim went shopping for fruits and vegetables in the bazaar, the Turkish women who ran the markets would no longer exchange greetings and smiles with her and, at times, were even quarrelsome. She became depressed. She recalled Haji Bey's advice to sell all their holdings and leave Smyrna. Unfortunately the Aga wouldn't hear of it. Sultan Hanim, being a woman, was forced to bow to his wishes. That's the way things were in those times.

When Sultan Hanim pleaded with him to heed Haji Bey's warning, he would get angry and shout, "This is my country! My land! The granite pits, the Turkish baths, the bakeries, my beautiful horses, and all the houses — they all belong to me. Me,

Sarkis Aga! No one will take them away! Not even the Turks if they come back."

You must remember, Nephew, even though he was nearing his one hundredth year, he still had a keen business sense. His ideas were young and fresh. Remember he was the one who wanted to build a movie theater to show films imported from Hollywood. Sarkis Aga should have been thinking about leaving everything behind, not starting new businesses. What Sarkis Aga didn't understand, however, was the political climate. What would happen to the Armenians if the Turkish nationalists defeated the Greeks? Things could get real bad.

Finally, after much thought, Haji Bey approached Sarkis Aga, "I have placed you in my heart as my own father. I've followed your advice in all business matters and I have married the wonderful lady you recommended to me. Please forgive me for saying it, but in one thing you are wrong, Effendi. Make no mistake about it. I am determined to take my wife and baby son and move them to safety in America. If you will not come with us, you should allow your family to leave, at least until we see what happens here."

Sarkis Aga was shocked. He acted as if he'd been stabbed in the back. "You mean to tell me that you're leaving? How can you possibly leave? After all I have done for you?"

"My mind is made up. We are leaving. I wish you would reconsider and come along with us."

The old man could see there was no changing Haji Bey's mind. The anger left his face and was replaced by a terrible sadness.

"No, my son, I won't come. What difference would it make whether I died here or there in your new land? You know I'm almost one hundred years old. I'm ready to meet my Maker.

"No, I will not leave, but I will think about allowing someone to go with you. I've been fortunate here among my Armenian, Greek, and Turkish friends. They have much respect for me. If the Turks come back, they won't harm one hair on my head. I have been too good to them. Go, if you must, but let me be."

■ ■ ■ ■

Haji Bey, of course, had no intention of leaving for America until he got his first son and young brother-in-law out of the orphanage in Syria. Your parents also wanted to have you baptized before their departure. As was the custom, you should have been baptized within forty days, so they sent word to Sarkis Aga asking him to be the godfather. He loved you so much, he reined in his anger and accepted.

You were to be baptized by the Armenian Primate of Smyrna, Bishop Levon Tourian. He had just returned from a trip to Jerusalem where he had a meeting with other religious dignitaries.

On the appointed day, the whole family went to the cathedral. When the Bishop was told that Sarkis Aga and his family had arrived, he went out to meet them on the steps. The Bishop smiled at his old friend Sarkis Aga and embraced him warmly.

"Welcome, welcome," the distinguished cleric greeted them. Then, with a twinkle in his eye, he addressed himself directly to the old man. "Do I owe you or do you owe me, my friend? I don't remember. If you owe me, perhaps you'll give me one of your bakeries so we can feed the children who survived the massacres. I will tell our Lord in heaven and He will go easy on you for your sins."

"No, Your Grace, I'm afraid it's you who owes me. And I'm here to collect."

"Oh, what can I do for you?"

"I want you to do me a favor, Your Grace. My granddaughter's new husband has a problem. He has a son by his first wife and a young brother-in-law who are in the Armenian orphanage in Aleppo. My grandson-in-law wants them brought here. As you know, it would be most dangerous for him to try to make the trip himself. Do you have a way of having the children brought to us via Jerusalem?"

The Bishop was not only one of the most brilliant of the princes of the church, he was also a kind-hearted man. He agreed to help if he could, and he took down the names and ages of the boys and gave them to his secretary.

They walked into the cathedral and began the age-old ceremony. At first, they all faced the rear of the temple and renounced "the devil and all his works" three times. Then they went over to the baptismal font. "What is this child's name," the Bishop asked.

"Harutiun [Paschal],[1] signifying the resurrection," your godfather answered. Your great-grandfather lifted you and handed you over to the Bishop. The Bishop asked Sarkis Aga, your godfather, three times what you came for. Your godfather answered "faith, hope, love, and baptism," three times in reply. Then the bishop immersed you in water reciting prayers: "Harutiun, child of God, I baptize you in the name of the Father, Son, and Holy Spirit and admit you to the company of the faithful."

Then you were chrismated, anointed with holy oil, on your head, your hands, your ears, eyes and nose, and on your feet. Finally, the Bishop went up on the *bema,* the berm on which the altar sat. Your godfather passed you up to the bishop and the bishop "presented" you before the altar. It was a beautiful ceremony, Son. By it you were made a new-born Christian and a member of the church, the most ancient national church in the world.

As the Bishop handed you back to Sarkis Aga, he laughed. and said, "Sarkis Aga, since you are the godfather, you owe the 'little baby' now. What will you do for him?"

The old man chuckled. "All right. All right. Tomorrow, Your Grace, in his honor, you shall have the deed to one of my bakeries for your Armenian orphans."

The kindly Bishop was overcome with joy, and he threw his arms around your great-grandfather and embraced him. Then he turned his face away so no one could see his tears. "All of you, please go now. Go! I'm very busy. I'll send word as soon as there's some news about the children in Aleppo."

Three weeks later, your parents were summoned to the cathedral. When they arrived, they saw the Bishop standing on the front steps holding the hands of two young boys in ragged

---

[1] Harutiun [Paschal] signifies the resurrection of Christ. The diminutive of Harutiun in Armenian is "Artin." The name is frequently transposed into the English name "Harry," because of their similar sound.

clothing. There they were, Garbis and Kourken! Safe and sound! Haji Bey's joy was boundless.

The boys were taken immediately to Sultan Hanim's house. Your grandmother took one look at them and called Victoria.

"Come quickly, daughter, these children are crawling with lice. Take them to the bathhouse and get them cleaned up. Then, for God's sake, get them some decent clothing."

When the boys were clean and properly dressed, everyone gathered around them to question them about what had happened on the death march and how they had managed to escape.

They were reluctant to talk about what they had been through. After all, it was a horrible nightmare for them. Garbis was only five years old and Kourken only seven when they, their families, their neighbors, and their friends were first driven from their village. Perhaps half of them survived in north Syria, with the help of the Arabs and American missionaries.

After the Ottoman Empire surrendered in October 1918, the few survivors struggled to get back to their homes. They were there only a few months when the Turkish nationalists approached and the Armenians had to flee again. By now the boys were ten and twelve.

After the second expulsion from Efkereh, Siranoush died of starvation and exposure. The boys managed to reach the outskirts of Aleppo with some of the survivors. There was almost no food in the town or the surrounding areas. The refugees were put in camps, which were hardly better than death camps. With the lack of food, water, proper shelter and sanitation, the refugees were dying like flies. The boys escaped to Aleppo and begged in the streets. That rarely gained them enough to eat since so many half-starved Armenian children were begging. There were so many Armenian beggars that the Arabs were running out of food themselves.

The police would walk through town and gather up the orphans and take them back to the camp. Kourken and Garbis were caught in just such a roundup. Finally, help came from America through Near East Relief and the orphanage was established. They were placed in the orphanage, where they were found only a few months later by Hakim Bey who had been searching the whole area for them. As soon as he had found them, he wrote Haji Bey the good news.

Their ordeal was still fresh in their memories, but they did not want to talk about it any further. To talk about it, was to relive it. That they were not willing, or able, to do.

■ ■ ■ ■

My uncle gazed at me for a long time. His face was filled with a deep sadness. I can see it as clearly now sixty years later as I did then sitting across the kitchen table from him when I was a boy of thirteen. "My boy," he finally said, you are thirteen years old, a man to my way of thinking. I believe that it is time for me to tell you the whole story of the Armenian genocide. When you have children, you must tell it to them. When they have children, they must pass the story along. We must never forget what happened to our people in the Ottoman Empire.

"In 1915, the Turks had decided to do something final about the 'Armenian question,' the problem of the Armenian minority. The Turks had been massacring our people for centuries, yet that wasn't fast enough for the Young Turk regime.

"So the leaders of the Young Turks came up with their relocation scam: Armenians would be deported to 'new homes,' but in reality, they would be driven to their death in the Syrian desert. First, the men of fighting age were drafted into the army, put in labor battalions, and eventually killed. Then the Turks went to the towns and villages all over the country demanding that the Armenians turn in their arms. All citizens had been allowed to own firearms since the revolution of 1908, but only a few Armenians really had any. If the Armenians didn't hand in a weapon, the man of the house was tortured until a family member brought one. Some people who had no weapons actually went to Turkish families and bought firearms from them so they would have something to turn in.

"After the people were disarmed, the Turks were free to do their dirty business. All remaining males aged fifteen to fifty-five were assembled. Then they were tied together and marched to a secluded place where they were killed.

"Then came the 'relocation' of those who remained. All women, children, and old men were ordered out of their homes with only what they could carry. They were formed into enormous convoys of thousands upon thousands of people from hundreds of Armenian cities and villages, and forced to march through the countryside, heading to the south, to the Syrian desert.

"Thousands of helpless souls were forced into these long winding caravans that stretched the length and breadth of Turkey. Mothers were separated from their children and then were raped repeatedly by whoever wanted to rape them. Babies were tossed onto bayonet tips. Those marchers who fell in exhaustion were forced back to their feet, forced to go on until they fell dead in their tracks. Pregnant women gave birth by the side of the road and were immediately made to get up and rejoin the marchers, leaving their babies to die. Kurds and Turks from villages through which the caravans passed were encouraged to prey upon the people, steal whatever they could find, carry off the women they might fancy, take the children they wanted, and kill and murder and maim whomever they wished.

"Thieves took the pitiful rags from the backs of the marchers in hopes that they might find gold coins hidden in the seams. After several weeks on the road, many of the people were stark naked. The women, feeling ashamed, bent over double as they staggered along in a feeble effort to conceal their exposed bodies.

"There was hardly any food or water. Even when they came to a stream or river, the gendarmes usually wouldn't let their prisoners drink from it. When the few survivors reached the desert, the sun burned their exposed bodies and the hot desert sands scorched their bare, swollen feet. They dropped like flies."

Suddenly, my uncle stopped. His face was wet with tears. He couldn't go on. I didn't press him.

CHAPTER SIXTEEN
A Family Greets the New Land

My family had to prepare to leave Smyrna in something of a rush. Once my father, Haji Bey, had found Garbis and Kourken, he wanted to get out of Smyrna as soon as possible. He learned the Turkish nationalists were scoring victories in the interior, and he feared it would be only a matter of time before they reached the city. Once the Greek army had been broken at the front, nothing remained to stop the Turks.

My mother Victoria told me about her trip to America. My dad had given his car to his brother Hovsep. The whole family had gathered at Sultan Hanim's house that last day in Smyrna — all of Sarkis Aga's children, grandchildren, and great-grandchildren, relatives and in-laws. Mother described the general confusion with people running around in all directions making last-minute decisions, doing last-minute packing, talking and crying, getting into each other's way. Her memory for details was sharp back then, and she related her account with a mixture of wit and melancholy. The following is my mother's story.

■ ■ ■ ■

My son, I'll never forget the chaos on the day when Haji Bey and I were getting ready to emigrate in the fall of 1920. The house was crowded with people and we were making final decisions about what clothes to take, what jewelry to pack, how much money we needed, double-checking our documents and tickets, and getting everything properly packed.

I embraced my beloved grandfather, and begged him for the last time to please come with us.

"No, my child," he said sadly, "my heartbeat is here, my roots are here. I'm part of this soil, it's part of me. If I were to leave this land, I would surely die."

He had, however, given two of my older sisters, your Aunt Artemis and your Aunt Arous, permission to come with us. So, our little group was finally made up of your father, you and me, my two sisters, and the two boys. Haji Bey was to take care of finding husbands in America for my sisters.

Grandfather continued to point out to everyone that there wasn't any trouble in the city with the Greeks in charge, and besides somebody has to stay and run the businesses. He promised the ones who stayed behind that he'd put them on the next boat to America if conditions got any worse.

Then, I begged my mother Sultan Hanim for the last time to come with us, too. She insisted that she had to stay and take care of grandfather. I think that deep in her heart she thought she would be able to change his mind before it was too late and get him out of there.

Your grandmother Sultan Hanim had a last-minute inspiration. She decided on the spur of the moment to send Sarkis Aga's property deeds with us for safekeeping in America. She feared that the Turks would return to Smyrna and there would be trouble. She thought the rest of them might have to flee on a moment's notice. If that happened, then after things settled down, we might be able to come back later and reclaim our properties. She told grandfather that she was adamant, she would stay and take care of him only on condition that the documents were sent with those who were leaving. He reluctantly agreed. She brought out the papers from the safe and stood at the dining room table sorting them into piles while a pathetic looking Sarkis Aga watched with an air of concern. We were running late, and your father Haji Bey was afraid we would miss our ship.

"Hurry, hurry!" he urged her on. "If we miss this ship, the next one won't be sailing for several days."

My mother, Sultan Hanim, gave a sigh of distress, then simply tied together the ends of the tablecloth on which the deeds were piled, pushed the bundle into a valise and handed it to me.

"Here, take care of these papers. They are important. Guard them with your life," she instructed me.

The carriages were waiting. We quickly loaded the baggage and jumped up to our places. When we arrived at the dock, we sent our things aboard with the porters.

We all walked down the pier to the waiting ship, the *Pannonia*. We embraced and shed tears, wondering if we would ever see each other again. Then our little group went aboard: I went first, clutching you to my breast, followed by my two sisters, Arous and Artemis, holding Garbis and Kourken by their hands, and Haji Bey bringing up the rear, shooing us along like some great sheepdog herding his flock.

We stood at the railing waving goodbye, tears running down our faces. Oh God, I thought, what will happen to the ones we are leaving, what will happen to us? I kept making the sign of the cross and praying to God for deliverance. What had we done to deserve this cross?

I took one look around and my heart sank. The boat was a creaky old tub, not like the great ships that grandfather and I used to visit. There were blasts from the ship's horn, and it slowly pulled away from the pier. Everyone crossed themselves and murmured prayers for a safe journey. I crossed myself, too, about thirty times, and looked up to heaven. "Oh, Lord, what will become of us?" All I knew for sure was that we were headed for Detroit where Haji Bey's brother Nazar awaited us.

For the first few days the weather was good and we got to know some of the other passengers. Some were businessmen, but most of the people were emigrants like us, going to America to find safety and a new life.

One dummy told me he was heading for California to find gold. Didn't he know the gold rush was long over? I wondered. Haji Bey had already lived in the United States and knew what to expect.

"Sure, there's gold in America all right," Haji Bey would explain, "but you have to earn it. Whether you are employed by someone else, or go into business for yourself, you have to work hard and earn yourself a pile of gold. That's the way it is."

I already had my gold, and I was leaving it behind. I had lived like a queen, the favorite granddaughter of one of the richest men in Smyrna. Oh, sure, I'd thought that maybe one day I would go to America, but it would be for a visit, for a holiday. I never dreamed I'd be going there to live for the rest of my life.

My life in Smyrna was much, much better than my life here. In Smyrna, everything I ever needed was at my fingertips. In normal times I would not have dreamed of moving to the United States. Of course, things were not *normal*, and so I came here.

We had a relatively pleasant journey to Marseilles. Then we passed through the Straits of Gibraltar and churned into the Atlantic. There the ocean became rough, and the ship rolled and bounced. Most of the passengers became violently ill, moaning and vomiting over the railings, cursing their stomachs for betraying them. I heard one woman groan, "It would have been better if we'd stayed behind and taken our chances with the Turks. Even if they killed us, it would be over quickly. This is torture."

I became sick, too, very sick. After about three days of vomiting, I really wanted to die. I went to the railing of the ship with you in my arms and tried to climb over it. I tell you frankly, my son, I was going to jump. Your aunts Arous and Artemis saw me and rushed over, grabbed you, and then pulled me away. They wouldn't let me hold you again until I had recovered. You can thank your aunts, my son, that you are still alive today; I suppose, I should, too.

Some days later the waters became calm, or maybe we were just getting our sea legs, who knows. Soon we heard Middle Eastern music being played. At first, the music was soft and nostalgic. Then the beat picked up. Soon, all the passengers were having a good time. After all, we were going to the promised land. The merrymakers joined hands and danced around the deck on their new-found sea legs. Perhaps life wasn't so bad after all.

Haji Bey went scurrying around the ship interviewing all the eligible ladies, finding out which ones were going to Detroit and taking down their names and addresses. He had promised his buddies back in Michigan that he would bring them wives, and he was not the kind of man to go back on his word. Anyway, he loved playing the matchmaker, bringing people together and making them feel good.

The days passed and we were drawing close to America. We were counting the days — four, three, two, one — the next day we would reach America. Everyone stayed up all night in anticipation. As dawn was breaking we could make out the harbor lights flickering in the distance. America! America! We were approaching America!

By midday, we could see the Statue of Liberty coming in to view. That great lady with the torch held high in her hand. "Send me your tired, your poor, your huddled masses, yearning to be free," she told the world. Of course, the favorite granddaughter of Doshchi Sarkis Aga Kouradjian didn't feel tired, or poor, or a part of the huddled masses. She just wanted a normal life, free of religious persecution and danger.

The captain blasted the ship's horns as it pulled up to a gigantic pier. We all shouted for joy — jumping, waving, and crying.

After passing through immigration at Ellis Island, we were ferried to Manhattan. Haji Bey hailed two taxicabs to transport us and our luggage — which was tied to the fenders and the roofs of the cabs — to Grand Central Station. We must have been some sight!

Your father knew the ropes this time. "Grand Central Station," he ordered with assurance. "We are going to take the train to Detroit."

Well, Artin my son, I had seen large cities before, but nothing like New York. No country in the world at that time had skyscrapers like New York. The place was a whirl of sights, sounds, and colors. I must admit that I became quite nervous. It was overwhelming.

When we arrived at Grand Central Station, the cabbies unloaded our baggage. I held on to you for dear life, while my sisters kept a grip on the boys. Your father, always wanting to look like a big shot, gave the cabbies generous tips. They smiled, thanked him, and drove off. We watched the cabs as they disappeared down 42nd Street.

Then Haji Bey called four porters over to lug our belongings into the depot. They put everything into a big pile, and we sat down on a bench in the waiting room while your father went to pick up our tickets. What an impressive sight that was. I had never seen such a cavernous and beautiful room. It seemed bigger than the sanctuary of Hagia Sofia.[1] After Haji got the tickets, we hired porters again to take our baggage to our train compartment. As we boarded the train, I was again filled with anxiety. Finally, the porter cried out, "All aboard, all aboard for Detroit, Ann Arbor, Pontiac, Michigan, and all stops in between."

"We are going home," Haji Bey announced with a big smile.

"Home?" My thoughts turned to the beautiful home we had recently left behind . . . the view of the harbor . . . our carriages . . . the fine restaurants . . . the servants . . . all our fine clothes . . . our. . . our everything. "Where is my home?"

As the train crept out of the tunnel from under New York, my sisters and I let out one big communal sigh and began to arrange the baggage and get comfortable.

Suddenly I shrieked and clutched my head in anguish. "Oh, my God! We left Sarkis Aga's deeds in the taxi!" I was almost hysterical, screaming loudly.

Haji Bey was calm. "Sarkis Aga does not need these deeds if the Greeks remain in Smyrna; and they will do him no good if the Turks return. So, don't worry yourself. That life is over, it is best to forget."

The train trip itself was uneventful. The American countryside looked beautiful. I couldn't help but be impressed by the richness of the land and the fertility of the soil.

We had wired ahead, and your uncle Nazar and Haji Bey's friend, Aram Bedrosian, were waiting at the Detroit train station to meet us. Aram's face was filled with anticipation and his eyes flitted from one to another of the women in our little group, searching for the "queen" your father had promised to bring him. He held a large bouquet of roses to present to his new Armenian bride.

"Aram, my friend, relax," Haji chuckled. "She is not here." After the men had embraced, Haji turned toward us and said to

---

[1] Hagia Sofia, the Church of Holy Wisdom (the Holy Spirit), the supreme masterpiece of Byzantine architecture. It was built (532-37 AD) by the emperor Justinian I and for centuries was the largest and most beautiful church in Christendom.

Aram, "I want you to meet my lovely wife Victoria, my son Garbis, and my young brother-in-law from my first marriage, Kourken. This sweet baby is my son Artin, who the officials at Ellis Island dubbed with an American name — Harry[1] . . . and these are my wife's sisters Artemis and Arous. They are spoken for."

Aram's face turned red, then, recovering his composure, he gallantly presented me with the roses and chucked you under the chin. He made a good impression on me.

Aram was darker than most Armenians, his nickname was *Kara Oğhlan* [Dark Youth], and a smile always lit up his face. He stood among us, smoking a long black cigar that was thick in the middle and tapered at both ends.

I could see that Aram was thinking of something. His bashful nature kept him from speaking out, but of course Haji Bey knew what his friend was waiting to hear. Haji was just teasing his friend.

"Your friend here is playing games with you, Mr. Bedrosian," I spoke up. "Please excuse him."

He blushed deeply. "Please, madam, call me Aram."

"All right, Aram. Your friend has indeed found you a queen. We met her while crossing the ocean; I'm sure you're going to fall in love with her as soon as your eyes behold her beauty."

"Yes," Haji Bey added, "She was even on the train with us. Her aunt and uncle are picking her up right now."

Aram flushed again with pleasure, then craned his neck around to stare at all the people milling about us.

"It's no use, Aram," Haji Bey laughed. "You'll never see her in this crowd. Don't worry, you'll meet her tomorrow. Come on, let's go."

Some of us got into Mr. Bedrosian's car while others got into two cabs where we also stashed our luggage. We were to stay at

---

[1] Actually, as stated earlier, Artin is the diminutive of Harutiun [Paschal]. The officials at Ellis Island often changed foreign names to their nearest-sounding English approximation. Thus, Harutiun became Harry.

Aram's until we got settled in our own home. Once we were in the car, Aram asked Haji Bey when he could meet the girl.

"Aram, please, the young lady has just completed a tiring journey from Smyrna. Give her a chance to relax and spend some time with her aunt and uncle."

"Yes, of course, you're right," Aram agreed, "but let's go to visit her the first thing in the morning. I have business in the afternoon."

Aram was impatient. He wanted to see the girl as soon as possible.

▪ ▪ ▪ ▪

My mother laughed. "Your father's big mouth got him into a lot of trouble, Harry. (By this time mother had gotten used to calling me Harry instead of Artin.) Yet he was irrepressible. He would scramble about and do whatever it took to make good on his promises, even if it meant going into his own pocket to back up his words. That's the way he was then and that's the way he still is today."

"But, Mom," I protested, "I think that's a great way to be. People must've really looked up to him."

"Your father is ruled by his vanity. He is often boastful. He would try to impress strangers before looking after his own family. There were a million things to do at that time for us to get settled. Haji Bey, however, ran around getting ladies lined up to meet the men to whom he'd promised brides. We argued a lot about this matchmaking obsession of his. I didn't like it. What can I say? He was that way."

I couldn't bear her criticism of my father and felt I had to say something in his defense. "Yes, but you have faults too, Mom, we all do."

Whew! Was *that* ever a mistake on my part. My mother's face clouded over in anger: I'd offended her ego.

"I don't ever want to hear you say that again," she scolded. "I'm your mother, and children don't speak that way to their mothers, understand?"

"Well, to tell you the truth," I rashly continued, "I think my father's a great man, and I'm proud of him. Someday, when I'm old enough, I'm going to write a book about him."

My mother was surprised by my outburst. "Write a book, you are going to write a book? Well, all right, that's fine. Write a book. But if you do, don't make me look bad," she laughed.

"I won't, Mom, I promise — although I'm going to have to try very, very hard to find nice things to say about you."

She laughed again. She knew I was pulling her leg and leaned over and kissed me on my cheek.

■ ■ ■ ■

Early the next morning, there was a knock on the door. It was Aram with a lame smile on his face. He hadn't slept all night, he explained, because he couldn't get his prospective wife off his mind. He'd showered and shaved and now wanted Haji Bey to get dressed and have his breakfast so they could be on their way.

Haji Bey threw up his hands. "All right! All right, for God's sake, let's go! I'll take just a cup of coffee, I don't want to choke on my food."

Haji Bey told me later that he didn't have the slightest idea of what he was going to do, he was really going to this meeting quite blind. He hadn't even told the girl they were coming, nor had he contacted the girl's aunt or uncle! Like I said, my son, your father's boasting got him into a lot of bizarre situations.

Anyway, he gave the address as they jumped into Aram's shiny new convertible. Haji Bey was barely in his seat when Aram roared away from the curb with little regard for oncoming traffic. He was on a mission of love and he was all excited. I am sure he broke every speed limit in the city of Detroit.

Wouldn't you know, they were stopped by a cop and given a $5.00 fine. That was a lot of money in those days. Ticket or no ticket, Aram wanted to meet his future bride. Nothing could dampen his spirits.

The two men found the house and Haji Bey had second thoughts. "Don't you think I should go first and talk to her relatives before you propose? She is an Armenian girl and we will have to deal with her family."

Aram was not to be put off. Haji Bey had promised him a queen, and by God he wanted her.

At their knock, an old man opened the door a crack, peered at them suspiciously, and asked what they wanted.

"Sir," Haji Bey ventured, "I believe you have a niece named Gulizar?"

"Yes, I do. Who are you?"

"My name is Haji Bey. I met your niece on the ship *Pannonia*."

"So? What is that to me? We don't deal with strangers."

"Please, Sir, I want to introduce my good friend here to meet your niece. I. . . I think they'd make a nice couple."

"Oh, you think so? Who are you? What business is it of yours?"

"We are Armenians, just like you. I am looking for brides for my friends."

"Oh, I see. You go around from door to door without an introduction looking for young ladies to pass out to your friends like candy. Is that it?"

Haji Bey was frustrated. He had almost decided to call it quits when Gulizar's aunt came to the door to see who her husband was talking to.

When she saw they were Armenians, she opened the door wide and said, "Come in, come in, gentlemen. Have a seat. Would you like a cup of Turkish coffee?" When Haji Bey told of his mission, the lady smiled sweetly. "My husband doesn't understand these things. Tell me about your friend."

"My countrymen, I want you to know that Mr. Bedrosian here has been in America for quite some time and is a reputable businessman. He owns a string of fine hotels and is already on the road to riches. That is his fine, new car outside. He also owns a house. He is of fine moral character and would make a good husband for some lucky girl."

The old man grumbled, "The girl has hardly gotten off the boat and you want to take her away in marriage already? She . . . ."

His wife interrupted before he could complete his sentence. "Let me handle this, my dear. Don't bother yourself with it."

In immigrant circles, it was not unusual for the wife to replace her husband as the dominant figure in the family. The husband, as a newcomer, had little or no status in the outside world; he was a greenhorn, a nobody. The wife, on the other hand, continued to have status as the mistress of the house. She hardly needed to know the local language, her skills were transferable.

After they had chatted for a while, the woman called Gulizar into the room. Gulizar was a slender, green-eyed, fair-haired beauty. She blushed as she came in and saw the two strangers. She had been listening at the door and knew it was the one with the cigar who was seeking her hand in marriage.

Aram was totally spellbound by Gulizar's girlish beauty. When he finally took his eyes off her, he said to Haji Bey, "Let us step outside for a moment, I need to talk to you."

Outside, Haji Bey was uneasy. "What's the matter. Didn't you like her? I've got other girls' addresses, you know, you're not obliged to take this one."

"Are you kidding," Aram protested. "I'm already deeply in love with her. But . . . but . . . I don't know what to say to her."

"Oh, that's nothing," Haji Bey replied, "just leave that to me. When do you want to marry her?"

Aram's face lit up like a light bulb. "As soon as possible!"

They returned to the house and within two hours the wedding date was set.

A month later, we went to Aram's wedding. Your father was godfather and I, godmother. Aram was so grateful that he turned over one of his hotels, the Lincoln, to your father.

"Haji Bey, you can pay me back out of your profits. There isn't any rush. You've made me a happy man, and I want to show my appreciation."

And that was it. We were now in the hotel business. There was no signing of contracts or any paperwork, just a solid handshake between two good friends. That's the way we made business deals in those days, my son. On trust.

The Lincoln Hotel was located on East Jefferson in downtown Detroit. Although it was rundown and needed plenty of work, it had a very good location. Your father and I worked day and night, cleaning and painting, to make the hotel more presentable. After a few weeks, the place was shining and ready for business.

World War I had been over for a few years and the factories were running day and night trying to catch up with consumer demand. The money was good, and so men were pouring into Detroit. They needed lodging, and we could take care of that. Our forty-eight rooms filled up quickly. Our bell kept ringing, despite the "No Vacancy" sign in the front window, with people begging us to place a few cots in the halls for them. They were willing to pay for sleeping space anywhere.

Even though I protested, your father put cots and chairs in the halls and took them in. "You can pay me when you get your first pay," he would tell them.

Within a short time, we had enough money put away to make a down payment on the hotel. Haji Bey made an appointment to see Aram to set up a payment plan, but Aram shrugged his shoulders. "What's the rush, Haji, take your time."

You see, Harry, we Armenians worked on trust. We didn't use lawyers. Lawyers are all crooks anyway.

■ ■ ■ ■

Well, my son, your father was not finished with the matchmaking business. He had promised my two sisters Arous and Artemis to two of his buddies, Harry Torossian and Garabed Warterian. We invited these men over to meet my sisters. Each man liked the girl Haji Bey had chosen for him, and the girls were pleased with the men, too. The wedding dates were set, and soon afterward they were joined in holy matrimony. To tell the truth, for the next five years, it seemed that we were going to somebody's wedding every month. Of course your dad didn't arrange all of them.

Life was good. I grew in the family way. When your sister Alice was born, we were elated! A great celebration was planned for her baptismal day. A female child was a rarity in the Yessaian clan, and Haji Bey went overboard in the preparations. We Armenians didn't have a church of our own at the time, so we used St. John's Episcopal Church downtown on Woodward. The pastor and congregation were good to the Armenians, and they let our people use the facility whenever we needed it. Haji Bey brought in an Armenian priest from out of town for the baptismal ceremony.

Your father joined together two rooms in the hotel and rented large tables and some chairs, enough to seat forty at a time for eating. Everyone we knew was invited to the party — more than a hundred and twenty people.

The hall was decorated beautifully. There were party favors on the long tables, and balloons and brightly-colored crepe paper strips were hung from the ceiling. Along one wall, we served a lavish buffet. For the children, there were games, like "Pin the Tail on the Donkey." A four-piece band played Armenian, Greek, and Turkish music.

Women pinned gold coins on your sister's dress as gifts and the dress got so heavy that we could hardly lift the baby. It wasn't like Smyrna, like your baptismal party, Harry, but I was growing reconciled to my new life and tried not to think of it. We had a good time.

Roomers came by to see what all the noise was about. We invited them all in to join the celebration. We all had a great time as we ate, drank, and danced until four in the morning. Haji Bey gave each roomer a quart jar of *raki* when they left.

Ah, yes, my dear son, looking back I can see that, despite the hardships, those were wonderful years. We were young and had so much fun and enjoyment . . . such *good* times. . . .

CHAPTER SEVENTEEN
Terror and Outrage in Smyrna

Yes, for our family, life was good in those days. In the 1920s, Detroit and several other American cities were attracting large numbers of Armenians from Turkey. Many of these folks came by way of Greece or Lebanon, where they wound up after the genocide.

It was 1921 and my mother Sultan Hanim and the others of our family were still in Smyrna. Since Sarkis Aga still would not think of leaving, we tried everything in our power to persuade mother to just leave him and come to us. We pleaded, we threatened, and we even sent her American money. Unfortunately, she simply wouldn't listen. She felt obliged to stay and care for the old man. In her letters, she wrote that things there were relatively calm. Of course, the Greeks were still in charge.

And then, my son, her letters took a frightening turn. There was bad news. Kemal Pasha's army was driving the Greeks out of Anatolia and those survivors of the death marches who had returned to their villages were being driven out for the second time. It was feared that the nationalist army would soon reach Smyrna.

"Did grandma ever convince the Aga to leave?" I asked. I saw anger flash in my mother's eyes.

No, my son. Only when it was too late did he see the light. When he finally admitted to himself that he should have listened to my husband and left Turkey with us, his end was near — he was over one hundred years old and had no strength left to do anything. He was ready to meet his Maker.

Yes, the news from Smyrna wasn't good. As I read the letters from my mother, I thanked God that at least we and our little band of relatives were safe in America.

■ ■ ■ ■

The Greek army withdrew from Smyrna without a fight and the Turks reoccupied the city. Life became difficult. The tension grew worse each day. The Turkish high command had given strict orders that all Armenians were to remain in their quarter. Those who left the quarter were liable for arrest, or might even be shot. Then the Turks arbitrarily began to arrest the Armenian men from about age sixteen to fifty-five.

Since we didn't live in the Armenian quarter, mother was worried. My brother Krikor was only fourteen at the time, tall and slim, and looked about eighteen. Mother made him wear short pants at all times, hoping to pass him off as a youngster in case the Turkish soldiers might see him. Of course, she kept him at home most of the time, almost locked up in the house.

Your Aunt Armenouhi suffered a grave loss at this time. She had married a widower, Stephan [Stephen] Terikian, with a seven-year-old son, Markar, and lived in our neighborhood. Her husband, Stephan, was one of the Armenian men arrested by the Turks and imprisoned. No one knew where he had gone or what had happened to him. Having no one to help support her and the boy, she was at my mother's place a good deal of the time, adding two more mouths to feed. The Turkish vendors brought food to sell only sporadically. Sarkis Aga had his stores boarded up in case the Turks decided to allow the soldiers to pillage Christian businesses, and so he couldn't get any food from them. The family was constantly hungry.

Of course, we in the United States kept sending wires and letters all the time — through a still friendly Turkish neighbor. We sent American money to buy food and begged Sultan Hanim to just leave the old man, and come. Of course by now, even if she had wanted to escape, she wouldn't have been able to leave the house to get the necessary documents and steamship tickets.

Krikor knew that his grandfather's boarded-up stores were loaded with cheese, olives, dates, figs, cakes, pies, bread, and other foods. One day, he could bear it no longer. He was so hungry he decided to risk his life for food. He waited until night, then went to the barn, saddled his fastest steed, and made his way through the back streets of Smyrna. He was being extremely cautious, of course, yet, as fate would have it, two foot soldiers spotted him when he turned a corner.

"Get down, Armenian bastard!" they shouted at him.

Krikor gave a smart kick to his horse's flank and took off at a gallop down the dark street. The soldiers opened fire and bullets whizzed by Krikor. One grazed his leg.

It was almost 2:00 am when the door burst open and Krikor came in, his arms filled with sacks of food. Although he tried to hide his wound from my mother, because of his short pants she saw the blood at once. She called for my sisters Zarmineh and Vartanoush. Together they poured *raki* on the wound and bandaged it.

Then they all had something to eat to quiet their grumbling stomachs. They made Krikor take a healthy shot of *raki* to help him get some sleep.

Unexpectedly, the silence was shattered by the hammering of rifle butts on the front door. My mother ran to the window. Peeking out the side of the heavy drape, she felt a sudden flush of panic. Standing on the porch were two Turkish soldiers and a captain!

"Hey, *gâvurlar* open up or we'll break down your door."

Sultan Hanim opened the door just a tiny crack to ask innocently what they wanted at this time of the night. Her answer was a bayonet jammed through the crack and used to force open the door. The soldiers forced their way in. One of them turned his rifle on mother and demanded to know if there were any males present. She caught her breath and replied, "No! Just my baby Sahag, Effendi, he's only six years old. There are no other males here."

At that moment, my baby brother Sahag ran into the room to mother's rescue. He put his backside against her and faced the Turk.

"Go away! Leave my mama alone!" he screamed as he burst into tears. "I'll fix you."

The soldier scowled at mother. "Whore of infidels! You better teach your bastard better manners or else!"

Mother didn't answer. She didn't want to provoke the soldier. Her main concern was to stay alive and somehow protect her children.

Meanwhile, Zarmineh and Vartanoush — remember, son, they were only nine and twelve at the time, younger than you are now — had hidden Sarkis Aga in a crawlspace under the servants' quarters. The space was very narrow and the old man grumbled. He was not used to such treatment. "Didn't I put food on the tables of these ungrateful dogs? Didn't I set so many of them up in business? Is this the thanks I get?" My sisters begged him to keep quiet.

The captain announced that his men would search the house. Mother lifted her head proudly. "You have no right to do this. We are honorable citizens," she said to the sergeant with great dignity. "We have many official friends."

Her words only served to anger the soldier further. "Madam, if you value your life, and the lives of your children, I order you to get out of our way. My men will search this house to see if you are telling the truth."

Praying that the old man and Krikor would stay in their hiding places, mother stepped out of the way. The Turkish troops began a methodical search, going from room to room, looking behind drapes, under furniture, and even under the lofty bed covers.

At this point a crowd of Turkish women suddenly invaded the house. While standing outside, they had seen the soldiers and presumed that the inhabitants were being arrested. They wanted to claim the house and all its furnishings for themselves. It was all so grotesque.

As the women began to collect valuables, linens, china, silverware, and the like, my mother tried to shoo them away. The captain heard the disturbance and returned to the living room.

"What do you people think you are doing," he asked angrily. "Get out of here this minute."

"We have come to claim this house, the house of an infidel. It should be ours."

"Do you have permission from Kemal Pasha? Do you have papers?"

"No. But this is the house of an infidel. We Turks should have it."

"This house will be taken by the government in good time. You have no business here. Leave those things and get out!"

The women gave the captain a look of resentment, but knew better than to talk back. They reluctantly backed off and left.

As the captain was speaking, mother glanced out the bay window at the side of the room. To her dismay, she caught a glimpse of Sarkis Aga and Krikor sneaking toward the horse barn. The Aga quietly eased his horse out of the barn and headed for the street. The two soldiers saw him and jumped off the balcony, aimed their guns, and shot the old man. Mother stifled a moan.

When the captain realized his men shot a man trying to escape, he was furious. "Madam, you lied to a Turkish officer!" As if to punish her, he grabbed little Sahag by the scruff of the neck and violently shook him. Sahag screamed in terror, demanding to be released. The Turk stared coldly at the child for a few moments, then gave him another hard shake and shoved him away.

"I order all of you to remain here," he shouted. "Don't come out of the house or you too will be shot!" Then he stormed out.

Mama ran over to the bay window and watched as the captain marched over to where Sarkis Aga had fallen. Sarkis Aga lifted himself with his elbow. The two men exchanged words which could not be overheard from inside the house. Another shot rang out and the old man fell back. Two bayonets were plunged into his chest. The Aga's blood gushed out on to the rich soil of his beloved garden. Sarkis Aga's life was ended. Death came to him by a Turkish bullet, a bullet of "his friends."

My mother, Sultan Hanim, stared in shock as the soldiers ripped open Sarkis Aga's jacket, exposing two long red velvet sacks. The soldiers slit open the sacks and out spilled a shower of gold coins and jewels. The men laughed uncontrollably and slapped each other on the back. The captain quieted them and took possession of the loot.

"*Eşekler!* [Jackasses!]," Mother heard him shout as she cracked open the door. "What were you going to do, keep this for yourselves? You're lucky I don't report you for even thinking about it."

The gold and jewels were scooped into a saddle bag and slung over the back of the captain's horse. He ordered one of his men to guard it, and returned to the house.

The captain grabbed Mother and shook her menacingly. "Madam, you saw what happens to those who don't obey. Now, for the last time, are there any other males in this house?"

We heard a scuffling in the hallway. The captain's men came in, dragging a trembling Krikor with them. They had found him sitting in the bathhouse. For some strange reason, he thought no one would look there. One soldier pulled him by the ear and told him to stand and face the captain. The short pants didn't fool the captain for a minute. He took one look at the light fuzz on my brother's face and decided that he was old enough. They tied Krikor's hands behind him and started to lead him away.

"Where are you taking my boy?" Mother cried out in anguish.

The captain was brusque. "That's our business!"

"No! Please, I beg you. Have mercy on my little boy, mercy! Don't take him!"

The captain turned his back and his men marched Krikor out of the house. My mother and sisters ran to the window and watched. Mother must have gone into shock. She fell to her knees and began screaming hysterically.

"Oh, Lord, what have we done to deserve your wrath! We who love you with every fiber in our bodies. These people are your enemies. Your enemies! Why are you allowing them to slaughter us? Mercy! Mercy!"

My sisters rushed to her side, trying to comfort her. They lay her down and told her to rest while they went to make a cup of mint tea on the kerosene stove in the kitchen.

After they had served tea to Mother, Vartanoush and Zarmineh decided that grandfather had to be buried. They snuck out of the house, wrapped his body in a carpet, and tied a rope to it. Then they hitched the rope to the pommel of the saddle of the Aga's horse and dragged the body into the orchard. They wrapped bed sheets around and around the corpse until it looked like a mummy.

Mother noticed that my little sisters were missing and went looking for them. She spotted the girls coming in from the orchard and grabbed them both.

"Are you mad!" she cried angrily. "Are you trying to get killed? Do you want us *all* killed!"

"We only wanted to bury our grandfather," they explained with bowed heads.

"Oh, your grandfather! He is dead and there is nothing we can do. It's all his fault. He is the reason we're still here in the first place! We would have been settled in America if it were not for him!"

Sultan Hanim's face twisted in pain, her shoulders sagged, and she began to sob uncontrollably. Her universe was completely destroyed in one day.

My sisters stared at mother, waiting. After a few moments, Sultan Hanim got a hold of herself. She straightened her back and took a deep breath.

"Where have you buried him?"

"In the orchard," they responded. Zarmineh and Vartanoush led their mother to Sarkis Aga's favorite fig tree and pointed at their handiwork. Sultan Hanim stared, aghast. She couldn't believe her eyes, and didn't know whether to laugh or cry.

Sarkis Aga's body was laid out in a shallow trench, with a thin layer of soil covering him from his neck down to his feet. His head was propped up on a rock. Mother gave each of the girls a hug, crossed herself, and they all recited the Lord's Prayer over Sarkis Aga's earthly remains.

As they walked back to the house, mother warned the girls not to leave the house again. That warning was for naught. Later that day, the girls, realizing that their mother had not approved of their work, went back to the grave to put more dirt on it. They took one look and went running back to the house, screaming. They each grabbed an arm of my mother, pleading with her to come with them and to see what had happened.

Sarkis Aga's body was now laying on top of the grave completely uncovered. The sheets and his clothes had been removed. A large rock had been placed in his mouth. Sultan Hanim understood at once. Robbers had uncovered the body in search of valuables. Finding nothing else, they had taken his clothes. They placed a stone in his mouth. She knew the superstitious robbers had put it there to prevent the spirit from leaving the body and taking revenge. They had desecrated the dead. Sultan Hanim shook her head sadly, so much for respect.

My mother stared down at her father-in-law's body for a long, long time. As she straightened up, her backbone went rigid and her jaw was set. Enough! She'd had enough. ***Now*** she would go to where the Turks could no longer hurt her and her family. She was convinced that she would also find a way to get Krikor back. If she were unsuccessful, he would have to fend for himself . . . that is, if he were still alive. My mother couldn't go to the authorities about Krikor because she could no longer leave the house. Anyway, who could she complain to? Who would help? It was a hopeless situation. Somehow, she had to get the rest of her children out before it was too late. Perhaps it already was too late, she didn't know. She would have to find out.

Every morning after that bloody night, your grandmother watched the street for signs of the bread delivery man. He hadn't delivered any bread to her since the Turks had invaded the house, but he was still making deliveries to nearby Greek and Jewish homes.

Sultan Hanim began to make ready to leave her homeland forever. At night, she sewed gold and jewels into the seams, hems and belts of four dresses. She gathered other personal necessities and placed them in valises, one each for Vartanoush, Zarmineh, and Sahag, and two each for Armenouhi and herself.

One day my mother finally spotted the bread delivery man plodding along in his rickety cart which was pulled by a scrawny donkey.

"*Ekmekci!* [Bread delivery man!] Please come over to the house a minute." She needed him for more than bread that morning.

The peddler reluctantly crossed the street and came up to the house. "Madam, I'm very sorry but I can't sell bread to you anymore."

Mother nodded her head. "Yes, I know. Let's not worry about that. I want something of much greater importance."

Almost as if he knew what was coming, the breadman started to back away. But Sultan Hanim quickly took hold of his arm. The look on her face compelled him to stop.

"Please. I must have your help. I know that you are a God-fearing man and completely trustworthy. I also know that you are going to help us." Her eyes burned into his. "I need you to get my children and me to the pier. We have to get away from Turkey."

"No . . . no . . . it's not possible," said the breadman almost in a state of shock. He tried to pull his arm away, while my mother held fast. "Madam, you're asking me to gamble with my life. The gendarmes are on the lookout for Armenians and might be only too happy to kill you, and me, too, if I were caught helping you. No. Not me, madam, you have the wrong man." He gave a mighty tug and yanked his arm from mother's grasp and began walking backward, shaking his head "no" with each step.

"*Please!*" Sultan Hanim's voice was a command. The breadman stopped in his tracks, again caught in her spell. "*Ekmekci*, your God will understand that you're doing this out of the kindness of your heart." As she spoke, she quickly counted out twenty-five of the American dollars your father and I had sent her. "God will look upon you with favor, prosperity will rain down upon you and yours." The breadman's eyes fastened desiringly on the green bills. She had him!

Mama walked forward, pulled the breadman's hand toward her and pressed the bills into it. "You will have seventy-five more of these after you have delivered us to the pier."

She held her breath until she felt the breadman's hand close tightly over the fresh green bills, then she released his hand and watched as he jammed the banknotes into his pocket.[1] His eyes darted around quickly to make sure no one had seen them.

"I have many young ones at home who depend on me. I must be careful. You must not betray me. Be ready at six o'clock tomorrow morning."

---

[1] A peddler such as this man would earn only a few *grosh*, a few cents, a day. Since the lower classes did not live on a cash economy, but bartered and made many of their own necessities, they could make do on the cash equivalent of less than a dollar a week.

Sultan Hanim watched as he scuttled back across the road. Renewed hope stirred in her heart.

That evening everyone bustled around, making ready to leave. Armenouhi arrived with her little boy, Markar, and mother made her put on one of the dresses. Mother, Zarmineh, and Vartanoush slipped on the others. The dresses hung strangely because of the heavy gold and jewels sewn in them. No matter, as long as they were not discovered. *If* the breadman kept his word. *If* they could get safely down to the port. *If* they could get on a boat. Oh *Lord*, there were so many *ifs*.

At that moment, the door opened and Krikor was standing there with a somber look on his face! Mother almost fainted. Joy surged in her heart. She rushed forward to embrace her son, then suddenly stopped. First, she offered a prayer of thanks to the Lord for His goodness. Only then did she allow herself to gather my brother to her bosom.

Krikor had been released. He had been away nearly three days. All he would tell them was he was taken down to the police station which the military officials had taken over. He was put in a cell with other Armenians and kept there with little food or water for two days. When pressed for more details, his face set into hard lines and he refused to speak.

Sadness filled his eyes. Whatever he had experienced in the last few days seemed to have aged him. Mother's heart grew heavy as she looked at her son. Where was her bright-eyed boy of three days ago?

Krikor was quickly brought up to date on the plan. Mother told him he must shave the fuzz from his face and put on a dress so that he could pass for a girl. Normally, he would have refused; now he obeyed without a murmur. He shaved and put on the dress, his face grim, his tongue silent.

At six in the morning, the *Ekmekci* tapped lightly on the door. My mother took little Sahag by the hand, followed by Zarmineh and Vartanoush, and hurried out to the donkey cart. Then came Armenouhi carrying her little boy. Krikor, clean-shaven and now wearing a dress, brought several valises to the cart and then closed the door of our house forever. They all lay down in the cart. The breadman piled their bundles around them and covered them with straw. Then he put his loaves of bread on top.

As my mother felt the cart start off down the road, she said her prayers and crossed herself. The wagon bounced and bumped down the cobblestone street that Sarkis Aga had built. After about fifteen minutes, they felt the cart turn toward the pier. They could hear the Turk murmuring his prayers over and over.

When the *Ekmekci* saw the pier come into view, he pulled his cart to the side of the road. He feared to go too close for soldiers were all over the area. When the cart stopped, Mother pushed aside their coverings and everyone hurriedly got out.

The breadman's face was streaked with sweat and his eyes darted nervously right and left. As he got down to help, my mother saw a puddle beneath his seat; he had urinated out of fright. Sultan Hanim pretended not to notice. She couldn't afford to embarrass this man now. She quickly doled out the seventy-five American dollars she owed him and thanked him.

The fellow's eyes moistened and he took my mother's hand. "Madam," he whispered, "may God see you through a safe passage. I feel sorry for you Armenians."

Mother and the children watched as the breadman disappeared up the street. "Thank you, Lord, for having sent that man to me," Sultan Hanim murmured gratefully. "It makes me feel good that he and his family can live well a year or two on that hundred dollars."

They picked up their baggage and walked toward the pier.

■ ■ ■ ■

You have to remember, Harry, they felt they had been in danger from the moment they set foot out of the door of their house. While the government told the rest of the world that everyone was free to come and go as they wished, and that no one was stopping them from leaving, the real truth was that it was difficult to get away. Even if Armenians were able to get to the docks, as thousands did in one way or another, there was no assurance that the soldiers would let them board a ship. The soldiers, it seemed, were arbitrary. They would shoot at random and kill whom they pleased.

The middle-class Armenians lived in a sector of the city which was just behind the large buildings facing the esplanade. The esplanade itself, which stretched for miles along the waterfront, was as wide as a boulevard. The Armenians fled their homes which were devastated, for the most part, by the great fire. Tens of thousands of refugees crowded the esplanade during the day. They would push and shove desperately in an attempt to get onto the piers where ships were docked and waiting. Periodically, the people would rush the guards like a herd of cattle. Some would get through, but most were pushed back. Those who could show a foreign passport were allowed to walk through without being molested, even though it must have been obvious that they were Armenian. Some of the refugees who managed to push past the guards would fall through broken or missing boards in the pier and plunge into the murky water below. The distance to the water might be from seven to fifteen feet, depending how far out you went.

Then the soldiers would often shoot at those who fell into the water. The water was filled with bodies, many riddled with bullets, floating between the pilings. A few who fell through the pier made it by swimming to a waiting ship. There were many out in the harbor waiting their turn to pull up to the piers. Those people who did swim to the side of a boat were usually hoisted aboard on ropes lowered by sailors. Some ships, of course, at first refused to board the refugees. The Turkish soldiers had orders not to fire near the ships because the Atatürk government didn't want to create an incident with a foreign power.

It was utter chaos — a scene from Dante's *Inferno*.

As to where the ships were going, my son, the refugees had no idea. Some were going to the nearby islands, some to Italy, some to Greece, some to France, others all the way to England. Destinations were not really important. What was important to them was that they *got out of Turkey*.

Mama watched the mad scene for a while and then decided that she must devise another plan. They would wait until the crowd thinned out at night, when people were either sleeping or had returned to their homes discouraged, and then try to bribe a guard. She still had a large sum of American money in the folds of her dress. She took her brood over to one side and sat them down.

They sat there for the entire day and well into the night. When at last things grew quiet, she decided to make her move. Mother rose to her feet, took a deep breath and, trembling from head to toe, started toward the checkpoint on the pier with her shabby looking band trailing behind.

A Turkish soldier barred the way and scowled: "What do you want, Armenian dogs?"

"No, Effendi, we are not Armenians." Sultan Hanim shook her head vehemently. "We are French. My daughters and I are on our way to Greece to meet my husband. From there, we will journey to France together."

This story didn't fool the guard for a moment. He could plainly see that they were Armenians. He could also see the wad of American dollars in mother's hand. As his eyes fastened on the money, mother's heart jumped with joy. He was going to bite.

The Turk proceeded to give mother a blistering tongue-lashing, telling her loudly that he was a loyal soldier of Mustafa Kemal Pasha. Frankly, mother didn't care who he was, but she was wily enough to tell him what he wanted to hear. "I'm sure you're a loyal soldier, and I'm also sure that you are a good man. If you help us, someday you will be glad that you had done a righteous deed for us. Let me put this money in your pocket and you let us through."

The guard looked around nervously.

"Go ahead, put the money in your pocket. What do you have to gain by turning us away?"

Once the guard was sure no one was watching, he signaled her his acceptance. "When I raise my gun over my head, pass through." He looked around again and after what seemed ages, raised his rifle.

"All right, *gâvurlar*!" he whispered. "Go! Go! Get the hell out of my sight!"

Mother and her little band carefully picked their way along the treacherous pier. A ship loomed up before them; it was a freighter. As soon as some people saw the Kouradjians walk out onto the pier, scores of refugees came rushing after them, pushing and shoving and clawing their way. Sultan Hanim urged her family to go faster. Because mother was in front of the crowd, she could avoid the holes in the pier.

As she reached the gangway, mama turned to make sure that everyone was with her. She panicked when she discovered that Vartanoush and Krikor were missing. Mother told Armenouhi to take her stepson, Markar, Zarmine and Sahag aboard and then turned to frantically search for her missing children. Suddenly, the ship's horn let out a series of ear-piercing blasts. They were going to pull up the gangplank!

Mother turned and made her way back to the freighter. Two deck hands yanked her aboard. As her foot touched the deck, she pleaded with them to hold the ship until she could find the rest of her family.

"Madam," one of the sailors said in French, holding her back, "we can't wait any longer. They'll probably come on the next boat."

Reluctantly mother gave up, and stood staring in anguish at the sea of faces below. As the ship slowly pulled away, she prayed that God would protect her unfortunate, lost children.

The deck was filled with people. There was hardly room to sit down and, of course, the ship being a freighter, there were no cabins or other facilities for passengers.

The captain appeared on the bridge and a mate blew his whistle to get the crowd's attention. A translator repeated the captain's words as he spoke.

"You are not yet safe," the captain said. "We must first make our way through the harbor and out of the gulf. We suspect that there are some mines which have not yet been cleared. Then we must find a country that will accept you. That will be difficult. We have no bedding and no food or water to give you. We will stop at the Greek islands two or three hours from here. Perhaps there you can buy food and drink. We shall try to land you in Greece, but we can't guarantee that Greece will take you. I wish you all good luck."

And with that not very encouraging speech by the captain, the engines shook to life, and the freighter slowly got under way. The crowd was quiet, praying silently, no one uttered a word.

After an hour or so, the children began begging mother for something to drink. There was not enough fresh water on board for the crowd and the sailors would not give them any. She was desperate. Where could she find water? Mother climbed up and down the ship searching. Finally, near the poop deck, she found a pipe with a pressure release valve. The valve discharged spurts of steam every ten or fifteen seconds. If only she had a tin cup she could catch some steam as it came from the valve. When the steam condensed, she would have water.

They all began to look for a tin cup. In a few minutes, Zarmineh came running. "Look at what I found. A tin can."

The can was rusty, but it would do. As mother saw the first few drops of water appear in the can she said, "This is a good omen. God is still watching over us. Vartanoush and Krikor must be alive somewhere. I know I will find them some day."

After the ship had traveled about another hour, crawling at a snail's pace, the captain came out on the bridge once again. "I have good news. We have cleared the harbor and are out of the narrow gulf. We are on our way to Greece. I think we can land you there. As I told you, we will first stop at one of the nearby Greek islands to see if you can buy some food."

The crowd of refugees sent out a cheer that would have awakened the angels in heaven. Where we were going didn't really matter, what did matter was that we had escaped from Turkey. Hopes were high.

A few hours later, the ship reached a small town on the eastern coast of one of the nearby Greek islands. The harbor was small and shallow, and the ship couldn't dock to allow the passengers to disembark. They would only be allowed to trade from the deck.

Merchants came out in small boats loaded with all sorts of food. The refugees lowered baskets with money in them and traders would load the baskets with grapes, cheese, olives, dried meat, bread, and bottled water. Some of the passengers were unlucky and didn't get anything in return when they lowered their baskets. The dishonest men would take the money and blow them a kiss goodbye. Fortunately, a decent man filled Mother's basket to overflowing and she hauled up all kinds of good things. All of them — Mother, Sahag, Zarmineh, Armenouhi, and little Markar — got enough to eat for the first time in days.

Mother was having strange dreams at night. Her two lost children were being chased by Turks on horseback. The children would scream, "Mother! Mother, wait for us! Don't leave without us. We will catch up with you." She took these dreams as a good sign.

The ship then continued on to Greece where the captain disembarked some of them at low tide at a spot just outside of Piraeus, the port of Athens. Others were taken, as my family was, through the Corinthian canal to Patras, on the west coast.

Greece not only had an open-door policy, it was actively concerned about the welfare of the Armenians in Smyrna. Once Greece received assurances from the Allies that their ships would be protected in the harbor of Smyrna, they began a regular shuttle to evacuate the Armenians.

Mother decided it made more sense to go to Piraeus, where the new "shuttle" was disembarking most of the Armenians, in order to meet the ships as they arrived. She hoped that she would find Krikor and Vartanoush. Armenouhi decided she would go also in the hope that her husband, Stephan, who had been taken captive by the Turks, might somehow have survived and then make it to Greece. In Piraeus they found a place to stay. It wasn't much, but it was a roof over their heads.

Some weeks later, Sultan Hanim's little band sat at a table at a sidewalk café in Piraeus. The proprietor would cook up great cauldrons of stew every day, which he sold by the potfuls to the refugees. Mother had bought a terracotta pot that she would take in everyday to have filled. As she emerged carrying the pot, a voice rang out. "Mama! Mama! Don't drop the pot."

"Don't drop the pot!" came a voice from across the street. It was little Vartanoush. She ran across the street to mother, crying and hugging her while at the same time trying to save the pot from falling out of her surprised mother's arms.

Well, my son, you can imagine the joy and laughter of that reunion. A part of my mother's prayers had been answered, her lost daughter had been found. Mother thanked God over and over again and prayed that she would find Krikor next. They sat around the table with the stew pot in the middle.

As they ate with gusto, Vartanoush told her story. This is Vartanoush's story as it was related by Mother to me.

■ ■ ■ ■

When Vartanoush got lost in the crowd on the pier, she became panic-stricken. The people behind were pushing hard and several times she almost stumbled through one of the gaps in the pier. Suddenly, a hand grabbed her and Vartanoush screamed in terror. Fortunately, it turned out to be one of her aunts, with all her family. Without hesitating, these relatives simply pulled Vartanoush along with them as they fought their way toward the ship.

The ship pulled away before they were even halfway there. The crowd milled around in bitter disappointment until someone shouted that another ship could be seen in the distance. A couple of hours later the new ship arrived and they pushed their way aboard. Vartanoush was crying for her mother. Her aunt tried to calm her, assuring Vartanoush that her mother was safe.

After awhile Vartanoush stopped crying. She understood that her mother had pushed ahead and was probably on the earlier ship. Somehow they would find each other.

They were all tired and hungry. The compassionate crew baked bread and gave loaves to the refugees. Vartanoush managed to get two and shared them with her aunt and her family.

Finally, their boat landed in Piraeus and they disembarked. A few days later, Vartanoush accidently spotted one of their neighbors from Smyrna sitting at a table at a sidewalk café. Vartanoush rushed over to the lady and asked if she knew anything of the whereabouts of her mother. When she was told that her mother was in Piraeus and searching everywhere for her, you can imagine her joy. In fact, the woman had just seen Sultan Hanim. She was not far down the street buying stew for her family! Vartanoush, overcome with excitement, ran and found them.

That was Vartanoush's story.

■ ■ ■ ■

"Gee, Mom, it's hard to think of Aunt Vartanoush experiencing all these things when she was only twelve. Burying her grandfather, going to the pier hidden in a wagon, and then getting lost and going on a ship without her mother . . . Wow! She was really something else, wasn't she?"

My mother laughed. "People grew up fast in those difficult times. Anyway, your Aunt Vartanoush is like that. She has had many escapades all her life and she is still having them."

"Uncle Krikor, Mom, what happened to Uncle Krikor?"

"Just wait, I'm getting to him."

■ ■ ■ ■

My mother Sultan Hanim contacted us from Piraeus, and we wired her more American money. Your father had learned of two Armenian brothers in Athens who sold coffee beans wholesale from their warehouse. He told Mother that these men would help her to find comfortable and inexpensive shelter. The family left for Athens that very day; after all, it was only a few miles away. The Armenian brothers fixed up a couple of rooms above their warehouse for Mother and the children, and they rented the rooms to them for a pittance, almost free. Haji Bey and I were overjoyed that at least a part of the family was safe, and we began to wire a certain sum to Mother each month for their upkeep.

Now Mother had to ask the Lord for one more favor. She hoped she wasn't making a pest of herself up in heaven as she prayed day and night asking for the safe return of her son Krikor. She believed he was alive and, with God's help, she would find him.

■ ■ ■ ■

A year and a half slipped by. Mama never gave up hope of finding Krikor, and never stopped searching, visiting Piraeus every day. She kept asking everywhere, bakeries, greengrocers, butchers, fish markets, shops, cafés and, most importantly, at the coffeehouses. Near the docks, she found an outdoor café where the younger people gathered. She went there every day to have coffee, feeling that if Krikor were in Athens, he would gravitate toward people his own age.

Mother got to know one of the waitresses, Maria, rather well. One afternoon, when business was slow, the two of them somehow began talking about figs. Mother insisted that the best figs came from Smyrna.

"You, too!" the waitress laughed, "my new boyfriend always talks about Smyrna. He thinks that the best of everything comes from there, especially the figs. I get sick of hearing about Smyrna, but I don't let on. Why antagonize him? He's so good to me. We started going together just six weeks ago."

Mother's ears perked up. "Tell me more about your boyfriend. What is his name? How old is he?"

"Gregorious. He's about seventeen or eighteen."

Mother pulled out a well-worn photograph of my brother Krikor and asked if the girl's boyfriend looked like him. "Yes," the girl replied, "in many ways."

Knowing that Gregorious would be Krikor's name in Greek,[1] mother asked the girl to tell her more about him.

"Well, madam, he is an Armenian refugee from Smyrna. He now drives a cab. In fact, Gregorious will stop by in a couple of hours to take me home."

Mother was now convinced that her beloved son Krikor was the girl's boyfriend. Mother stuck a five-dollar tip in the girl's apron, ordered another cup of coffee, and settled back to wait for "Gregorious."

Eight cups of coffee and several visits to the lavatory later, mother shook with anticipation as she watched a cab pull up in front of the restaurant. The driver hopped out. Mother was in a state of shock. It *was* Krikor!

You really have to know Krikor to appreciate his peculiar humor. He's funny in an unusual sort of way. Of course this

---

[1] Krikor, or Grigor, is the Armenian variant of Gregory, which would be Gregorious in Greek.

strange humor became characteristic of him after he had been arrested by the Turks. That did something to him. When he saw mother, he called out farcically: "Hey, lady, *you* over there. What are you doing here? Looking for your dog?"

Then he rushed over to her and they embraced, crying tears of happiness. Mother persuaded the café owner to let the waitress off a bit early, and Krikor drove them both to the coffee warehouse to meet with the rest of our family.

Krikor had changed. He had grown up. He was tall and handsome and sported a moustache. He was no longer a boy, he was a man.

Krikor had a lot of hurt inside of him. He was unhappy, ill-tempered, and bitter. Whatever had happened to him in Smyrna when the Turks took him away had burned its way into his heart, leaving scars that it seemed would remain forever. Mother thought it would be better if he could only talk about it. She pleaded with him time and again to get it out of his guts. He just refused. "No, Mother, I can't. I won't. Please, let me be. I'm okay."

Mother would hug him and say, "I know, my son, but the good Lord wants us to spit out the bile that eats away at our hearts. Then He can heal us."

My brother would only shake his head firmly and walk away. Later, he would come back and crack one of his silly jokes.

Once Mother had found my sister Vartanoush and then my brother Krikor, my sister Armenouhi hoped that she would someday find her husband, Stephan Terikian, as well. One day Armenouhi received word that her husband was still alive and perhaps somewhere in the city. He had been imprisoned, not killed, by the Turks. When the Greeks and Turks decided to exchange populations, apparently he was released.

Well, there is no denying it: except for the problem with Krikor and her missing son-in-law, Stephan, Mother was happy and content. Part of her family was safe in America and the rest of them, with only one exception, were with her in Athens. She would give thanks to the Lord and murmur, "Dear Lord, by your will, next stop, America!"

CHAPTER EIGHTEEN
Krikor's Ordeal

My Uncle Krikor never did tell his mother what he had suffered when the Turks took him prisoner. He kept the story bottled up for years. I had to beg him time and time again before he finally agreed to confide in me. He was by then twenty-six years old. This is his story as I remember it.

■ ■ ■ ■

Harry, my dear nephew, it pains me to tell this story, it brings back terrible memories. Yet perhaps you're right. Maybe it will do me good to tell someone instead of keeping it locked up inside. I get sick every time I think of it.

I was just fourteen when the soldiers arrested me. They took me, and a bunch of other Armenian men, and they put us in a fenced-in area outside the gendarme station, which was being used as the headquarters of the soldiers. They brought us into a room, about thirty at a time, and questioned us. If they felt anyone was lying, that person would be taken to be tortured. In my case, they beat me and locked me in a room that was jammed full of other Armenians. We could hardly breathe, had no toilet, and were given gruel only once a day. In a couple of days, they took some of the men away and released the rest of us. I was in bad shape from hunger, lack of sleep, and the beating I had received.

I started to make my way home. I decided to pass through the Armenian quarter on my way to the section of town, near the bay, where we lived among the rich Armenians, Greeks, Jews, and Turks.

As I walked toward the Armenian quarter, from a distance I could see that it was burning. The flames lit up the sky. The Turks did nothing to stop the fires. In fact, I was told later, all the fire wagons were taken to the Turkish quarter to protect that section from the spreading flames.

The old wooden houses in the Armenian quarter were close together, built right next to each other. These houses were engulfed by flames as the fires jumped from one to the other. It was a regular inferno. The whole quarter was going up in flames. Even the stone houses, and there were several streets of them, were being scorched. You could hear the screams of people being roasted alive. You could smell the stench of burning flesh. The streets were narrow and the heat was unbearable. Those who could, were fleeing; but many were trapped and died.

I saw a group of Armenians run into a church to pray for deliverance. The flames spread to the church. Many of the people inside were trapped. There must have been two or three hundred people packed in there. When they began to rush to the doors at the same time, many were trampled. There was no way more than just a few could get out. The church was made of stone, but the rafters were made of timbers. Soon, the church was engulfed in flames. It was a holocaust. The roof finally gave in and the burning timbers fell on those who remained inside. It was like they were caught in a brick oven — roasting alive. I wondered how many of my friends might be in there.

I heard all the screams, Nephew, and I still hear them today. I also see the inferno that devoured the Armenian quarter. Many nights I break out in a cold sweat when I see those flames in my dreams. What my eyes saw would drive anyone mad.

I finally made it home and found that, except for grandfather, my family was still alive. I was relieved. But who knew what lay in wait for us. I was so powerless. It is hard to imagine the depth of my frustration. Thank God, Mother had a plan. You already know how she saved us. I am proud of her.

When Mother got us down to the harbor and we were running out on the pier to the ship, I was overtaken by the frantic crowd behind us. The desperate people pushed and shoved with such force that I fell through a hole left by a missing plank. Down I went into the water. I panicked. There were bloated and stinking corpses floating all around me. I still shudder thinking of it.

Turkish soldiers were shooting at those who had fallen in the water. I hid myself as best I could behind a corpse. Its flesh was bloated and clammy to my touch. I never touched a dead person before, much less one that had been floating in water for hours. How I held on I still don't know.

I was in the water for what seemed to be hours, holding on to this dead woman. I saw a ship leave that I intuitively felt my family had boarded. Another ship came and went. What was to become of me? Then I saw the outline of a third ship drawing close. This was it, I thought. How much longer could I last in the water? I have to risk it. I must try to swim to that ship.

I heard the people above me on the pier swarming toward the incoming ship. I pushed away from the bodies around me and swam as fast and as hard as I could. A rope was dangling from the ship's railing, dancing on the waves like a beautiful dream. I wrapped the end of the rope around one of my legs and began climbing up. As I climbed, I kept slamming into the side of the ship. Someone on deck saw me and hoisted me up.

I looked up and saw a beautiful red, white, and blue flag: an American ship! Chills of excitement swept through my body like electricity. The sailors took hold of my hands and pulled me aboard like a wet fish, still in the dress my mother made me wear. They asked me my name. I said "Krikor."

One of them laughed and said, "He must be a boy, let's call him 'George.'"

I laughed, too, and said, "Yeah, George." I didn't really know what they were saying for sure; what I did know was that they were saving my life, and I was grateful.

There were several hundred Armenian refugees aboard. Some of them knew English. I was shivering with cold and my body was turning blue. They must have believed that I was suffering from hypothermia, so the medic took me down below, made me take a hot shower, and gave me some dry clothes and a sailor's hat to wear. Then they wrapped me in a blanket, gave me a shot, and lay me in a hammock in the sick bay. Just before I was about to fall asleep from exhaustion, I remembered something. I reached over and grabbed the dress my mother had made me wear when we escaped and tore open the hem. The gold coins and jewels Mama had sewn in it were still there. I put them under my pillow.

I awoke early the next morning to find we were cruising through the blue Mediterranean. I learned that we were bound for Greece.

When I got to Athens, I found a room and got a job to take care of myself. I didn't even think about my family. Sure, I know I should have looked for them, Nephew, but I didn't want to see anyone, to talk to anyone. I was still in shock from what I had experienced. I felt depressed all the time. I had passed through hell and I wanted to forget, not to be reminded. To this day, I can still smell the stench of death in my nostrils. The nightmares still haunt me. It is painful for me to talk about it even now.

My only pleasure was the young Greek girl I had met. Then, you know the story, my mother found me and wired Haji Bey. He wired back: "Now that Krikor is found, it is time for you to board the next ship to America."

My older sister Armenouhi, however, didn't want to leave. Once she had learned that her husband Stephan was still alive, she decided it was better for her and her little son Markar to wait in Greece until he arrived.

Mother took just one week to settle her affairs, pack our belongings, and book passage on the next ship to the United States.

Sure enough, Armenouhi was right; not long after the rest of the family left Greece, she was reunited with her husband. Unfortunately, my brother-in-law Stephan had been so starved and abused in prison that he lived only a few months in Greece before he died.

When the family learned of Stephan's untimely death, they encouraged Haji Bey to find Armenouhi a suitable match in America so that she and her son could join them. In fact, Haji Bey located an Armenian lawyer who was willing to accept the match.

As it turns out, by the time Armenouhi learned of the offer from America, she had already accepted a proposal from another man. The two of them decided to take her son and go to Armenia to make a new life for themselves. Perhaps it was not a bad choice; they seemed to have found happiness and managed somehow to keep in touch with us by mail.

■ ■ ■ ■

Uncle Krikor looked drained. Telling his story had taken a lot out of him. Still, I think he was relieved that after all those years he had finally gotten it off his chest. I understood that it hurt him to recall all those dreadful experiences, and I was proud that he had chosen me as his confidant. I loved him very much; he was like a real hero to me.

I remember so clearly when I first met him. It was in 1923, and we had just celebrated my third birthday. The atmosphere in our little hotel on East Jefferson was charged with expectation. Mother had said that my grandmother Sultan Hanim, my uncles Krikor and Sahag, and my aunts Vartanoush and Zarmineh were on their way to America. They would arrive at any moment. "Keep an eye out for them," she told me. That was probably her way of keeping me busy and out of her hair.

I kept running back and forth, first to the front window, looking down into the street to see if there was a cab pulling up to our front door, and then to the stairway to look down and see if they were coming up the stairs. Thirty or forty trips, back and forth. I soon got pretty tired and lay on the couch where I fell asleep.

Suddenly Mother was waking me. "I hear funny noises. Go see who's coming up our stairs." She had a big grin on her face, and tears of joy were rolling down her cheeks.

When I reached the head of the stairs, I could hear them giggling as they shuffled up.

An older lady, who I later learned was my grandmother, Sultan Hanim, was calling from the landing below, "*Yavrum! Yavrum! Asdvadz! Asdvadz!* . . . *Yegank! Yegank!* . . . [My dear ones! My dear ones! Oh, God! God! We have arrived! We have arrived!]

What a celebration we had! No one slept that night. We talked and talked. Grandma's stories about close escapes and memories of dear friends filled the air. So did the aroma of the delicious *monte* baking in the kitchen.

It had taken several hours to roll out the dough for the *monte*, and many hands to make the little canoe-shaped pastas filled with spiced ground beef and lamb. Mother would always insist that all the relatives in the house wash their hands and pitch in to help. It was a lot of work, but it was sure worth it.

We all sat around the large dining room table, the Kouradjians and the Yessaians united at last. While the adults continued filling and shaping the *monte,* their conversation rang out happily. Although, I was only three and too young to take part in making the *monte*, I was still allowed to be seated at the table. I sat against my mother's side, my head nodding in the warmth and happiness and well-being of that evening, so very many years ago.

CHAPTER NINETEEN
Business As Usual

The year was 1928. Haji Bey was bored again. He wanted out of the hotel business. He needed a new challenge. When other Armenians were adding to their holdings, Father was selling off our little gold mine. He, his cousin Simone, and Uncle Nazar formed the Yessaian Construction Company. They began building houses. The Italians had a lock on the market, however, and the three of them weren't doing very well. They were barely making a living.

My father wanted to do better. He talked his partners into building a hotel for single men near the Ford Rouge Plant. The hotel site was not far from the large house that Haji Bey and his brothers had bought when they first came to the United States. The area brought back warm memories of the good times he'd had there with his friends from the old country. He felt good whenever he thought about having helped those men escape with their lives from Turkey.

The three partners invested almost all of their capital in the hotel project. They borrowed $60,000 more from the banks. That was a great deal of money in those days. The foundation was poured and the framework started. Then, in October of 1929, came the great crash. The collapse of Wall Street caused the Yessaian Construction Company to go bust. Father was able to salvage only $4,000. I will never forget the tense conversations that went on during dinners after the big crash.

Mother was worried. How was the family going to make a living? What could Father do now? She would go on and on, badgering him about all his big ideas and how his latest one had ruined us financially. One night, Father became furious.

"If you'd just keep your mouth shut for a minute," he screamed, "I might think of something." He grabbed a pad and pencil and stalked off into the living room. It was the first time I ever heard him shout in anger at Mother.

A couple of hours later, he came back to the kitchen and, with a broad smile on his face, settled into his usual chair. He was back in charge again. He had received a challenge, a new mountain to climb, and he had it all worked out.

"We're going to get a farm, Victoria," he announced firmly. "We'll lease one somewhere on the outskirts of town and produce vegetables, chickens, eggs, *madzoon, basterma,* and *raki*. I'm going to introduce this country to our own fine Armenian foods, particularly *madzoon* [yogurt]!"

"*MADZOON*! Americans have never heard of *madzoon*!" Mother just stared at him, shaking her head in disbelief. The man was mad.

"Well, it's about time they learned to enjoy this nutritious food," Haji Bey continued, impervious to Mother's cold, scathing stare. "Americans need to know about the medicinal benefits of yogurt. Anyway, we will sell the other things, too."

"You belong in the nut house!" Mother exploded. "You want to take me out to a farm far away from my sisters, try to get Americans to eat foreign foods, and then make *raki* — something that's against the law in this country! You are completely out of your mind!"

Father flew into a rage. "Listen! There's no work out there, there is a depression going on, no way to make money. Everything is at a standstill. We either move or we starve. Which do you want?"

There were no two ways about it, we had to go. We moved to a farm near Utica, about seventeen miles from downtown Detroit. It was a beautiful farm. It had thirty-two acres of low-grade soil, which of course was of little concern to my father. After all, he was not interested in regular crops.

The farmhouse had five bedrooms. There was a large parlor and a large dining room, with French doors separating the two areas. Heat was supplied by a steam boiler. It had an inside toilet and its own well for water. It was quite modern for a farmhouse. To me, it looked like a mansion.

Since Father knew absolutely nothing about raising chickens, he ordered some books from Michigan State University's Agriculture Extension Service. When the books arrived, I brought them to my father. Naturally, all the books were written for educated readers. He stared at the books for a moment or two, surely wondering how he would understand what was written in them.

"Fine," he declared, then thrust the books back at me. "Now read them and translate them for me. The baby chicks will be here in about two weeks and I want to be ready to house them and do whatever is necessary to raise them into healthy layers."

I told him I couldn't translate the books because they had agricultural terms in them which I didn't know in Armenian, Turkish, or English. It was 1930 and I was only ten years old; besides, I had been held back from going to school until I was almost eight.

Father looked at me sternly. "You can't explain these books to me? What good are you? You're not going to amount to much."

Father's criticism hurt me. I was very sensitive. His disparaging words stripped away whatever little self-esteem I possessed at the time. At the age of ten, I didn't understand that my father might ridicule me only because he was frustrated with his own shortcomings.

Father snatched the books back. He announced that he was going to Detroit. And off he went. He returned a few hours later with Mr. Babik Babikian whom he had fished out of the Armenian coffeehouse.

Mr. Babikian carried a suitcase. We were told he was to be our guest for a while. We later learned that he was a graduate pharmacist. But the way things were, with the Depression and all that, he couldn't find a job.

Dad had got Babikian because he could read and understand the agricultural books. He explained every operation in detail to Dad. Babikian told him how to raise the chicks, what diseases to watch for, everything. Father listened intently, taking notes in Armenian.

Two weeks later, two thousand baby chicks arrived. Father was ready for them. Following Babikian's instructions from the university books, we had washed and scrubbed the chicken house and then whitewashed it inside and out. We changed the straw on the floor every three days. Each night the chicks would gather around the electrical brooders and snuggle down to sleep.

Three months later, Mr. Babikian was still with us. He had been sending letters to pharmaceutical houses and drugstores all over the area for the entire time, looking for a job. His diligence finally paid off. He got an interview and was hired on the spot. He thanked us for letting him stay with us after his work with Father had been finished in the first week. Father, always playing the big man, stuck a hundred-dollar bill in Babikian's shirt pocket.

"You're going to need a place to stay and food to eat. They won't pay you for a week or two so this will come in handy."

Mr. Babikian's eyes filled with tears of appreciation. He thanked us all, tossed his suitcase in our car, and Dad drove him off to Detroit.

The State Agriculture Department sent out an inspector every three months. He would pick out a chicken, kill it, and cut it open to inspect it for disease. On one of his visits, the inspector said to me, "Your dad is doing a great job. These chickens are very healthy. He should have a productive stock of layers."

Well, to make a long story short, Father won second prize in Macomb County for the most productive and healthiest chickens. He received a certificate, which he proudly framed — though he could hardly read a word of it — and hung on the wall of the chicken house.

Soon there were relatives and friends of Father's living with us. They were out of work and needed a place to stay. Father hired a man named Medzig. Father taught Medzig to save all the ashes from the boiler in the winter and use them all year long to wash Mason jars until they were crystal clear. The jars were then filled with yogurt and placed in large metal containers Father had made. Each metal container held ten Mason jars, and dry ice was placed around the jars to keep the yogurt fresh until my brother Garbis, who was now called Charlie, could get it to the food markets.

Father went around to Armenian and Greek doctors to persuade them to recommend yogurt to their patients. The doctors were well aware of the beneficial value of yogurt, so that wasn't really the point; Father wanted those patients to buy from *us*. The patients would come to our farm every week for a new supply. While they were there, we also sold them eggs, cheese, butter, canned Armenian-style pickles, and *basterma*. Now *basterma* is another story.

Basterma is the tenderloin of beef, cut four inches wide and two inches thick. The length of the loin can be anywhere from two-and-a-half feet to three feet. Father would pierce a hole near one end of each piece and loop a thick string through it. He had a large press made to help process the meat. Pressure was applied to the press with a large, irregular wheel that would bring down the top plate on the salted beef, wrapped in cloth, to squeeze the blood out. It took about a week for us to bleed dry two thousand pounds of meat. This was done only during the winter months, when the environment was free of insects, since the next step was to cure the meat outdoors.

Father hammered nails all over the outside wall of our three-story barn where he hung the pieces of beef in good weather. They looked like two-by-fours swinging from the side of the barn in the winter wind. Our neighbors would drive by and wonder what the hell that Armenian was up to now.

Father had leak-proof wooden boxes made. We put a dozen or more of the tenderloins into each box, which we then placed in the basement. The *basterma* was so cold we had to use gloves to handle them. Father mixed different spices and herbs with water, salt, vegetable coloring, pepper, garlic, and cumin powder — to make a paste that is called *chaman*. He blended these ingredients until they had the consistency of red mud, then he would pour buckets of this mixture over the meat in the wooden boxes. Then we had to spread the *chaman* carefully on all sides of each tenderloin. About four weeks later, some of the paste would be absorbed, leaving an uneven coating on top. The excess *chaman* would be scraped off the tenderloins, which were then hung for the coating to dry. The *basterma* was then ready.

Now and then Father would take a loin out for our own use. He'd cut it in half with a sharp knife and slice the *basterma* so thin it was almost transparent.

When Dad was pleased with me and feeling fatherly, he would call me Artin. "Go ahead, Artin," he'd say affectionately, "Make yourself a *basterma* sandwich and tell me how you like it."

"It's great, Dad, really great," I would say as I would eat three sandwiches at a time.

We would sell the *basterma* on weekends at Detroit's Eastern Market on Gratiot. Father's customers were Armenians, Greeks, Lebanese, and other Middle Eastern peoples. The market was colorful, filled with stands where farmers from all over the state came to sell their produce.

The huge market-square was surrounded by all kinds of shops where exotic foods and spices were sold. Buyers came from all over the area to stock up on food for the coming week.

One Saturday, on our way home from the market, we stopped to pick up a big copper still that Father had ordered. In fact, the still was made by the same man who had built the very first still for Father when he and my uncles Nazar and Mardiros had first come to America.

The still was a beautiful piece of work. It stood about five feet high and was about eight feet in diameter. The project was very exciting to me because I knew that it was illegal to distill liquor, although each family was allowed, by law, to make a few gallons for home consumption. Every time we had to pick up a load of brewing supplies, Father would borrow Mr. Schoenherr's pick-up truck. While driving, we had to be careful not to let policemen too close to our neighbor's truck lest we be discovered.

You should have seen the production work going on in our basement. Two men were cutting the *basterma* into one to five-pound pieces, weighing them and wrapping them in heavy wax paper, and writing the weight on a label. These pieces were then placed in boxes for shipment or for sale at the market. Mother was making cheese in another part of the basement. My Father's friend, Arsen, was churning butter. And I was washing "droppings" off the eggs we had gathered that morning. We put the eggs into cartons and then placed the cartons into crates which held twelve dozen each. Still other workers were busy making yogurt, my father's second most popular product.

The making of *raki,* however, took up most of my father's time. The *raki* was ready after six weeks of brewing and then being distilled. I must have lugged out over a hundred gallons of the stuff, taking out six one-gallon jugs at a time in a wheelbarrow and wheeling them out to the vegetable patch. There Father would be busy digging holes every two feet, each hole just deep enough to hold a gallon jug. The holes were filled in and the tops of the jugs were then covered with rich fertilized soil, where we planted Michigan beefsteak tomato seedlings. Father was very proud of his "tomato patch." When the next batch of booze was ready, he would repeat the same burial operation in another part of the "vegetable garden."

Whenever visitors came to the farm, Father made sure they took a tour of his tomato patch. Tongue in cheek, he would boast to his guests that his garden was his work of art, the best money-maker on the whole farm. He would turn to me and wink. "Isn't that right, Son?"

I would wink back and answer, "For sure, Dad!"

The *raki* was poured into one-quart jars and sold for $5.50 a quart. That was a lot of money in those days. Dad never forgot to tell his customers to mix the powerful drink one-to-one with water when they were ready to imbibe it.

Yogurt orders increased each month. The milk came from our neighbors' cows at ten cents a gallon. Nearly half the milk was cream, and as a result our yogurt was overly rich. Realizing the yogurt was excessively rich, Father separated much of the milk from the cream, which we then used to make the butter.

Then Father had the bright idea of building a dance pavilion out in the field. With the help of his carpenter friends, they put down a three-thousand-square-foot floor and crowned it with a peaked canvas roof. Next to the pavilion, he set up a stand from which he sold his products. Dances were held on weekends during the warm months of the year.

The dance music was Armenian, Turkish, Greek, and Arabic. For our Greek friends we often played *bazooki* music. After church on Sundays, our pious German neighbors would stop by and join the festivities. The band would always play a polka or two for their benefit.

Fridays were "guess-who's-coming" and "guess-what's-going-to-happen" evenings. I would run out to the front yard at eight p.m. and watch for any signs of cars coming. If there were more than five or six cars coming down the road in a row, each following the other, then it was a sure thing that they were the Armenians.

When they arrived, it was party time from Friday night to Sunday evening. People called my father a *kefgi*.[1] Some of the visitors slept in the house: the older folks and children got the beds in the rooms upstairs, other people slept on the *yourghans*[2] on the floors. The overflow slept in their cars.

Mother would set a gourmet table, with all kinds of foods imaginable: *basterma, sujukh* [spiced Armenian sausage], stuffed grape leaves, caviar, black olives, pickles, anchovies, several different cheeses, salads, deviled eggs, and what have you. The relatives would bring food, too. What a spread we would have!

There would be talk about the old country, the Armenian genocide, the bad times of the Depression. After a few tears, someone would start the singing of heart-wrenching songs about the "old country" and lost loved ones. All those who were within hearing range would cry.

Father, after a while, would signal the boys to strike up the band. The tears would be forgotten and our hearts would sing with joy. Then Dad would ask for an exuberant *zeybek*. The women would start singing and clapping in rhythm, easily persuading my father to dance.

It wouldn't take much coaxing to get my father up because he loved to dance, and was proud of the figure he cut on the dance floor. Haji Bey was a wonderful dancer. I can see him now, hands held high above his head, fingers snapping, his body moving in syncopated rhythm, dancing like Zorba the Greek.

---

[1] One who enjoys the pleasures of life.

[2] Heavy woolen quilts. In the "old country," when people came to visit they would often spend a few days with the family. Travel was difficult and hotels and motels nonexistent. Inns were infrequent and often dangerous. Immigrants, of course, often carried these customs to the New World.

The women would cheer, "*Yel, Haji Bey, Yel*!" [Go, Haji Bey, go!]. In the next moment, he would be atop the table, whirling and turning, never touching any of the dishes below with his feet. Then the climax — a hop back, slapping one knee with the palm of his hand and then bringing it down on the table, then rising sharply, and slapping his other knee, raising his other foot up high and giving a smart slap to his shoe. One had to be agile to do the *zeybek*. You should have seen him!

If any of the men drank too much and became a nuisance, the others would get together and haul him over to a tall stepladder they had placed up against the side of the house. There they would persuade the drunk to climb about five or six steps, and make him turn around to face forward. They would tie him there, rain or shine, it didn't matter. Every so often one of the men would come over and check to see if he were all right. If he had sobered up, they would let him down to rejoin the festivities. Those guys sure knew how to enjoy life. They were real *kefgis*!

Guests kept arriving every Friday and staying the weekend. They sang, they danced, they drank, and they ate. When they were ready to leave, they would buy Dad's products. To those who couldn't afford it, he would say, "Don't worry about it. Pay me later." So, as I said, there wasn't any Depression for us. The good times rolled on month after month. Mother was busy buying more and more things. There wasn't any money being put away for a rainy day.

My dad, Haji Bey, had climbed halfway up his new mountain and there was no stopping him now.

Then tragedy struck. I came down with typhoid fever. Father was alarmed because one of my cousins, the son of Aunt Arous, had just died from the dreaded disease. Father rushed me to the Herman Kiefer Hospital in Detroit.

The doctors told Father that I had gotten the fever from the farm's well water. That did it for him. When I was released from the hospital forty days later, I found that he had already moved us back to the city. Anyway, he was bored with the farm and all the work involved. He needed a new challenge, a different mountain to climb.

He bought a rooming house, but it didn't work out. Too many people were out of jobs. In a short time, he had to sell it. After paying off his debts, he had a paltry $400 left in his pocket. We fell on real tough times.

"What was to become of us?" I wondered. "What could Dad think of next?"

Sure, there was welfare. Yet to accept welfare would be a dishonor for an Armenian. Father wouldn't even consider it. Then, he found a hotel in the black section of town, and went around to his friends trying to borrow enough money for the down payment. The property was tied up in the courts and the deal dragged on for months. Soon the last of Father's money was gone.

It was a humiliating time for him. At the age of sixty-one, Father had climbed his final mountain and had to come down again. He would never be able to regain his former status as breadwinner for his family and a leader among his compatriots. He fell into the valley of despair.

Father made one more attempt at business. He found a friend to lend him enough money for a down payment on a third-rate hotel in downtown Detroit. It wasn't much, but it brought in some income. To help out with expenses, I sold newspapers and would bring every penny I made back to my parents. We managed to pay the bills and we ate well, but that was about all.

It was 1936. I was sixteen then. I figured it was my turn to support the family, so I decided to quit school and look for a factory job.

CHAPTER TWENTY
Adding Up a Life

My father was only fifteen when all four of his brothers marveled at the brash kid who had led them out of Efkereh and masterminded the establishment of a thriving iron-working business in Smyrna. With the clear eye of a visionary, he had taken the destiny of the Yessaian brothers in his young hands. And he succeeded. Had the entire family understood his vision, he would have saved them all.

Not only had he led his older brothers from the hamlet of Efkereh to the great city of Smyrna, he had managed to persuade two of them to leave Smyrna and come with him to America. Then he helped them to find jobs, to move to a new city, and then helped other Armenians escape out of Turkey and to find jobs or establish businesses in the New World. He found them wives, lent them money, and showed them how to have a good time.

As an immigrant, he had done remarkably well in those days. He helped to improve production in the shoe factory, helped young girls in need, opened a boarding house, hotel, started a construction business, and managed a farm.

He had always helped so many people and had also provided for his family's needs. At age sixty-one, it was over. Now he himself was in dire need.

He felt he had failed his wife and children because he had run to the aid of other people and not provided for the future of his own flesh and blood.

He felt guilty about his failure to come up with something else to do to make a living. At times, when my mother was out of hearing range, he would mumble, "I haven't done well for my family. I should have put my family first. Saved money. Provided for the future."

He would confide in me: "Harry, I don't know what went wrong. I always found the answers. When we left the farm, I figured I still had time to start fresh, to establish a new business.

I wanted to do it for you. To let you take it over. I don't know why I couldn't do it again. I failed myself and the family."

Then he began to blame our hard times and his deteriorating health on others. He blamed the big bankers in New York and the politicians in Washington, "the legal crooks," as he would call them. "They've undermined the health of this country. They rob and steal through the loopholes in the laws. They have no concern for the common man. They are doing nothing about this Depression." He was drained, deteriorating before my very eyes.

He would rattle on and on, complaining and blaming, and then would look up, as if talking to his Maker. "Give me one more chance," he'd plead. "Give me one more chance."

Just before he died he said to me, "My son, what's to become of you? You left school to support the family. You haven't had a chance to get a good education. To learn a real trade. And I, myself, have taught you nothing."

I loved my father. I knew about his generous nature. His kindheartedness. He hated to see injustice done to any person, and he was always of help to those in need.

I wanted to comfort him. "Father," I replied, "don't say that. You've taught us all a lot. You showed us that hard work and a clear vision can help a man be a success in this country. But times have changed. Big business runs this country. There is not much room for the little man anymore. It takes more money and skill to go into business now. We should have stuck with the farm and the yogurt business. We could have made it an even greater success."

He slowly shook his head and gave me his faraway look. "Of course I was afraid for our health, yet we could have cleaned up the water. I know that. But I guess I was looking for a new challenge. Frankly, I was tired of the farm. My brother Nazar would often bawl me out. 'Donik,' he would say, 'follow through! Follow through! You are a genius, but you don't follow through.' I would laugh at him and say, 'Don't worry, when I find what I really want to do, I'll hang on to it. You will see.'

"I guess I was having too much fun sniffing out pots of gold. I was having fun showing others how it could be done. Maybe I was just being a show-off. My brothers and I were blessed with many talents. Why should we have feared hard times? Then, it all caught up with us.

"I'm afraid I have wasted my life. I wanted something better for you. I wanted to leave you something. People need an education today. You need a trade. You also have to understand the ways of the world so that you can be in control of your destiny. What's to become of you, Artin?"

Tears rolled down Dad's face. This was the second time I had seen my father cry. The first time was when he struck me in anger because I'd caused him to be late for an important appointment. He repented immediately and cried.

My father often complained of a bad pain. I took him to see Dr. Hippocrates Kuprie, a Greek doctor in Detroit, a very compassionate man. Dr. Kuprie would get angry with his patients if they didn't follow his instructions. If they didn't do as they were told, he would tell them not to come back.

He always made jokes about his parents' foresight, having named him Hippocrates.[1] He was a kind man, too. If his patients didn't have money to pay, he would treat them free of charge.

He gave Father an extensive examination. Then Dr. Kuprie announced his diagnosis. "Son, I'm afraid your father has leakage of the lymphatic vessels, sometimes called dropsy. I'm sorry, but it will only get worse in time. There is nothing that I can do."

■ ■ ■ ■

Father passed away in 1956 at the age of seventy-six. By that time he had become disenchanted with God and had become an atheist. He flirted with Marxism as did so many Americans during the Depression. He attended church only for weddings and funerals. Mother decided, however, that he had to have a church burial. The priest chanted in Armenian as he read the Bible over my father's casket. His words seemed rushed to me. For him, I

[1] Hippocrates, of course, is considered the father of medicine. Doctors still swear the Hippocratic Oath to do no harm to their patients.

thought, it was just one more funeral service to get over with; for me, it was my father's last rite.

They locked Father's casket and presented the key to Mother. What use was there for a key? Death isn't a lock that can be reopened.

On the way to the cemetery, the funeral procession snaked its way through the many twists and turns of the winding streets. Every turn reminded me of another chapter in my father's life as it was told to me so many years ago by Uncle Nazar. I remember thinking, so this is how that once proud and adventurous man ends his life — locked in a box by an indifferent hand.

EPILOGUE

In 1948, my Uncle Nazar felt himself failing. His last wish was to return to his native soil and be buried in the land of his ancestors. He was not alone in his desire. There were many Armenians, after World War II, who wanted to spend their remaining days in the homeland.

Armenians, of course, could not return to Turkey. Their only choice was to go to Soviet Armenia,[1] in the Caucasus. Most of them had never been there, but for them it was the only Armenia left to return to. Uncle Nazar was one of the Armenians from the Detroit area who decided to go. "I am determined to go, Nephew. From that sacred soil one can see Mt. Ararat, the symbol of Armenia. Noah's ark landed there after the Great Flood."

I remember pleading with Uncle Nazar not to leave. "Who do you know there? What will you do there? Who will care for you?" I argued.

"Nephew," he said simply, "Let me go in peace. I have no other desire in life."

Uncle Nazar left as he had determined. We received word from a relative living in Armenia that Uncle Nazar was carried off the ship in Batum on his deathbed. They took him to Armenia where he passed on. He was laid to rest under historic Armenian soil. He slept in the holy ground of his forefathers.

His final wish had been granted.

■ ■ ■ ■

Some years later, in 1980, I retired to Florida and found a place not far from where my mother lived with my sister, Alice,

---

[1] The Armenian SSR was one of the fifteen Soviet Republics. It was ethnically homogeneous and culturally, but not politically, independent. Its leaders encouraged "repatriation" after World War II, and many Armenians from all over the world, as Nazar Yessaian, went to the "homeland."

in Clearwater. My sister worked; and as my mother became more dependent, it became increasingly difficult for Alice to care for her.

Finally, when Mother was eighty-nine, we were forced to place her in a nursing home in Safety Harbor, Florida. Mother remained in the nursing home until she died in 1988.

I recall that whenever we visited her, Mother would reminisce about her happy days in Smyrna. "Those were the good days. Those were precious days," she would say. "They vanished all too quickly. Nothing ever replaced my paradise. It's not fair. Life is not fair. Why were we forced to leave our homeland? Why did we have to endure such hardships?" she wept.

Then, in the next moment, a faraway look would come over her face. She would gaze out the window. "See, see!" she'd call out, her eyes dancing with excitement, "Grandfather is walking past the window! His workmen are following him. I know where they're going . . . I know. I know where they're going!" Still staring out the window, she'd wave excitedly, "Grandfather! I'll be ready Saturday morning! Remember, you promised to take me to the fashion shops!"

"How is your brother?" Mother asked me. "Why doesn't Artin come to visit me?"

"But, Mom, I *am* Artin, and this is your daughter Alice."

"No, No!" Mother shook her head back and forth. "You can't fool me. That's my sister Vartanoush . . . Grandfather is coming on Saturday to pick me up. We're going shopping again!"

"Mom, your grandfather died over sixty-five years ago."

"Stop, Stop!" She would become very agitated. "He promised! He's coming to take me shopping for my new wardrobe. And Sunday, Grandfather and I will visit the Russian ship. We are invited to a magnificent dinner. We'll be seated at the captain's table. Afterwards, there will be music and dancing for all the guests! All the best people from the city will be there — wealthy businessmen, their wives, their children, even the consular officials — all invited to spend the afternoon aboard the ship. It's my duty to accompany Grandfather to such elegant parties. Since

Grandmother passed away, *I* have taken her place at these special functions.

"And next month, we're scheduled to visit a French ship. I have the latest gown from Paris for the occasion. Look!" Mother pointed to the tiny closet beside her wheelchair. "Go ahead, take a look! They're all there. Grandfather has bought all my outfits for our visits to foreign ships."

Then she switched her thoughts to Sarkis Aga's quarry. "Sssh, sssh! Can't you hear it? Can't you hear the workmen hammering? Listen. Chig, Chug! Chig, Chug! They're drilling holes in the granite. Soon, they'll insert dynamite into the holes. Any moment now, there will be explosions, and tons of granite will be loosened for excavating. The only chore remaining will be to load the stone onto wagons for transport."

The first time she did this, Alice and I stared sadly at each other, deeply concerned. Our poor mother was hallucinating. Her mind was slipping. It hurt to listen to her ramblings. We wanted to bring her back to reality. But we were told to let her be. She was happy in her reveries.

My sister wept when we left the nursing home. I put my arm around her and said, "Don't cry, Alice. She's happy. Don't cry, she's living her youth all over again. We must remember Mom and Dad as they were in their prime. You and I know they were special people.

"And, as Haji Bey would have said, 'Let's go and live.' We have children and grandchildren to think about . . . . We have a future. They are our future."

AFTERWORD

by Dennis R. Papazian

This Afterword is written for those readers who want to know more about the Armenians and the Armenian genocide. Part I, an Outline of Early Armenian History, is provided for those who know little or nothing about the Armenians and their heritage. It briefly covers the period from the beginnings of the Armenian people up to the Ottoman invasion of the 16th century. Those who have some idea about Armenian history may choose to skip it altogether and go directly to Part II.

Part II, the Armenian Genocide, is provided for those who want to place the events mentioned by Harry Yessaian in historical context. Part II covers in brief the history of the Armenians in the Ottoman Empire, the massacres of 1894-1896 by Sultan Abdul Hamid (Abdülhamit) II, the genocide of 1915-16 by the Young Turks, and the final burning of Smyrna by the Turkish nationalists in 1922.

A few paragraphs have been appended to this section on the current situation in Armenia and the struggle of the Armenians of Nagorno-Karabakh for independence from the Azerbaijani Turks.

For those who would like even more information, we have appended a brief bibliography. The annotated bibliography is worth perusal by any reader who would like to know of the rich materials on Armenian history currently available.

Part I

OUTLINE OF EARLY ARMENIAN HISTORY

Early Times

The origin of the Armenian people can be traced back to the early dawn of history. They are one of the few ancient peoples whose history, although too extensive and complicated to relate here in detail, extends from ancient to modern times when Armenia — or at least a small fraction of it — once more became an independent state in 1991.

Historic Armenia is located in eastern Anatolia, what is today called Turkey, and in the southern Caucasus, an area called the "Armenian Plateau" by geographers. Its center is Mt. Ararat, where we are told Noah's ark landed, and it is defined by the presence of three lakes — Van (now in Turkey), Sevan (in Armenia), and Urmia (in northern Iran).

Present-day independent Armenia is located on the territory which comprised former Soviet Armenia (11,620 sq. miles), in Transcaucasia, and occupies only ten percent of the historic homeland.

Armenia was located near one of the four known centers of ancient civilization, that of Mesopotamia, and eventually became connected by trade routes to the other three — Egypt, India, and China. Armenia's early history is tied by culture with Mesopotamia, for the headwaters of both the Tigris and Euphrates rise in historic Armenia. Armenia was known generically to the Mesopotamians as the "north country" and the "land of Ararat."

The Armenian highlands are transversed by several mountain ranges that lie on an east-west axis, the valleys of which have provided easy routes for both trade caravans and invading armies. Being located at the crossroads of East and West, Asia and Europe, Armenia not only enjoyed the stimulation of relating to various civilizations throughout history but also suffered from their frequent conflicts. Armenia has aptly been called "the crossroads of civilizations" and a "theater of perpetual war."

Later, Armenia was related by culture, trade, warfare and conquest to the Persian Empire. Xenophon gives a fine description of Armenia during that period in his *Anabasis*.[1] When the Persian Empire fell to the armies of Alexander the Great, Armenia was associated with the empire of the Seleucids, one of Alexander's four successors, and entered its Hellenistic period. For a brief time, with the weakening of the Seleucids, the Armenian King Tigran II (95-55 B.C.), with the help of Mithradates of Pontus, managed to carve out an empire of his own which stretched from the Caspian Sea to Cilicia and from the Black Sea to Lebanon.

Rome meanwhile had conquered the West and had become interested in the East. A new Persian Empire, that of the Parthians, had arisen in the East. The vast expanse between the Black Sea and Egypt, in other words Armenia and the Near East, now became an area of contention between the two great powers.

Armenia was invaded by the Roman generals Lucullus (69-68 B.C.), Pompey (66 B.C.), and Mark Antony (35 B.C.). It was Mark Antony who finally captured the Armenian king, Artavazd, and took him in golden chains to Egypt for a triumphal march to impress his lover Cleopatra and the Senate in Rome. Mark Anthony then proclaimed his luckless son by Cleopatra as king of Armenia.

Some of the Armenian nobles turned for aid to Augustus, who was by then ruler of the Roman world, while others turned to Parthia. Augustus soon took Armenia under Roman suzerainty for the next half century. The Roman general Corbulo found it necessary to invade a recalcitrant Armenia again in 58 A.D. In 66 A.D., Tirdat I established the Arshakuni dynasty, which was to rule until 428, although Lesser Armenia was invaded by the Roman Emperor Vespasian in 72 A.D. and Greater Armenia by Trajan in 114. The Roman-Parthian wars in Armenia (161-163) caused Armenia to be fragmented into various parts for a generation.

[1] Sometimes translated as, "The March Upcountry."

Christianity in Armenia

In the first century of the Christian era, Armenia was evangelized by the apostles Thaddeus and Bartholomew, although those who converted were subject to persecution. It should be remembered that Christianity originated as an Eastern religion in Palestine. The Apostles, who were of course Jews, spread the gospel along the trade routes in cities and towns which had Jewish communities. Several of those trade routes passed through Armenia, and it is therefore not surprising that Christianity should have taken root there at an early date. Eusebius, the great church historian, speaks of an Armenian bishop, Mitrozanes (Mehroojan), in Armenia during the middle of the third century.

It was not, however, until sometime between 301 and 314 A.D., the exact year has not been determined, that the king of Armenia declared Christianity to be the state religion, making Armenia the first nation in history to do so. It was not until 391 that the Roman Empire adopted Christianity as its state religion. In 387, Armenia became partitioned between the Eastern Roman Empire (sometimes called the Byzantine Empire) and the Persian Sassanid Empire, and Western Armenia came under Roman rule.

In 404 A.D., the Armenians devised their own alphabet of 36 letters to accurately express their language. Thereupon followed the Golden Age of Armenian culture, with teams of learned scholars translating virtually all important manuscripts to be found in Greek, Latin, or Syriac, as well as writing many original works. Many of these translations from Greek, Latin, and Syriac can be found today only in their Armenian renditions.

Heretofore, the Armenians had used Greek and Syriac as liturgical languages, reflecting the influence of Byzantium and Syria in the early Christian church, rendered into Armenian by an Order of Translators. Accordingly, the Armenians had trained translators when they embarked on their massive intellectual project. Furthermore, they sent their most promising young men to study at the major centers of Greek, Roman, and Syrian learning to perfect their knowledge and equip themselves for their monumental task.

Many Persian subjects, particularly in western Persia and Mesopotamia, had been converted at an early date to Christianity. The Nestorian heresy, which was rejected by both halves of the Roman Empire at the Council of Ephesus in 431, took root in Persia and was at first encouraged by the Sassanids who welcomed the Nestorians as enemies of Rome.[1]

In 439, the new ruler of Persia decided that his state should be solidified by imposing the Zoroastrian religion on all his subjects, including those in Eastern Armenia. When most Armenian nobles refused to lead their people into submission, the Persians sent a vast army, which defeated the Armenians on the plain of Avarayr in 451. Armenian resistance continued for thirty years, however, until the Persians signed the Treaty of Nuvasak granting them freedom of conscience.

Rise of Islam

The beginning of the Muslim era is marked by the Hijra (622 A.D.), the flight of Muhammad from Mecca to Medina, by which the Muslim calendar is dated. Muhammad and his followers soon took over Arabia. Following his death, Muhammad's successors conquered the whole of the Middle East, North Africa, Spain, Sicily, Cyprus, and Armenia. Many of the indigenous peoples of these areas, particularly the Nestorian Christians of the Middle East, were quick to convert to Islam. Most Eastern Orthodox and Roman Catholic Christians, however, remained loyal to their faith. The Arabs were finally halted in the east at the gates of Constantinople and in the west at Tours in France. The Arab conquest of Armenia first began to alter the ethnographic homogeneity of the Armenian plateau, for the Arabs settled their followers among the native Armenian population. The Armenians, upon the payment

---

[1] Nestorianism was a 5th century heresy proffered by Nestorius, patriarch of Constantinople. Its followers held that Jesus was two distinct persons, one human and one divine. Nestorius opposed the title Mother of God for the Virgin Mary, since he claimed she had borne only Jesus the man. The Nestorian Church that was formed in Persia has few connections today with Nestorianism.

of a head tax, however, were allowed to retain and practice their Christian religion.

The Medieval Kingdom of Armenia

Armenia remained an area of contention, this time between the Byzantines and the Arabs, and its history during this period — both internal and external — is complicated. Suffice it to say, it was that period which witnessed the rise of the house of the Bagratunis who established a magnificent medieval kingdom with its capital at Ani, which became a prominent Armenian manufacturing, trading, and cultural center.

Ani, because of its many beautiful religious edifices, has been called "the city of a thousand and one churches." It was also during this period that Armenians began to migrate into the Byzantine Empire, as far as Cilicia in southwestern Anatolia, to escape the chaos in the east which developed after the fall of the Bagratunis.

Cilician Armenia (1096-1375)

About the time of the First Crusade (1096-1099), the Rupenids, a branch of the Bagratunis, succeeded in establishing an independent kingdom in Cilicia, on the Mediterranean coast. The Armenians fraternized with the Crusaders and there were frequent intermarriages between the Armenian and European nobility. Cilician Armenia was enriched by trade and commerce with the Europeans, and served as middleman between European merchants and the merchants of the Middle and Far East. The resulting wealth supported the Silver Age of Armenian literature and culture. With the fall of Cilicia in 1375 to the Egyptian Mamelukes, the Armenians lost the last of their kingdoms. The Armenian king, Levon, was ransomed by his friends in France and is buried in St. Denis Cathedral with his relatives — the kings of France.

Arrival of Turks, Turkmen, and Mongols

Turkic bands from Central Asia began to force their way into parts of Transcaucasia and the Middle East from the 11th century. One of these Turkish chiefs eventually conquered Persia. Other Turkish bands invaded and settled in Armenia, thus adding to the alien populations in the Armenian homeland. The Armenian nobles in Nagorno-Karabakh (Artsakh), Siunik (Zangezur), Gugark (Lori), Sasun, and other mountainous regions managed, however, to preserve their autonomy.

There was also a revival of eastern Armenia under the Zakarids as vassals of the Bagratunis, the Armenian dynasty of Georgia. The final blow, which effectively destroyed Armenian political and military power in the homeland, was the depredations of the Mongols and the conquest of Tamerlane, which reduced the land of Armenia to ruins. It was perhaps a hundred and fifty years later when the Ottoman Turks arrived on the scene.

Part II

THE ARMENIAN GENOCIDE

The Ottoman Turks

The Ottoman Turks originated in Central Asia, the homeland of the Turkic peoples. In the late 13th century, the Ottomans invaded Anatolia, bypassing Armenia and encircled Constantinople. They then moved north into Europe, conquering the Balkan peninsula. While they established their first capital in Asia Minor in Brusa (1326), in less than fifty years they moved their capital to Europe, to Adrianople [Edirne] in the Balkans.

It was one hundred and fifty years later that the Ottomans returned to conquer the Armenian homeland, so as to secure their eastern flank against Persia, before attacking the powerful Hungarians in Europe.[1] The idea that historic Armenia was somehow a central part of the Ottoman Empire is a 19th-century invention by the Turks.

By the time the Ottomans invaded Armenia, it had been laid waste first by the Mongols and then later by Tamerlane. Cities, towns, villages, and farms had been destroyed. Once prosperous Armenia — rich in culture, agriculture, manufacturing, and trade — had become a grazing ground for the flocks of the nomadic invaders. Under these circumstances, the arrival of the Ottomans in Armenia at first brought peace and stability.

Then, in order to further dilute the indigenous Armenian population and to serve as border guards against Persia, the Ottomans began to settle Muslim Kurds in Armenia and gave the Kurds special privileges over the native Christians.

---

[1] At that time, Hungary was one of the preeminent states of Europe and was respected for its military power made famous by Hunyadi.

The *Millet* System

When Sultan Mehmed II, the Conqueror, overpowered Constantinople in 1453, he needed an administrative system to govern the complex mix of peoples within his expanded empire. Islam is both a political as well as a religious system. Only Muslims may be involved in the body politic. Its natural result, as seen in Iran today, is a theocracy. Since Mehmed II presided over millions of Christians and Jews in his Empire, he decided by analogy with his own religion, and a precedent set by the Prophet Muhammad, that the minorities should be governed in their internal affairs — civil and religious — by their own clerical leaders. This system of having people governed according to their religion, and not by their physical location in the Empire, was called the *millet* system.

Consequently, Mehmed II appointed the Greek Orthodox Patriarch as ruler over all Orthodox Christians throughout the Empire and likewise appointed an Armenian bishop as Patriarch and ruler over all Lesser-Orthodox Christians — the Armenians, the Assyrians, the Egyptian Copts, and the Ethiopians.

These Christian patriarchs had to be approved by the Sultan with an imperial edict, a *firman,* since they were responsible directly to him for law and order among their people. The minorities who belonged to the *millets* were called *rayahs*, or flocks: sheep to be protected by their Muslim shepherds. After all, Christians and Jews were "Peoples of The Book (the Bible)," and not genuine infidels.[1]

This *millet* system, in theory, was rather progressive in its day and worked reasonably well until the Ottoman Empire began its

[1] Judaism, Christianity, and Islam are all considered "Abrahamic" religions, since they all accept the Old Testament as their common root. The Muslims honor the Old and New Testaments as God's revelations and accept Jesus as a prophet, but only one of the series of twenty-seven who led up to Muhammad, the greatest and the "Seal of the Prophets."

decline. As time passed, the flaws in the system were to become more onerous. Christian testimony, for example, was ignored in Muslim religious courts; Christians were not allowed to bear arms; they were required to pay an annual "boy-tax," that is, to give up a certain number of Christian boys to be converted to Islam and placed in the imperial shock-troops (*Janissaries*) and civil service; they were required to pay a head tax; and the Armenians in particular were required to give free winter quarters to the nomadic Kurds.

The boy-tax died out in the mid-18th century, but the other burdens were continued into the 20th century. The *millet* system, progressive in its conception, slowly deteriorated into a practice of repression and exploitation.

All these burdens of servitude began to reduce most Armenian peasants, some 80 percent of the Armenian population, to a life of constant humiliation and grinding poverty. Some Armenians in the larger cities, such as Constantinople (present day Istanbul) and Smyrna [İzmir], often became wealthy through government service, banking, manufacturing, and trade. In provincial towns, Armenians often held supportive positions in the administration, such as municipal engineers, secretaries, bookkeepers, translators, administrative assistants, and telegraph operators. Other Armenian townspeople were doctors, pharmacists, craftsmen, shopkeepers, and entrepreneurs.

Christopher Walker in his book, *Armenia: Survival of a Nation*,[1] gives some examples of prominent Armenians in the wealthy *amira* class in Constantinople and Smyrna. The position of superintendent of the Ottoman mint, for example, was always chosen from the Duzian family. The Duzians, and their Armenian employees, even kept the records in Armenian. "The few factories which were established in the Ottoman Empire before the Crimean War [that is, before European capitalists arrived in Turkey], were almost all funded by Armenian capital."

The Dadian family managed the gunpowder factory, the imperial paper mill, the imperial silk mill, an iron foundry, a

---

[1] New York, St. Martin's Press, second edition, 1990.

small-arms manufacturing plant, a tannery, and two cloth factories. The Kavafian family "managed a shipyard in Constantinople." The "Balian family dominated Ottoman architecture." Some of its members built the Nusretiye Mosque, the Dolmabahche Palace, the Chiragan Palace, and the Beylerbey Palace.[1] Other Armenian families were equally prominent in the major cities of the Empire, such as the Kouradjians of Smyrna.

Harry Yessaian rightly senses that the animosity directed against the Armenians by various classes of Turks had more to do with the uneven rate of modernization between the Turks and the Armenians than with the Armenians' Christian religion *per se*.

Not only did the Armenians begin their modernization before the Turks, they more readily espoused the progressive values, industry, and attitudes of their co-religionists in Europe. As the Turks grew angry with European domination of their economy at the turn of the century, the Armenians would serve as convenient scapegoats for Turkish frustration.

The precise status of the Armenians in various parts of the Empire often depended on the whims of local governors and military commanders. In some provinces, for example, speaking Armenian in public was prohibited. In others, the practice of Christianity was restrained. The rights of the *millets* were often abridged by officials at all levels. In reality, by the 19th century, no Armenian in the Empire was secure in his life or property.

The Eastern Question

As the Ottoman Empire grew old and became corrupt, the fortunes of its Muslim and non-Muslim inhabitants deteriorated. The Russian Empire, ostensibly to protect Christian minorities, began to make encroachments on the Ottoman Empire both in Europe (the Balkans) and in Asia (historic Armenia).

Slowly the other European powers began to take a self-serving interest in the far-flung Ottoman territories in southeastern Europe, North Africa, and the Middle East. Many non-Turkish Muslim

---

[1] Walker, pp. 97-98.

minorities, including the Kurds, Egyptians, and the Arabs, sought autonomy and even independence. The issue of what to do with the rotting Ottoman Empire became known in Europe as the "Eastern Question."

Europeans not only had their eyes on acquiring Ottoman territories, they also wanted to gain economic concessions in those parts of the Empire they could not occupy. By the end of the 19th century, the Ottoman government was deeply in debt to the Europeans, especially the French and the British (and later the Germans), who effectively took control of the Ottoman economy in their own interest.

As the Ottoman Empire declined, it could no longer offer economic or even personal security to its inhabitants. The Sultans, in order to meet their growing debts, began the practice of "tax-farming," that is, auctioning the privilege of collecting taxes to the highest bidder. This system led to the further impoverishment of the population, particularly among the minorities on whom most of the tax burden fell.

Freeing the Balkans

The Russian Empire in a series of wars dating from the early 17th century, began to drive the Ottomans out of Ukraine, the Crimea, the Balkans, and the Caucasus. One after the other, the Greeks, Rumanians, Bulgarians, and others were given autonomy or independence. In the Caucasus, the Russians occupied Georgia and the eastern part of Armenia, and by the 19th century had marched as far west as Kars, Ardahan, and Bayazid. These wars, and the loss of extensive territories, produced a crisis in the Ottoman government.

Ottoman Reform Movement (*Tanzimat*)

Progressive sultans decided that reform of the government was the only way to save the decaying Empire. In the 19th century, they, with the aid of notable Turkish statesmen, introduced the *Tanzimat*, or the constitutional reform movement. The idea was to introduce a European-type constitution for the Empire, giving full civil rights to the ethnic and religious minorities and correcting the numerous abuses in the administration.

In other words, they wanted to construct a democratic, multinational state in place of the medieval, theocratic-militaristic state then in existence. Unfortunately for all concerned, this attempt to reform the government and save the state met ultimate failure.

Abdul Hamid II and the Armenian Massacres of the 1890s

When Sultan Abdul Hamid II came to the throne in 1876, he had two alternatives to save his moribund empire in light of the aspirations of the European powers regarding Turkish territories and of Turkey's economic, political, and military decline. He could either seriously reinstate the earlier reforms and strengthen the Empire, or massacre his Christian minorities and remove the major excuse for European intervention. For reasons that can only be surmised, he chose the latter.

The dreadful massacres of Christians which took place in the Balkans in 1876 attracted Russian intervention against Turkey. During the ensuing Russo-Turkish War of 1877-78, the Russians attacked the Turks in the west and the east; that is, both in Europe and in historic Armenia.

The Russian army reached the outskirts of Constantinople in Europe, at San Stefano, and captured Erzerum in eastern Anatolia (historic Armenia). The Armenians sent a delegation to the Russians in San Stefano to seek protection from the rampages, looting, and murders which had become commonplace in the Armenian-inhabited provinces. Harry Yessaian's account of the attack on Efkereh in 1885, which begins this book, was in some ways typical of such raids.

The Russians obligingly wrote protections for the Armenians into the Treaty of San Stefano. The other European Powers (led by a recently reunited Germany), now jealous of Russian successes, overturned the agreement and imposed a new treaty drawn up in Berlin. The Armenians were again abandoned to the mercy of an even more disgruntled Sultan.

The Armenian Question

The issue of what to do about the Armenians in the Ottoman Empire became known as the "Armenian Question." Abdul Hamid, angered by the Armenian appeal to the Russians, decided to punish them. He created the *Hamidiye*, an irregular cavalry on the model of the Cossacks of Russia, to carry out *pogroms* against the Armenians, just as the Tsar used his irregulars to persecute the Jews.

Abdul Hamid massacred hundreds of thousands of Armenians between 1894-1896. These massacres took place particularly in those rural regions where the Armenians were numerous and self-reliant.

The Sultan also encouraged his *Hamidiye* brigands to rove among Christian villages killing, raping, and looting at random. It is no wonder that Abdul Hamid is known in history as "the Damned" or "the Bloody Sultan."

The Young Turk Revolution

Enlightened Turks were every bit as distressed by the continued misrule of Abdul Hamid as were the Armenians and the European powers. Young Turkish patriots began to organize a revolutionary movement in the 1890s, the members of which were called the Young Turks.[1] Later they organized the *Ittihat ve Terakki Çemiyeti* [Committee for Union and Progress (C.U.P.)] to give leadership to the movement.

The Committee for Union and Progress was also known popularly in Europe and America as the "Young Turks." In their early days, the Young Turks had many factions. Some Young Turks were reformists, while others were nationalists or even proto-fascists. Haji Bey's experience in the café might be used to illustrate their differing views, although we are not sure if any of that group of young Turkish men were actually members of the

---

[1] Undoubtedly this name came from the Italian unification movement under Garibaldi, whose *Carbonari* organization was called "Young Italy."

Young Turk party. Ibrahim Pasha, a moderate, wanted to befriend the brash young Armenian who entered the café, while Keskin Oglu, a radical, wanted to kill the Armenian for his audacity.

About the same time as the Young Turks organized, the young Armenians also began to establish political action societies. Two of the most popular, the *Dashnaks*[1] and the *Hunchaks*,[2] were organized in the Russian Empire, but soon thereafter sent cohorts into Turkey to defend the civil rights and the personal security of the Armenian population. Contrary to present general opinion, the Hunchaks were more militant at that time than the Dashnaks.

The Dashnak party, realizing that reform of the Turkish government was perhaps the only genuine answer to the Armenian plight, took part in the reformist First Congress of Ottoman Liberals in 1902 and in similar meetings of constitutionalists after that. The Dashnaks even offered to collaborate with the Committee of Union and Progress to seize the Sultan's power by revolution and to reinstate the liberal constitution of 1876.

The faction of the Young Turks which consisted mostly of young Turkish army officers finally carried out a successful *coup d'etat* in 1908 against Sultan Abdul Hamid and made a show of reinstating the constitution of 1876. Turks, Armenians, Greeks, and Jews embraced in the streets. A new era seemed to be dawning.

The Young Turk Genocide of the Armenians

The Committee of Union and Progress took power from the Sultan in 1908, in the name of Ottomanism, a kind of multi-nationalism with all peoples of the Empire equal under the law. Conservatives staged a counterrevolution in 1909, at the time of

---

[1] The Armenian Revolutionary Federation.

[2] The Hunchaks were inspired by the Russian Populist movement. Their very name, meaning tocsin, or alarm bell, comes from the Russian *kolokol*. The Hunchaks were divided into reformist and radical wings, just as the Populists were.

the great massacre in Adana,[1] but the Young Turks quickly regained power. In 1912, the leaders of the Young Turks were forced out by a revolution of the "Savior Officers," a military *junta*.

In 1913, however, a new clique of Young Turks took power, led by Talat, Çemal, and Enver pashas.[2] These three men and their numerous followers were rabid racists and Pan-Turkist in their political philosophy. They wanted to establish a new Turkish empire that would stretch from the borders of Europe through Anatolia into Central Asia, the Turkish homeland. The Christian minorities of the Ottoman Empire had no place in their vision of the new Turkish state.

Accordingly, the new leaders, who were unequivocally irreligious, decided on a "final solution" to the "Armenian Question": the annihilation of the Ottoman Armenians in a state-sponsored genocide. The Armenian genocide was to be followed by the forced assimilation of the Muslim Kurds and the expulsion of the Christian Greeks.

When the Turks joined Germany against the Allies in World War I, the Turkish leaders were able to carry out their plan of genocide in 1915-16 under the cover of war and when the Allies could do nothing to stop them. Recent scholarship suggests that the decision to destroy the Ottoman Armenians arose from the frustration of the Turks at their early defeats in the war on the Russian front. Since the Turks could not defeat their external enemies, they created an "internal enemy" as a scapegoat.

The Armenian genocide was carried out by a covert and secret "Special Organization [*Teskilati Mahsusa*]" created by the C.U.P. separate from the state structure but in control of it, similar to the way the Communist Party of the Soviet Union controlled the USSR

---

[1] The Armenians of Adana, interestingly, were among the most progressive people in the Ottoman Empire. They had begun to introduce mechanized farming, with equipment imported from Europe, and were considered an economic and social threat by conservative Turks.

[2] *Pasha* is a high title of respect reserved for high-ranking leaders such as governors or generals.

without official status for some sixty years. Brigands, as well as thugs and murderers taken from prisons, were organized into butcher battalions (*çetes*) to carry out the killings.

Humane Turkish and Arab officials who refused to cooperate with the agents of the *Teskilati Mahsusa* were dismissed from their posts or even put to death.

Early massacres on the Russian front in the Caucasus seemed to be "practice" for the systematic slaughter which was soon to follow. In April of 1915, the Turks killed Armenian notables in Constantinople, including members of parliament, to deprive the Armenian people of leadership. The Turks then drafted the remaining Armenian men of fighting age into the army where they were disarmed and slaughtered.

Armenians in the villages were commanded to give up their arms, which they had been allowed to possess legally since 1908. Then those males from 16 to 55 who had not been drafted were forcibly taken out of cities, towns, and villages to be slaughtered. Finally, the old men, women, and children were driven from their homes to be "relocated" in the Syrian desert. Only a few Armenians, mostly children, survived these death marches. This was, of course, the case of Harry Yessaian's two young relatives. All the adults in the family had been killed.

The atheistic Young Turks, ironically, inflamed the incipient religious prejudice among the masses to entice them to kill Armenians as they were driven through Turkish and Kurdish villages. The higher Muslim clergy was embarrassed by the Young Turk ploy and the gullibility of the Turkish and Kurdish masses.

The Sheik-ul-Islam, the highest Muslim religious authority in the Ottoman Empire, resigned his position in anger. Arab Muslims were not at all deceived by Young Turk propaganda and universally gave refuge to the Armenian victims of the deportations. As a matter of fact, most of the Armenians who survived were given aid by pious Turks, Kurds, and especially Arabs.

The Armenians were driven out and annihilated not only from their historic homeland in the east, but across the whole length and breadth of Ottoman Anatolia, with the exception of the Aegean coast where German General Liman von Sanders was in control of the Turkish army. Their turn would come in 1922, as we shall see.

Smyrna, the Jewel of the Aegean.

Smyrna (present-day İzmir), the scene of much of Harry Yessaian's story, is an ancient seaport attractively located on the beautiful coast of the Aegean Sea in Asia Minor. It has one of the finest harbors in the whole of the Middle East, located at the end of a narrow gulf. First settled around 3,000 B.C., it was colonized ca. 1,000 B.C. by Ionian Greeks and experienced its first era of glory. Enjoying a mild climate and an excellent location, it continued to prosper under Seleucid and Roman rule and, after a complex history, fell to the Ottoman Turks in the 15th century.

Under early Ottoman rule, it continued to be a thriving and cosmopolitan seaport and commercial center inhabited chiefly by Greeks, Armenians, and Turks, with a significant number of Jews, Persians, Egyptians, Arabs, and those of many other nationalities.

The Greeks made up the single largest segment of the population, followed by the Armenians and the Turks. Most of the population spoke Greek, which served as Smyrna's commercial and cultural language before the arrival of the Europeans. Next to Constantinople, Smyrna was the largest and most dynamic seaport in what is today Turkey. Smyrna was noted for its wealth, its splendor, and the sophistication of its people. Tradition has it that the most beautiful women and the most spirited men of all Asia Minor lived there.

By the end of the 19th century, Smyrna had a thriving European colony that included Britons, Americans, Dutch, Italians, Germans and others. The Europeans engaged in manufacturing and extensive trading, particularly in oil and tobacco. The American consulate in Smyrna was one of the most important in the Middle East; all the European powers had extensive official representation.

The Europeans and Americans enjoyed a district of the city that was noted for its handsome villas and lavish country clubs; and the wealthy Greeks, Armenians, Turks, and Jews had their own quarters which were no less luxurious. The Onassis family, for example, lived in an opulent abode. The less well off of all nationalities lived in their own, separate quarters of the crowded old city.

Smyrna, the Destruction of the City, 1922

The European powers — Britain, France, tsarist Russia, and Italy — had multiple and often contradictory schemes for the division of the Ottoman Empire after the war. They had made conflicting promises among themselves and with the Arabs, the Armenians, the Greeks, and others.

Furthermore, since Allied armies did not actually occupy Anatolia, Turkish armies remained armed after the armistice at Mudros on 30 October 1918. Soon after, many of the Allies, as well as the United States, began to flirt with the Turks for post-war economic concessions, particularly for oil which was to fuel modern industry and transportation.

It was in this atmosphere of political intrigue and double cross that small British, French, Italian, and Greek armies moved into the wider area. No brief account can possibly do justice to the complex mix of events; in this short exposition we can only give the reader some idea of what was happening as it related to Smyrna.

Although the British effectively controlled Constantinople after the war, the Turkish armies in the east had not been disarmed by the Russians because of the fall of the Tsar. Mustafa Kemal Pasha, later to adopt the surname Atatürk, was naïvely sent by the British-backed Ottoman government to demand that the Turkish eastern army give up its weapons and disband. Instead, Kemal took control of the army and organized the Turkish National Movement. His aim, under the slogan "Turkey for the Turks," was to drive the Europeans out of Anatolia and create a Turkish nation-state.

Meanwhile, the European Allies, not able to come to some accommodation among themselves, sent the Greek army from Smyrna into the interior of Anatolia to disarm the Turks. The Greeks, who had landed in Smyrna on 15 May 1919, surprised most observers by their successes in defeating the Turkish armies.

It was during this period of the Greek occupation of Smyrna that Haji Bey Yessaian was able to return to and enjoy the city even though the Armenians of Efkereh, his native town in the interior, had long since been massacred.

Many wealthy Armenians and Greeks took advantage of the Greek presence in Smyrna to flee the city. Unfortunately, Harry Yessaian's grandmother, Sultan Hanim Kouradjian, his great-grandfather Sarkis Aga Kouradjian, and their families did not. Most minorities apparently believed the Greeks would remain in control.

Despite their victories over the Turks, or perhaps because of them, the Greeks were soon sabotaged by the French and the Italians, abandoned by the British, and forced to retreat toward Smyrna. The Greeks finally evacuated that city on 9 September 1922, as Mustafa Kemal Atatürk's nationalist army reached its environs, without a fight. The Greeks hoped thereby to save the city from destruction. Within days of the Turkish occupation of the city, the tragedy began.

The destruction of Smyrna, and the slaughter and flight of the Armenians, was witnessed by thousands of Europeans of all nationalities. In fact the day Atatürk's army entered the city, there were, as described by Marjorie Housepian Dobkin in her moving book *Smyrna 1922: The Destruction of a City:*

> Besides twenty-one warships — two British battleships, three cruisers, and six destroyers; three French cruisers and two destroyers; an Italian cruiser and destroyer; and three American destroyers — the harbor was massed with virtually every sort of vessel that could float, from tiny Levantine caïques to massive freighters bearing the flags of all the maritime nations on earth — except Greece. The last Greek ship had pulled down its flag and slid away before dawn.[1]

[1] Kent State University Press, 1988, p. 101.

The European and American warships were in the harbor to shield the Greek troopships while they evacuated the Greek army, to safeguard their own nationals and their extensive business properties in the city, and to curry favor with and acquire commercial concessions from Atatürk — who was then effectively the new ruler of Turkey — when he arrived.

The massacres of Armenians by the Turks, the burning of the Armenian quarter — and shortly thereafter the Greek and European quarters — and the flight of the pitiful survivors to the quay defy description even though many eyewitnesses have left memoirs and diaries attempting to portray the impossible.

What is particularly tragic about this terrible affair is that Mustafa Kemal apparently expected the Allies to rid him of the Armenian population by taking them away from Smyrna, while the Allies refused to remove the Armenians for fear of offending Kemal and losing his favor.

This confusion of expectations made the affair all the more macabre inasmuch as thousands died in the most horrifying ways while the Americans and Europeans dallied and played politics. Although perhaps half a million Armenians — including refugees from the interior — struggled to flee the burning of their homes, the massacres, the indiscriminate and episodic murders, and the deadly debacle on the docks, at least 100,000 died.

Despite the indifference of the co-religionists of the Armenians, the Americans and Europeans, the lone Japanese ship in the harbor threw its cargo overboard to make room for the maximum number of refugees.[1]

George Horton, the American consul in Smyrna, penned a moving memoir on his life in the Ottoman Empire, entitled *The Blight of Asia*. Referring to it, Marjorie Housepian Dobkin wrote:

> George Horton thought that only the destruction of Carthage by the Romans could compare to the finale of Smyrna in the extent of its horror, savagery, and human suffering.

---

[1] Dobkin, p. 174.

> "As the destroyer moved away from the fearful scene and darkness descended, the flames, raging now over a vast area, grew brighter and brighter, presenting a scene of awful and sinister beauty. Yet there was no fleet of Christian battleships at Carthage looking on at a situation for which their governments were responsible." The Turks had plundered, slaughtered, and now burned the city "because they had been systematically led to believe that they would not be interfered with."
>
> "One of the keenest impressions which I brought away with me from Smyrna was a feeling of shame that I belonged to the human race."[1]

Refuge in Greece

Once the Americans, British, and some other Europeans realized that Atatürk actually expected the Europeans to help their fellow Christians and to rid Smyrna of Armenians, the Allies and the Americans finally moved to evacuate the Armenians and to provide protection for a large fleet of Greek troopships sent by the Greek government to rescue the Armenian refugees.

By 1 October 1922, some one-quarter-million Armenian refugees had been removed to temporary safety, mostly to nearby Greek islands or to Greece proper. According to the description given by Harry Yessaian's grandmother, Sultan Hanim Kouradjian, of the conditions on the dock, she and her family must have been among the last to escape.

To the everlasting credit of Greece, no Armenian refugees were turned away, although Greece itself was groaning under the burden of an economy devastated by the war and was soon to be awash with Greek refugees from Anatolia.

Many have wondered why the Greeks were spared the horrors of a genocide in Anatolia and the destruction of Smyrna. The answer came only days after the Armenians were driven out. Atatürk wanted to exchange the Greeks of Anatolia, as well as the

---

[1] From Horton as referenced in Dobkin, p. 167.

piteous Armenian remnant of Asia Minor, for the Muslims in Thrace.[1] In essence, he and the Young Turks had all along considered the Muslims of Europe, namely those in Grecian Thrace, as hostages for the safety of the Greeks in Asia. The depressing story of the exchange of populations cannot be told here. Yet despite their grave suffering, most of the Greeks — totaling over a million — managed to escape Turkey.

There is a definite advantage for a people to have their own state to defend them. Armenians and Jews, unfortunately, have been taught this lesson well. Fortunately, the story of the Armenians does not end here.

The Armenian Republic

The Russian revolution of 1917 and the fall of the Russian Empire gave an opportunity to the subject peoples of Transcaucasia — the Georgians, Armenians, and Azerbaijanis — to establish an independent Transcaucasian Federation.

Still bent on establishing a new pan-Turkish empire, the Turkish army invaded Transcaucasia and encouraged the Azerbaijanis to pull out of the Federation, leaving Georgia and Armenia to declare their precarious independence.[2]

A determined Turkish army then invaded the small and helpless independent Armenian Republic to finish off the genocide.

The Armenians of the Republic — many of them survivors of the genocide — conscious of their impending doom, arose *en masse* — men, women, and children — and fought heroically to check the advancing Turkish army which was finally halted at Sardarabad, Karakilisa, and Bash Abaran. Thus this tiny piece of land, later further constricted by an imposed treaty, was all that remained of Armenia for the Armenians.

---

[1] There was approximately 1.25 million Greeks, 100,000 Armenians, and 390,000 Turks involved in these massive exchanges.

[2] 28 May 1918 is Armenian Independence Day.

Armenian SSR

While the Turks were invading the Transcaucasus from the west, the Bolsheviks were winning the Russian Civil War (1918-1920) and sent their army over the Caucasus from the north. The independent Armenian Republic, beset by insuperable problems, was caught between a menacing, unrepentant Turkey and the approaching Bolshevik armies. The Armenians, denied significant aid by the Allies and the United States,[1] and unable to resist on their own, decided to cast in their lot with Soviet Russia as the lesser of two evils.[2] Bolshevik power in the Caucasus was finally to give Armenia a modicum of respite, which it so desperately needed.

While accepting Russia's rule guaranteed the survival of Armenia, it also brought all the problems of Bolshevization. At first, the three Transcaucasian republics were united by the Bolsheviks into one state in 1922, the Transcaucasian Federation, but in 1936 each was made a separate "Union Republic." Thus, the Armenian SSR was born. The advantage of Soviet rule was that Armenia received protection, was able to save and develop its language and culture, experience industrialization, and, more importantly, was able to preserve and solidify its Armenian national identity. The disadvantages are well enough known not to need repeating here.

Lenin and Stalin, in their eagerness to appease Atatürk, attached the Armenian provinces of Nakhichevan and Nagorno-Karabakh to Azerbaijan. The Azerbaijanis drove most of the Armenians out of Nakhichevan and persecuted the Armenians of Nagorno-Karabakh. This persecution became known

---

[1] It should be noted that the European powers asked the United States to accept a mandate (protectorate) over Armenia. On 24 May 1920, President Wilson sent Senate a request to do so. The Senate, by then in an isolationist mood, rejected President Wilson's request.

[2] 29 November 1920 is the traditional date for the "Sovietization" of Armenia.

world-wide when Mikhail Gorbachev came to power in 1985 and instituted *glasnost*.

Free and Independent Armenia and the Nagorno-Karabakh Struggle

When Mikhail Gorbachev came to power in the USSR there was some hope that he would revitalize the Soviet Union, including the Armenian SSR, with his ideas of restructuring (*perestroika*), openness (*glasnost*), and democratization (*demokratizatsia*). There was some early hope that Gorbachev might be willing to settle the Nagorno-Karabakh problem by giving the Armenians there more autonomy, making it a part of the Russian Federation, or perhaps even attaching it to Armenia. Those hopes were dashed after the immense peaceful demonstrations in Yerevan, capital of Armenia, during the winter of 1987-88. These demonstrations, even though they were in the name of *glasnost*, seemed to displease Gorbachev, who was not known for his ethnic sensibilities.

Shortly after massive pro-Nagorno-Karabakh demonstrations in Yerevan, a series of massacres of Armenians took place in Azerbaijan — in Sumgait (February 1988), in Ganja (former Kirovabad, November 1988), and in Baku (January 1990). It seems likely that these massacres were approved, if not instigated, by Soviet leaders in Moscow.

Then came the devastating Armenian earthquake of December 1988, in which tens of thousands of Armenians died. The outpouring of aid from the West, the first time it was accepted since 1921, and the wealthy Armenian *diaspora* (dispersion), probably made a positive impression on many leaders in the Kremlin. To befriend Armenia might be good politics. Yet others in the Russian power elite, probably including Gorbachev, remained indifferent to the plight of the Armenians of Karabakh.

The Soviet Union, after a power struggle at the top, fell apart in August 1991. This momentous event opened a new page of Armenian history. On 23 September 1991, Armenia declared its independence and held democratic elections. Levon Ter Petrosian was elected president. The people of Nagorno-Karabakh, given new hope by Armenia's democratic success, revitalized their struggle for freedom.

Azerbaijan and Georgia also declared their independence. The republic of Turkey, seeking to spread its influence into Central Asia to establish a pan-Turkic realm, sent aid to Azerbaijan and agents into the Turkish heartland. The leaders of Turkey, however, were soon disabused of their ambitious plan. Russian influence in Central Asia, particularly within the ruling elites, remained paramount.

Turkey then decided to concentrate on Azerbaijan. Most of the inhabitants of Azerbaijan, some 5.5 million out of 7 million people, were Turks, too. Furthermore, Turkey had close relations with the post-World War I Azerbaijani republic and the Azerbaijanis had no love for the Russians. For decades, Russians had taken Azerbaijani oil and given little in return.

Abulfez Elçhibey, the Azeri nationalist who had been elected president of Azerbaijan, cooperated with the Turks of Turkey. He also encouraged the wealthy international petroleum companies of Europe and America to flock to Azerbaijan to acquire oil concessions. Azerbaijan, with the cooperation of Turkey, also tightened a four-year-old blockade against Armenia.

The wealth of Armenia lies in the education, talent, and industry of its people and the advanced technology of its enterprises. Armenia, however, is not self-sufficient in food, raw materials, and fuel. The major railway line bringing food and raw materials to Armenia from Russia comes through Baku, the capital of Azerbaijan; a lesser line comes through Georgia, Armenia's neighbor to the north. There is also a small-gauge line through Turkey, which had not been in use for decades, however, because of the Cold War. Iran is presently connected to Armenia only by a pontoon bridge over the Arax River.

Oil, which is vital to all industrialized countries, provided Armenia with heat, light, and industrial feed stock. Without oil, Armenia, like most industrialized countries, cannot survive. Here again, the main oil pipelines to Armenia come from Baku, although there is also a smaller line that comes through Georgia.

Accordingly, the rail and pipeline blockade of Armenia by Azerbaijan and Turkey effectively cuts Armenia's lifelines. For the past several years the economy of Armenia has been in ruins. Food is in short supply, electricity is almost non-existent, and fuel has been cut down to a trickle. The Armenians have suffered through several unbearable winters with much pain, suffering, and loss of life. An observer has said, "It looks like the Turks want to finish off the Armenians and complete the Armenian genocide. It is 1918 all over again."

Fortunately, the Armenians have been aided with food and supplies by both Russia and the United States. Without this help, thousands more would have died.

Recently Haidar Aliev, former KGB general and former Communist leader of Azerbaijan, returned to Baku and took power. While Aliev, a reborn nationalist, felt it necessary to join the Russian-backed Commonwealth of Independent States (CIS), he is also trying to flirt with the West. Azerbaijan, however, is politically unstable. We may yet see it fragment into several small "republics."

Eduard Shevardnadze, former general of the Soviet Ministry of Internal Affairs (MVD) and former Communist leader of Georgia, drove out the democratically elected president of Georgia, and has taken over Georgia. Georgia, too, belatedly joined the CIS. Yet Georgia is also unstable like Azerbaijan. Abkhazia has broken away from Georgia, Ossetia is effectively in Russian hands, and we may in the future see the departure of Adjaria, and perhaps even Dagistan.

Control of an "independent" Abkhazia moves the Russians farther south and closer to Armenia. Control of a "united" Ossetia will give them dominance over the pass through the Caucasus Mountains and move them closer to both Armenia and Azerbaijan. Adjaria, which contains the seaport of Batum, would provide a port on the Black Sea near Armenia.

The recent military success of the Armenian freedom fighters in Nagorno-Karabakh after several years of heavy losses gives them renewed hope of liberation. Military successes alone, however, do not bring victory. The political battle, to win the peace, is still being fought. Much suffering may still lie ahead.

It remains to be seen if Armenia can survive the Turkish blockade and continue on its road to democracy and free enterprise. It also remains to be seen if Nagorno-Karabakh can retain the freedom for which it has endured so much suffering and shed so much blood.

Armenia is effectively under siege. The misery is overwhelming. The children and the old are especially vulnerable. If sufficient help does not arrive in time, if the blockade is not lifted, those who have survived the past few years may yet succumb. Large quantities of aid are needed.

Yet there is no turning back the clock. The current problems of Armenia must be confronted. If Armenia does not receive help, it will not survive, and the genocide will be completed. A long and glorious history will have been brought to an ignominious end. If help comes and Armenia does survive, as we must hope it will, the story of the Armenians will have a new chapter that continues into the next century.

Dennis R. Papazian, Ph.D.
The University of Michigan-Dearborn
April 1994

BIBLIOGRAPHY FOR READING

General Overviews

The four European atlases of Colin McEvedy give an excellent view of Armenia's changing position in the Middle East and how it fits in with its neighbors. Those who read Armenian history should keep these atlases close at hand in order to make reference to changes in Armenia's territory or to Armenia's neighbors. They are kept in print continually by Penguin Books (*The Penguin Atlas of Ancient History*, *The Penguin Atlas of Modern History*, *The Penguin Atlas of Recent History*, and *The New Penguin Atlas of Medieval History*).

An excellent book for adult beginners is George A. Bournoutian's *A History of the Armenian People, Volume I: Pre-History to 1500 A.D.* (Costa Mesa, CA: Mazda Publishers, 1993). It gives an excellent overview of early Armenian history placed in the context of contemporary areas of importance, such as the Fertile Crescent, Greece, Rome, Byzantium, India and China, Europe, the Americas, and the like.

General Armenian Histories

There is no satisfactory general history of Armenia, although several are useful. From the Soviet point of view, we have M.G. Nersisyan, ed., *Istoriia armianskogo naroda* [History of the Armenian People, in Russian] (Erevan, 1980).

A dependable overview of Armenian history, especially political relations with Russia and the Ottoman Empire and the genocide, is Christopher J. Walker, *Armenia: The Survival of a Nation*, Revised Second Edition (New York: St. Martin's Press, 1990).

A general work, based on secondary sources, is Vahan M. Kurkjian, *A History of Armenia* (New York: Lydian Press, 1964), which contains a useful bibliography. Another general work, by an outstanding scholar, is Sirarpie Der Nersessian, *The Armenians* (New

York: Praeger Publishers, 1970). This book covers art, architecture, religion, and literature as well as history. An excellent book to read. Useful in general, especially for the early period, is David Marshall Lang, *Armenia: Cradle of Civilization* (London: George Allen & Unwin Ltd, 1970). Highly recommended.

Somewhat old-fashioned and outdated but based on good scholarship, is Jacques de Morgan, *The History of the Armenian People* (French edition, Paris, 1919; various English editions; reprint, Boston: Hairenik Association, 1965). Also useful, for a contextual view of Armenia, is Charles Allen Burney and David Marshall Lang, *The Peoples of the Hills: Ancient Ararat and the Caucasus* (New York: Praeger Publishers, 1971).

Armenian Chroniclers

A full, but not always accurate, history of early Armenia up to the fifth century is the classical history of Armenia by Moses of Khoren, *History of the Armenians* (tr. with comm. by Robert W. Thomson; Cambridge, MA: Harvard University Press, 1978), who gives us some insight into pre-Christian pagan Armenian religion.

More dependable in detail, perhaps, than Moses of Khoren is the not readily identifiable author Agathangelos, who wrote *Patmowtiwn hayots* [History of the Armenians] (a facsimile reproduction of the 1909 Tiflis edition with an introduction by Robert W. Thomson; Delmar, NY: Caravan Books, 1980). It describes the pre-Christian pagan cults in Armenia and gives the story of the conversion of Armenia to Christianity by Gregory the Enlightener. An excellent English translation of this work is Agathangelos, *History of the Armenians* (tr. and comm. by R.W. Thomson; Albany, NY: State University of New York Press, 1976).

Elishe, *History of Vardan and the Armenian War* (tr. and comm. by Robert W. Thomson; Cambridge, MA: Harvard University Press, 1982), gives the classical account of the Armenian war for religious independence against the Persians. It is an excellent source for understanding Christianity in Armenia in the fifth century.

For the Arab period we have the work of Hovannes Draskhanakertsi, *Patmutiwn hayots* [History of the Armenians] (a facsimile reproduction of the 1912 Tiflis edition, with an introduction by Krikor Maksoudian; Delmar, NY: Caravan Books, 1980). Krikor Maksoudian also translated it into English as Yovhannes Drasxanakertc'i's (a different system of transliteration) *History of Armenia* (Atlanta: Scholars Press, 1987).

Also for the Arab period, but from the point of view of the Armenian kingdom of Vaspurakan, we have Thomas Artsruni, *History of the House of the Artsrunik* (tr. and comm. by Robert W. Thomson; Detroit: Wayne State University Press, 1985).

Leading on to the invasion of the Mongols, we have a most valuable work by Grigor of Akanc, *History of the Nation of the Archers (The Mongols)* (Armenian text edited with an English translation and notes by Robert P. Blake and Richard N. Frye; Cambridge, MA: Harvard University Press, 1954).

Our knowledge of the life and work of Mesrob Mashtots, the inventor of the Armenian alphabet, comes chiefly from the classical historian Koriun, *The Life of Mashtots* (New York: Armenian General Benevolent Union, 1964).

From the Bagratid period, we have Gregory of Narek, *Matean oghbergutean* [Book of Lamentations] (in Armenian, a facsimile reproduction of the 1948 Buenos Aires Edition with an introduction by James R. Russell; Delmar, NY: Caravan Books, 1981).

Ancient Armenian History

Armenian archeology is covered by Lang in *Armenia*, but the specialist should also consult a series of scholarly articles written by various Soviet Armenian experts and translated from the Russian by Arlene Krimgold and edited by Henry Field, *Contributions to the Archaeology of Armenia* (Cambridge, MA, 1968). Boris B. Piotrovsky's, *Urartu* (English translation by James Hogarth; New York: Frederick A. Praeger, 1967) is a classic of good scholarship on the

Urartian period. Paul E. Zimansky's *Ecology and Empire: The Structure of the Urartian State* (Chicago: University of Chicago Press, 1985) is another.

Xenophon, *Anabasis* (The March Upcountry), has a great deal about the society, economy, and folkways of the pre-Christian Armenians. This is kept in print both by Penguin Books and by Harvard University (the Loeb Classics series).

Two excellent books which help to place Armenia in the context of the ancient world are Malcolm A.R. Colledge, *The Parthians* (New York: Frederick A. Praeger, 1967) and David Marshall Lang, *The Georgians* (New York: Frederick A. Praeger, 1966). To put Armenian history in the context of Rome, see D. Magie, *Roman Rule in Asia Minor* (Princeton: Princeton University Press, 1950).

An interesting perspective on Armenian history c. 180 B.C. to the early A.D. years can be found in Paul Bedoukian's *Coinage of the Artaxiads of Armenia* (London: Royal Numismatic Society, 1978). While most historians look at written records, a numismologist looks at the coins which various rulers commissioned and what the coins say about the ruler.

A magisterial work on Armenian history in the early Christian era is Nicholas Adontz, *Armenia in the Period of Justinian* (tr. with partial revisions and bibliographical notes by Nina G. Garsoïan; Lisbon: Calouste Gulbenkian Foundation, 1970).

Medieval Armenian History

An excellent essay that puts Armenian history in the context of the Dark Ages in Europe is Sirarpie Der Nersessian, "Between East and West: Armenia and Its Divided History," in *The Dark Ages*, ed by W.P. Ker (New York: New American Library, 1958), pp. 63-82.

An important book that is based on the most significant sources is A. Ter Ghewondyan, *The Arab Emirates in Bagratid Armenia*, tr. by Nina Garsoïan (Lisbon: Calouste Gulbenkian Foundation, 1976).

A brief but very readable and dependable book on the Armenians and Byzantium is Sirarpie Der Nersessian, *Armenia and the Byzantine Empire* (Cambridge, MA: Harvard University Press, 1947).

A heavier work on the same topic is Peter Charanis, *The Armenians in the Byzantine Empire* (Lisbon: Calouste Gulbenkian Foundation, 1964)

Many insights can be gained for Armenian as well as Middle Eastern history from Avedis K. Sanjian, *Colophons of Armenian Manuscripts, 1301-1480* (selected, translated, and annotated; Cambridge, MA: Harvard University Press, 1969).

For the Cilician period, a useful book is T.S.R. Boase, ed., *The Cilician Kingdom of Armenia* (New York: St. Martin's Press, 1978). Also covered in Der Nersessian, *The Armenians*.

A more inclusive book is T.S.R. Boase, *Kingdoms and Strongholds of the Crusaders* (New York: The Bobbs-Merrill Company, 1971).

An interesting perspective on Cilician Armenia can be found in Paul Bedoukian's *Coinage of Cilician Armenia* (Danbury: Paul Z. Bedoukian, 1979).

Armenian relations with other nations, cultures, and societies can best be studied by tracing the paths of Armenian merchants and travelers. Two excellent books on that subject are H.A. Manandian, *The Trade and Cities of Armenia in Relation to Ancient World Trade* (tr. by Nina G. Garsoïan; Lisbon: Calouste Gulbenkian Foundation, 1965) and K.S. Papazian, *Merchants from Ararat: A Brief Survey of Armenian Trade through the Ages* (edited and revised by P.M. Manuelian; New York: Ararat Press, 1979).

Leading to the Ottoman period, a controversial but insightful study of the *dhimmi* and the *dhimma* is Bat Ye'or, *The Dhimmi: Jews and Christians under Islam* (Rutherford, NJ: Farleigh Dickinson, 1985). Well worth looking at.

Modern History

An excellent study of the Armenians and the Armenian church in the Ottoman Empire, and a definitive source on Armenian rights and privileges over the Holy Places in Jerusalem, is Avedis K. Sanjian, *The Armenian Communities in Syria Under Ottoman Dominion* (Cambridge, MA: Harvard University Press, 1965).

Light reading on the Ottoman Turks is Noel Barber, *The Sultans* (New York, 1973). More serious is Lord Kinross, *The Ottoman Centuries: The Rise and Fall of the Turkish Empire* (New York: Morrow Quill Paperbacks, 1977).

The classical story of the conditions of Armenians just before the turn of the century is H.F.B. Lynch, *Armenia: Travels and Studies*, Vol. I, *The Russian Provinces*, and Vol. II, *The Turkish Provinces* (1901; reprint, New York: Prelacy of the Armenian Church of America, 1990). Also suitable for reading on that topic is Mary Kilbourne Matossian and Susan Hoogasian-Villa, *Armenian Village Life Before 1914* (Detroit: Wayne State University Press, 1982).

A good book on various aspects of Caucasian history throughout history is *Transcaucasia: Nationalism and Social Change* (edited by Ronald Grigor Suny, Ann Arbor: Michigan Slavic Publications, 1983). Its emphasis, though, is on the 1800-1923 period.

The American missionary activity in historic Armenia is covered by Frank Andrews Stone, *Academies for Anatolia* (Lanham, MD: University Press of America, 1984), Joseph L. Grabill, *Protestant Diplomacy and the Near East* (Minneapolis: University of Minnesota Press, 1971), and James B. Gidney, *A Mandate for Armenia* (Kent, OH: Kent State University Press, 1967).

Two of the very first academic studies of the Armenian question were done by A.O. Sarkissian in his *History of the Armenian Question to 1885* (Urbana: University of Illinois Press, 1938) and by Mary Mangigian Tarzian in her 1935 dissertation *The Armenian Minority Problem, 1914-1934* (Atlanta: Scholars Press, 1992).

The pioneering work on the Armenian resistance movement is Louise Nalbandian, *The Armenian Revolutionary Movement: The Development of Armenian Political Parties through the Nineteenth Century* (Berkeley: University of California Press, 1963).

Richard G. Hovannisian, *Armenia on the Road to Independence, 1918* (Berkeley: University of California Press, 1969), deals extensively with the aftermath of the genocide and the rise of the short-lived Armenian republic.

The history of the Armenian Republic and the international politics surrounding its establishment is told in great detail, with superb archival scholarship, by Richard G. Hovannisian in *The Republic of Armenia* (Berkeley: University of California Press, 1971, 1985). The first two volumes have appeared so far.

A good book on efforts to influence the U.S. government in ways beneficial to the new republic of Armenia is *Armenia, Vision of a Republic: The Independence Lobby in America* by Gregory Aftandilian (Boston: Charles River Books, 1981).

The Sovietization of Armenia is covered in Firuz Kazemzadeh, *The Struggle for Transcaucasia* (New York: Philosophical Library, 1951), in the somewhat dated book by Mary Kilbourne Matossian, *The Impact of Soviet Policies in Armenia* (Leiden: E.J. Brill, 1962), and in the book by Manuel Sarkisyantz, *A Modern History of Transcaucasian Armenia* (Leiden: E.J. Brill, 1975), which focuses on the economic history of Armenia after Sovietization.

Armenian Church History

There is no satisfactory up-to-date work in English, or any other language, on the Armenian Church. Perhaps one of the most useful, although it contains some anachronisms, is Malachia Ormanian (Armenian Patriarch of Constantinople), *The Church of Armenia: Her History, Doctrine, Rule, Discipline, Liturgy, Literature, and Existing Condition* (London, 1912; 1955; reprint, New York: St. Vartan Press, 1988). An early Armenian bishop is mentioned in the important history of the early church by Eusebius, *Ecclesiastical History,* but there is not much more about the Armenians.

A most useful book, although written with a slight protestant bias, is Leon Arpee, *A History of Armenian Christianity* (Princeton: Princeton University Press, 1946). A more radical protestant position is presented by G.H. Chopourian, *The Armenian Evangelical Reformation: Causes and Effects* (New York: Armenian Missionary Association of America, 1972). A more benevolent exposition of the Armenian protestant movement is Vahan H. Tootikian, *The Armenian Evangelical Church* (Southfield, MI: Armenian Heritage Press, 1982).

One of the earliest works in English, although not fully dependable, is Paul Rycaut, *The Present State of the Greek and Armenian Churches* (London, 1679; facsimile reprint, London, 1970). A more dependable early work, something of a classic, is E.F.K. Fortescue, *The Armenian Church* (London, n.d. [c. 1872]; reprint, New York: AMS Press, 1970). A rather good book, although written from the Roman Catholic point of view, is Aziz S. Atiya, *History of Eastern Christianity* (London: Methuen, 1968).

A valuable, although dated, work on the Armenian catechism is Archbishop Khoren Narbey, *A Catechism of Christian Instruction* (Istanbul [in Armenian], 1882; first English edition, Calcutta, 1898; corrected and revised by Archbishop Tiran Nersoyan, New York, n.d. [1955]).

An excellent study of the Armenians and the Armenian church in the Ottoman Empire, and a definitive source on Armenian rights and privileges over the Holy Places in Jerusalem, is Avedis K. Sanjian, *The Armenian Communities in Syria Under Ottoman Dominion* (Cambridge, MA: Harvard University Press, 1965).

A magisterial study of the eucharist, including the Armenian, showing the fundamental similarity of the traditional forms, is Dom Gregory Dix, *The Shape of the Liturgy* (Westminster: Dacre Press, 1945).

A most valuable bilingual edition of the liturgy of the Armenian church, which is a definitive source on current practice and which has a great deal of useful information on all aspects of liturgical dress and vessels, is [Tiran Archbishop Nersoyan], *The Divine Liturgy of the Armenian Apostolic Orthodox Church* (New York, 1950). English editions of the other offices of the church are also available.

The battle of Vardanantz for religious freedom in Armenia (AD 451) was taking place at the same time as the Council of Chalcedon. For the Armenian attitude toward the Acts of the Council we have [Bishop] Karekin Sarkissian, *The Council of Chalcedon and the Armenian Church* (New York: Prelacy of the Armenian Apostolic Church of America, 1975).

A little book useful for its references is Karekin Sarkissian, *A Brief Introduction to Armenian Christian Literature* (Bergenfield, NJ: Michael Barour Publications, 1974).

An interesting book on the influence of the Arabs on Armenian Christology is Hagop A. Chakmakjian, *Armenian Christology and Evangelization of Islam: A survey of the relevance of the Christology of the Armenian Apostolic Church to Armenian relations with its Muslim environment* (Leiden: E.J. Brill, 1965).

An excellent study of the Paulician heresy in Armenia can be found in Nina G. Garsoïan, *The Paulician Heresy* (The Hague: Mouton & Company, 1967).

An important comparative study of early Armenian Christianity is Cyril Toumanoff, *Studies in Christian Caucasian History* (Washington, DC: Georgetown University Press, 1963).

Armenian Art and Architecture

Jean-Michel Thierry and Patrick Donabedian, *Armenian Art* (tr. by Celestine Dars, New York: Harry N. Abrams, 1989).

Sirarpie Der Nersessian, *The Armenians* (New York: Praeger Publishers, 1970). This book covers art, architecture, religion, and literature as well as history.

Aram Ayvazian, *The Historical Monuments of Nakhichevan* (Detroit: Wayne State University Press, 1990).

Documents of Armenian Architecture (Milan, Faculty of Architecture of the Milan Polytechnic, 1968 onwards). Twenty-one volumes published to date, each concentrating on one particular region of historic Armenia.

Armenians in America

For Armenians in America, we have the thorough book by Robert Mirak, *Torn Between Two Lands, The Story of Armenian Immigration in America* (Cambridge, MA: Harvard University Press, 1983). A sociological approach is taken by Anny Bakalian, *Armenian-Americans: From Being to Feeling Armenian* (New Brunswick, NJ: Transaction Publishers, 1993).

Armenian Genocide

The first year of the Armenian genocide is well substantiated in the collection of documents by Viscount Bryce, *The Treatment of Armenians in the Ottoman Empire, 1915-1916* (London, Sir Joseph Causton and Sons Ltd, 1916; reprinted, New York: J.C. & A.L. Fawcett, 1990; and reprinted with special witness and place identification, Beirut: G. Doniguian & Sons, 1972), which was edited by Arnold Toynbee.

Several works that deal with the genocide through the window of the military tribunals which tried many of the criminals are Vahakn N. Dadrians's "The Naim-Adonian Documents on the World War I Destruction of the Ottoman Armenians: The Anatomy of a Genocide," *International Journal of Middle East Studies*, Vol. 18, No. 3 (August 1986), Dadrian's "The Documentation of the World War I Armenian Massacres in the Proceedings of the Turkish Military Tribunal," *International Journal of Middle East Studies*, Vol. 23, No. 4 (November 1991), and Dadrian's "A Textual Analysis of the Key Indictment of the Turkish Military Tribunal Investigating the Armenian Genocide," *Armenian Review*, Vol. 44, No. 1/173 (Spring 1991), as well as Vartkes Yeghiayan's *The Armenian Genocide and the Trials of the Young Turks*, (La Verne, CA: American Armenian International College Press, 1990), and *British Foreign Office Dossiers on Turkish War Criminals* (La Verne CA, American Armenian International College Press, 1991), also by Vartkes Yeghiayan.

The *Armenian Review* devoted a whole issue (Vol. 37, No. 1, Spring 1984) to various aspects of the Armenian genocide. Also in the *Armenian Review* (Vol. 39, No. 4, Winter 1986) is an article by Dennis Papazian on "The Changing American View of the Armenian Question: An Interpretation."

Two other short works on the Armenian genocide are Vahakn Dadrian's "Documentation of the Armenian Genocide in Turkish Sources," *Genocide: A Critical Bibliographic Review*, Volume 2 (edited by Israel Charney, New York, 1991) and "The Role of Turkish Physicians in the World War I Genocide of Ottoman Armenians," *Holocaust and Genocide Studies*, Vol. 1, No. 2 (1986), also by Vahakn Dadrian.

The Armenian genocide as an issue in International Law is taken up in *The Armenian Question and International Law* (La Verne, CA: American Armenian International College Press, 1988) by Shavarsh Toriguian and in "Genocide as a Problem of National and International Law: The World War I Armenian Case and Its Contemporary Legal Ramifications," *Yale Journal of International Law*, Vol. 14, No. 2 (1989) by Vahakn Dadrian.

An easy-reading work on the Armenian genocide is Edward Alexander's *A Crime of Vengeance: An Armenian Struggle for Justice* (New York: The Free Press, 1991). Two other works on the assassinations of the Turkish war criminals are Jacques Derogy's *Resistance and Revenge: The Armenian Assassination of the Turkish Leaders Responsible for the 1915 Massacres and Deportations* (trans. by A.M. Berrett, New Brunswick, NJ: Transaction Publishers, 1990), and *The Case of Soghomon Tehlirian* (trans. by Vartkes Yeghiayan, Los Angeles, 1985), which also has a timeline in the back of the book.

No study on the Armenian genocide is complete without reading Henry Morgenthau, *Ambassador Morgenthau's Story* (Garden City, NY: Doubleday, Page Co., 1918) and Leslie Davis, *The Slaughterhouse Province* (edited by Susan K. Blair, New Rochelle, NY: Aristide D. Caratzas, Publisher, 1990).

Two good anthologies on the Armenian genocide are *The Armenian Genocide in Perspective* (New Brunswick, NJ: Transaction Publishers, 1986) and *The Armenian Genocide: History, Politics, Ethics* (New York: St. Martin's Press, 1992), both edited by Richard Hovannisian.

Donald E. Miller and Lorna Touryan Miller, *Survivors: An Oral History of the Armenian Genocide* (Berkeley: University of California Press, 1993).

Clarence D. Ussher, *An American Physician in Turkey: A Narrative of Adventures in Peace and in War* (Boston: Houghton Mifflin Company, 1917).

George Horton, *The Blight of Asia: An Account of the Systematic Extermination of Christian Populations by Mohammedans and of the Culpability of Certain Great Powers; with the True Story of the Burning of Smyrna* (Indianapolis: Bobbs-Merrill, 1926).

Marjorie Housepian Dobkin, *Smyrna 1922: The Destruction of a City* (Kent: Kent State University Press, 1988).

Also to be read is an article by Dennis Papazian on "'Misplaced Credulity': Contemporary Turkish Attempts to Refute the Armenian Genocide," *Armenian Review* (Vol. 45, No. 1-2, Spring/Summer 1993).

Current Issues

A brief overview of Karabagh's history can be found in *Armenia and Karabagh: The Struggle for Unity* by Christopher J. Walker (London: Minority Rights Publications, 1991). For a look at the twentieth-century history of Karabagh through documents, we have the book *The Karabagh File* edited by Gerard Libaridian (Cambridge: Zoryan Institute, 1988)

Firsthand accounts of the Sumgait massacre can be found in *The Sumgait Massacre: Pogroms against Armenians in Soviet Azerbaijan, Volume I* (edited by Samvel Shahmuratian, New Rochelle, NY: Aristide D. Caratzas, Publisher, 1990) and in Yuri Rost's book, *Armenian Tragedy: An Eye-Witness Account of Human Conflict and Natural Disaster in Armenia and Azerbaijan* (New York: St. Martin's Press, 1990). Rost's book also narrates the conflict over Karabagh in its early stages and covers the December 1988 earthquake.

Stephen Brook, *Claws of the Crab: Georgia and Armenia in Crisis* (London: Sinclair-Stevenson, 1992).